THE COUNTRYSIDE DIARY

THE COUNTRYSIDE DIARY

A RURAL YEAR

Richard Brigham

BLANDFORD

Blandford
An imprint of Cassell
Villiers House, London WC2N 5JE

First published 1990

Distributed in the United States by
Sterling Publishing Co. Inc.
387 Park Avenue, New York, NY 10016–8810

Distributed in Australia by
Capricorn Link (Australia) Pty Ltd
PO Box 665, Lane Grove, NSW 2066

British Library Cataloguing in Publication Data
Brigham, Richard
    The countryside diary.
    1. Great Britain. Rural regions. Organisms. Seasonal
    variation.
    I. Title
    574.5′43′0941

ISBN 0–7137–2109–X

Typeset in 10½ on 12pt. Ehrhardt by Fakenham Photosetting Ltd.

Printed and bound in Great Britain by Courier International, Tiptree, Essex

The line illustrations of edible plants are by Vanessa Luff and are taken from Blandford's *Nature's Wild Harvest*, an essential guide to the wealth of free natural food available from Britain's countryside.

Contents

Acknowledgements

To my wife Barbara, and children Jennifer and Michael, whose co-operation and understanding allows me to lead an interesting and infinitely varied way of life.

To John Wilson, to whom my grateful thanks are extended for true friendship and much helpful advice and enthusiasm.

Introduction

An acquaintance of mine once admitted that, although he thoroughly enjoyed an occasional day out in the country, he could never bring himself to actually live there, for the general run of daily life seemed far too quiet, uneventful and even lonely compared to his normally busy urban way of life. Nothing could be further from the truth, for to the countryman with open eyes the countryside never stands still, and as each new season unfolds it brings a wealth of new pleasures, an everchanging pattern of bird, animal, plant and insect life that provides a constant source of wonderment and delight.

The first signs of an awakening year transform spring's stark skeletons of trees and hedgerows into verdant lushness, hordes of birds flock to our shores from foreign parts to nest and rear their young and, as the weather improves, the countryside begins to teem with all kinds of new life as emerging crops thrust through the bare earth to add to the general greenness. Sadly, it is time to rest the hunting hawk for her summer moult, but as the trout begin to stir and feed, it is also time for the fly rod to come out of hibernation and for the gun to be taken up as hordes of woodpigeons and rabbits pilfer the growing crops—providing the opportunity for sporting forays and a chance to stock up the game larder.

By summertime the corn has grown tall, a sea of green stirred by the gentle summer breezes above which swallows hawk the myriad insect life all day, and the fragrant smell of new-mown grass fills the air. Coarse fishing begins before the longest day, and swarms of biting mosquitoes are braved as one spends entire nights mesmerized by a tiny float or line bobbin, waiting expectantly for that first electrifying pull of a fish.

Autumn brings many rewards. It is a time for harvest, a coming to fruition of the bounty the land provides for the bleak, unproductive months that lie ahead, and all is activity in the fields as crops are gathered in while the weather holds fair. It is time for a wild harvest also for, as the mists of autumn gather on the low marshes, the duck venture out at evening to glean the shorn stubbles, growing fat on the barley and wheat spilled by the harvester and providing an exciting hour or two as they drop on arched pinions against a full harvest moon. In the woods the first pheasant days begin, as stinging frosts cut back the cover, and the birds test the skill of the guns against a backcloth of trees resplendent in their full autumn glory.

Even the depth of winter holds its pleasures. Inhospitable though the weather may be, one can always find a sheltered spot in which to tuck oneself up at the waterside and cast a bait beside the dwindling reedbed, hoping for a specimen pike; and there is little to match the anticipation of a float gliding slowly away to the pull of a fish, save for the stoop of a trained hawk closing fast upon its quarry. In this season the countryside appears dormant and dead, but it is merely resting, recharging its batteries in preparation to burst forth once more as the days begin to lengthen and the whole process begins again.

I have kept a diary of these events for as long as I can remember, at first amounting to nothing more elaborate than brief accounts of how I fared on shooting, fishing and hawking days, though gradually other events began to creep in: the vagaries of the weather, the state of crops around the farm, and the many and varied sightings of wildlife and odd occurrences that form part of an intricately varied life. I am luckier than most in being able literally to step out of my back door with gun, fishing rod or binoculars, or to take up a hawk from the mews and share with it the thrills of hunting, possibly the most fulfilling of all my pleasures.

There are days when all goes well, and others sooner forgotten, but even the most fruitless day provides much food for thought, the little hints and signs there for all to see if one can read them, and on this measure the enjoyment of the day instead of putting too much emphasis on the bag. In the following pages I have attempted to convey some of these pleasures, though it would take an abler pen than mine to recapture the full atmosphere and excitement one feels when deeply involved with the countryside. The pleasures and rewards are many, the senses of sight, scent and sound constantly indulged. The thrill of parting the foliage to reveal the first bird's nest of spring. The heart-stopping glimpse of a big trout rising to one's fly on a summer evening. The babel of geese approaching through the murk on a misty autumn dawn or the chortling of a late winter cock pheasant approaching at height above the beeches, as a watery sun glints metallically upon his plumage. There is much to savour, stimulate and excite.

Quiet, lonely and uneventful? If this be so, long may it continue. I could wish for nothing more.

R. B.

January

JANUARY 1ST

From the point of view of the weather, it was a rather depressing start to a brand-new year. Having returned home from a party at about half past four in the morning under cloudless skies illuminated by a brilliant full moon, I was surprised to awake in the late morning to the sound of buffeting winds and heavy rain lashing against the window panes. Easing myself reluctantly out of bed, I became aware of being doubly under the weather—the pleasures and excesses of seeing in the New Year not being without its disadvantages. Everything appeared to be happening in slow motion, and judging by the way I felt, we must assuredly have enjoyed a good time during the early hours, though any particular details of the event remain rather hazy.

Spectre, the buzzard, was screaming as I went to feed her in the mews, her high-pitched voice seeming just that much more piercing than usual and the pair of snowy owls huddled disconsolately in the far corner of their aviary. Coming from the far frozen north, the birds can stand any amount of snow and cold weather, but rain they dislike intensely. The pair spent almost the entire day standing on a log with feathers fluffed up, looking thoroughly fed up and miserable. I knew exactly how they felt!

The downpour continued almost throughout the day, relenting only for an hour or so as I plodded across the saturated field of winter barley to feed my collection of waterfowl on the nearby duck ponds. The fresh air gradually began to make me feel more human again, and on the return journey, my enthusiasm was aroused by the sight of a small flock of about fifty wood-pigeons that rose from the little strip of maize stubble running from West Lake to the bottom of my garden. With hopes of a few birds for the table, I hurriedly erected a rough hide in a patch of standing maize on the downwind edge of the field, planning a brief foray for tomorrow morning. I am certainly feeling the need to get out after today's spell of self-inflicted inactivity, though the very thought of firing a gun in my present state seems rather horrifying.

JANUARY 2ND

Arrived at the strip of maize stubble just as dawn was breaking. The strong winds of yesterday had, if anything, increased overnight, though the air was mild and low grey skies held the promise of yet more rain. Staked out half a dozen decoys slightly upwind of the hide, for in such a high wind any birds dropping in to join them would do so by pitching into the wind prior to landing. This forces them to pass within range of a hide sited downwind and can have a marked effect on the success or otherwise of a day's shooting.

9

Nothing moved for quite some time after first light, except an almost continuous stream of blackheaded gulls leaving their lakeside roost to spend the day scavenging for food, and an occasional ragged line of cormorants beating resolutely into the gale towards their favourite fishing grounds further up the valley.

The first pigeons arrived unnoticed over the decoys, as my attention was focused on a goosander coming from the opposite direction—a fully coloured drake resembling a rather ungainly mallard as it fought to maintain a steady path against the wind, eventually passing within 60 yards before being lost from view over the high bank behind me. Turning back to the decoys, I was surprised to see three pigeon take off 40 yards away, being blown quickly out of range before I could raise the gun.

After this rather sorry start, a steady little trickle of birds began arriving from the distant fir woods towards the decoy area, some providing testing shots as they lifted and fell on the gale. I began to get a few and at intervals propped them up to add to the decoy pattern, but the flight soon subsided with only an occasional bird arriving to provide further sport until the rain began and blotted out any hopes of remaining.

I finally picked up fourteen birds—unlike normal January pigeon—all plump and in good order due to the unusually open weather of the past few weeks. Plucked and dressed, there was enough for many a good meal later, and without exception all were well larded with fat and in prime condition for the table.

JANUARY 3RD

Caught up a male Hawaiian goose from the pond collection, for I have been meaning to bring him home and have been trying to get him an adult mate for some time. This would have given me a potential breeding pair for the coming season. I had previously bred with the pair a few times but last year the female was lost during the moulting period and there is an apparent shortage of mature females. As it is, the best I can achieve is to replace her with a last year's young bird from a breeder friend.

The Hawaiian goose or 'Ne-Ne' is one of the success stories of modern captive breeding programmes, for by 1949 the birds were on the very brink of total extinction, their numbers believed to be no more than about forty specimens left worldwide. By careful breeding and rearing in captivity, the geese were increased to a few thousand and later many were returned to re-populate their islands of origin. At the moment there is a healthy nucleus of birds in collections throughout the world and the future of this handsome goose—at least for the time being—seems reasonably assured.

I travelled down to Bungay in the afternoon to collect the goose and to see my old friend Trevor, who breeds and sells ornamental waterfowl as a means of earning a living. As usual he was late, but I amused myself before he arrived by watching the antics of a couple of pairs of smew—small and attractive sea ducks that occasionally frequent our coastline and salt marshes during the winter months. The birds are extremely difficult to breed in captivity but the drakes, the 'white nuns' of the old-time Norfolk coastal fowlers, were busily engaged in showing off their finery to a couple of unresponsive females, erecting their crests repeatedly and assuming an air of greatly exaggerated self-importance.

By the time Trevor turned up, the two birds had completed their showing off and the females had wandered to the bank to preen, thus making it quite clear to their potential suitors that they were simply not interested. I expect it will be a different story once a few short weeks have passed.

Like me, this year Trevor is also having a problem with rats, and as we walked around giving his birds a late feed, I noticed a number of holes and tracks in his pens despite the use of poison and traps. There seems to have been a widespread population explosion in the last few months.

Besides the goose, I also collected a lesser whitefronted gander and a female wigeon, both to replace birds lost over the last year, but as it was dark by the time I returned home, I put the new arrivals in the fenced orchard at the back of the house ready for taking to their new homes tomorrow.

JANUARY 4TH

It was still blowing a gale from the south-west, and as such the weather continues to prevent me from hunting Spectre on the marshes. Instead I took two of the new birds acquired yesterday to the ponds for introducing to their future partners. As I crossed the field a shrill piping heralded the return of a few wintering golden plover, and I was just able to discern about a dozen of the smaller streamlined birds milling around with a huge squadron of lapwings in the distance, wheeling and circling in disarray as they played on the gusting wind. A dog fox had crossed the barley overnight only 30 yards from the pond, his padmarks easily visible on the damp earth and discernible from the vixen's track by the widely splayed toes and greater size, altogether a different shape from the neat, pointed padmarks of a vixen.

The cock wigeon was obviously delighted to see his new mate, and immediately I released her on the water the pair joined up, the drake wolf-whistling in excitement while he swam around her and the female responding in her low growling tones. It was also a case of love at first sight for the geese, the pair running to join one another amidst raucous greetings and a bout of introductory neck stretches and bowings. This was followed by a sustained shuffling and rousing of feathers until the pair eventually took to the water together. I now have everything paired up and ready for the breeding season, over forty species, and with luck these should produce a good number of youngsters.

The effect of the recent rains has now raised the water level dramatically, flooding several of the basement rat-holes along the steep pond banks, though rats are competent swimmers and this will only prove a temporary setback. I will soon need to make an intensive effort to reduce their ranks. The problem is an annual headache in late winter, though never before have I been troubled with such a drastic upsurge in their numbers.

11

JANUARY 6TH

After a brief respite the gales have returned with a vengeance, uprooting yet more trees to add to the destruction of last autumn's big blow and leaving another trail of wreckage in its wake.

About sixty Canada geese were feeding on the recently harvested sugar-beet field above the farmhouse. As the situation looked quite promising, I decided to seek a position well upwind on their expected path of flight towards the lakes, hoping for the chance of a goose at evening flight. The main problem was to judge exactly where to hide. I was at least half a mile from the feeding ground, but it was a fair bet on such a rough night that they would head directly into the wind towards West Lake, where they have recently been spending the long hours of darkness sheltering under its steep banks.

After assessing the situation, I finally narrowed it down to a 100-yard stretch along the edge of Blackthorn Copse, eventually settling for an ivy-draped elm trunk halfway along the hedge. At least there it was relatively sheltered from the weather, and after slipping a couple of BBs into the gun, I settled down to spend an uncomfortable hour or so before the light began to fade. The wind showed no sign of abating, and after enduring its powers and the added discomfort of heavy showers of icy rain it began to get even more unpleasant. By the time the light decreased enough to move the geese, I was shaking visibly and my entire body felt stiff and cold with the effects of the freezing wind.

But all was soon forgotten as the first flight of geese, about fifteen in all, came beating low across the pasture, the line rising and falling with each gust of wind. At first they appeared to be coming within range, but even the flankers passed just too far upwind of where I crouched low among the ivy. As soon as the last goose had cleared the copse I raced along the hedge to the same position, arriving just in time to drop to the ground as the main flight of about forty birds battled determinedly along the path of the leaders. The geese still appeared to be a little too wide, but a sudden squally gust of wind brought them curling directly overhead at the last moment, the first shot dropping the leader into a dense tangle of blackthorn bushes and the second crumpling a goose that bounced heavily on the grass behind me—a satisfying double and well worth enduring the discomforts of the wind and rain. All thoughts of the cold were gone as I stumbled home with the well-earned burden on my back.

JANUARY 7TH

The, by now, monotonous high winds and rain are still making life a misery, except for an all too short interval this morning when a weak sun filtered briefly through the thick cloud. I was therefore amazed to hear the chirpy springtime notes of a song thrush echoing from the top of the garden, the valiant bird perched somewhat precariously at the very top of an ash tree fully exposed to the gale, but somehow managing to fill the air with a promise of spring to come. Its migrant cousins, the fieldfare and redwing, have virtually disappeared at the moment, despite a larger-than-normal influx during the cold days of late autumn. They normally spend the winter months around the local orchards, where rotting apples provide them with sustenance during the worst days of their long winter stay.

JANUARY 9TH

We began our end-of-season shoot by working out a strip of kale situated above the farmyard. As expected, there were not many pheasants present but those that came out with the wind in their tails provided some excellent shooting, all good birds heading for the safety of the woods behind us that curled over very fast as we stood well back on an adjoining grass field. Most were flushed from one end of the kale, but standing in the middle of three guns I swung up and blotted out a very good hen that came directly overhead, having the satisfaction of seeing it fold up and bounce on the grass fully 80 yards behind. This gave us half a dozen birds for the first short drive.

The walking guns then attempted to bring in a few partridges from a large area of high ground above the Roughground Copse, but as we stood fully 80 yards apart and partridges are renowned for finding any gap in the line, the three of us stood little chance as they swerved to avoid us. I did manage to topple one as it sneaked along the edge of the copse, and minutes later followed this with one of the best pheasants I have shot for some time, dropping it almost behind the next gun in line. Charles had just emptied both barrels without success at a very high jay, and when the pheasant screamed over the line gaining height, he was frantically trying to reload. Almost without thinking I swung the gun through it and fired, resulting in a stone-dead pheasant at extreme range. It was a very satisfying shot and fell a long way behind us down the valley.

Following a welcome break for lunch at the local public house, the rest of the day was spent hunting out the few remaining patches of rough cover left at this time of year, most places providing us with a shot or two to help make up the bag. Cock pheasants are especially cunning by the end of the season, by which time several attempts have already been made to put them in the bag, but we did manage to eject a few from the roughest places, the credit for which must go to a team of hardworking dogs. The final tally was just over twenty head including a dozen pheasants, three partridges and the odd pigeon, rabbit, and snipe thrown in for good measure. An enjoyable winter's day that was much improved by good company.

JANUARY 10TH

There was only a slight, very mild breeze, just the weather for hunting Spectre around the marshes. Unfortunately it was also ideal weather for building, and as the day had been earmarked for working on Barbara's new goat shed I thought it prudent to slip away early in the morning while the going was comparatively good. I succeeded in sneaking out of the garden without arousing too much wifely suspicion, and we were soon on our way along the road rejoicing in our freedom and nurturing hopes of finding a moorhen or two to chase. Our first brief encounter was with a tiny male sparrowhawk winging his way along the road towards us. He zoomed along just above the surface but on spotting us flipped over the hedge with a flick of his tail and was gone, a little blue thunderbolt looking hardly bigger than a thrush. Spectre watched it out of sight.

The marsh appeared empty as we stood on the old iron bridge surveying our surroundings, but in the event things turned out well, for no sooner had we crossed the bridge onto the marsh than a moorhen scuttled out from a patch of rushes barely 20 yards away, its wings a blur as it fought to pick up speed. Spectre was away immediately, her bells jangling as she followed it across the marsh, but before she could get to grips, the bird dived for safety in another patch of thick sedge below a leafless oak. Spectre alighted in the bare branches of the tree and peered below waiting for me to flush her prey, but it was several minutes before it was ejected below her and she again gave chase. This time she had the advantage of height to lend her speed, and gained on it sufficiently to allow her to snatch it just before it reached the river, banking around to miss the water and slumping heavily on the grass with her prize. We had made an exciting start to what had promised to be a rather trying day.

JANUARY 12TH

Found a bit of spare time at midday so I took Spectre along to Spring Marsh again when I went to feed the ducks, planning to hunt out the small drainage channel that runs adjacent to Marsh Wood that has been left undisturbed for some time. The black shapes of two moorhen ran into cover as we approached, and one was flushed almost immediately, twisting around behind us to seek sanctuary in the depths of the wood. Spectre followed fast, zig-zagging through the trees until the pair reached a tangle of withered brambles into which the moorhen rapidly disappeared. Spectre alighted on the ground beside the bush, bouncing back and forth and craning her neck forward to establish where her prey had gone. I took her up and cast her high into an overhanging alder, and then made my way carefully into the prickly jungle of thorns in the hope of flushing the bird. Halfway through my nostrils were filled with a familiar reek. Beneath a fallen trunk a shallow, leaf-lined depression in the earth betrayed the daytime layup of a fox, situated snug and dry and normally undisturbed in the twilight of the wood.

Progressing with all due respect for the thorns, there was a sudden flapping of wings just in front of me as the moorhen scuttled out, the sound quickly followed by an urgent rattle of bells as Spectre dived in pursuit. The pair were soon lost from sight among the maze of trees and the only link between us was the sound of Spectre's bells gradually receding into the distance. All was quiet by the time I had disentangled myself from the bush and I had no idea in

Spectre waiting impatiently for
the author to flush her prey.

which direction the chase had gone. I stood listening for a few tense minutes and presently could just make out the faint tinkling of bells. By following the sound through the trees I finally came up with her where the struggle had ended in a large bed of nettle stalks. Spectre was outstretched on the ground, tail fanned and wings spread wide, clutching the reward of our labours.

JANUARY 13TH

Following a dull beginning, the sun broke through a layer of light cloud to give a really glorious day, more reminiscent of early April than the expected cold depths of midwinter. The recent unseasonable weather has certainly confused the local wildlife. As I walked to the ponds there seemed to be a thrush singing from every copse and all around the field echoed to the first musical orchestrations of spring. Marsh Wood has now become a regular hive of activity as the resident herons set about the task of repairing their huge nesting platforms in preparation for the breeding season. The heronry contains about a dozen nests on this side of the river, with a small overflow in the pine trees on the far bank. Sited in the tallest trees, the nests are normally re-used each season, though last year many were badly damaged by the severe autumn gales and some were completely demolished in the more exposed sites hit by the full force of the wind. I suspect there will be much squabbling and argument over the ownership of suitable nest-building materials and already the wood begins to echo to their wild ringing cries. Apart from the mallard, the graceful heron is our earliest nesting species, for I have even seen youngsters huddling in the bottom of the huge, stick nests while late winter snows still carpet the ground—although they continue to thrive and their numbers have shown a healthy increase over the years.

JANUARY 14TH

As there was little or no wind it seemed to be an ideal day for gassing some of the rat-holes in the waterfowl enclosure. Normally the rats are easily cleared by the regular use of poison, but this year—despite topping up the bait tins almost daily for several weeks—there appears to be little significant reduction in their numbers. I wonder if they have built up an immunity?

I selected the worst area where a veritable maze of freshly used runs lead to half a dozen well-tenanted holes hidden beneath the rotting roots of an old alder stump beside the water. After clearing the area of vegetation, I spooned a small amount of cyanide powder into each of the holes, blocking the entrance with a sod of grass to prevent any attempts at escape. One hole was almost out of reach between two large roots, but being part of the main burrow I left it open and settled down with the fourten to await the outcome.

There was not long to wait. Within minutes the first whiskered nose appeared at the mouth of the hole, the fourten barked, and the career of an old doe rat was over. Almost immediately another bolted, plunging headlong into the pond and moving swiftly beneath the water towards another set of holes further along the bank. Its head popped up beneath an overhanging root but before it could make good its escape, the gun again did its deadly work.

Although I gave it another half an hour nothing further emerged from the bolt-hole, but just to be on the safe side I blocked up the exit before leaving to prevent any remaining inmates from escaping. There should be no further trouble from that particular warren.

JANUARY 16TH

There was a thick fog again at dawn, the visibility only slightly improved from yesterday when I had seen over fifty geese feeding on the sugar-beet field. As I plodded across the sticky, cultivated earth towards the far end of the field, a tawny owl hooted close by in the twilight, and seconds later I met him on his rounds, skimming along the hedgetop on soundless wings, only spotting me at the last moment before twisting silently over the bushes out of sight.

There was only the semblance of a breeze, but I stationed myself on the downwind edge of the field hoping any geese arriving would pass over me as they glided down to alight in the centre of the field. As the sky brightened almost imperceptibly in the fog, I could just make out the first gabble of awakening geese half a mile away—Canada, greylag and Egyptian—preparing themselves for the dawn move from West Lake to their daytime feeding grounds. It seemed to take an age to get fully light, and for at least half an hour nothing moved, although goose voices rose and fell repeatedly as if the birds were working themselves up for flight, but then fell silent as if unsure of their directions in the poor light.

Standing beneath the refuge of the dripping hedge, the cool breeze was just beginning to penetrate when a greylag suddenly cackled somewhere beside me. Swinging round I was just in time to make out three blurred shapes passing well wide, barely on the limit of my vision and far too distant to risk a shot. Although obviously not alarmed, they quickly melted back into the fog to circle the field once before leaving, their cackling contact calls gradually diminishing as they receded into the distance. Minutes later the Canadas took wing, their bugling voices reaching a crescendo as they lifted from the water. They appeared to circle the lake as if to get their bearings but then, their minds made up, they apparently steered a path in my direction, their voices growing louder and more urgent with each passing second. To me there is no sound more thrilling or evocative than the clamour of approaching geese, and I huddled tighter in the bushes, eyes strained and heart thumping as the long string of birds suddenly materialized out of the gloom. The main pack were moving wide to my right, but a small bunch of four set their wings to glide purposefully in my direction, veering off sharply as I stood to raise the gun. They had seen me too late. The nearest bird crumpled to the first shot, closely followed by the next in line, the two geese hitting the ground 20 yards behind and only a few feet apart. As the sound of the flock scattered into the distance, more geese came from the rear, finally

17

appearing as dark blobs looming out of the swirling mist but passing at extreme range and very high. I selected a tail-ender carefully and swung through hard, my single shot bringing it planing down to crash at the far side of the hedge where it lay, its white belly uppermost and standing out conspicuously against the darkness of the freshly tilled earth.

JANUARY 17TH

Had a short piking session on Bulrush Lake this morning, when a bitter chill from the south-west carried darkened clouds that from time to time released a light squally shower of rain to add to its unpleasantness. I began by wobbling a dead smelt on snap tackle at the open end of the lake, but after a fishless half an hour exposed to the wind I was prompted to seek out the refuge of a high gravel bank on the upwind edge where it was far more comfortable beneath the shelter of a clump of leafless alders growing somewhat precariously on the sloping bank.

Bulrush Lake itself covers approximately eight acres. Left as a lake following the extraction of gravel, it is roughly crescent shaped, almost 600 yards long by 200 yards wide, the monotony of the open water tastefully relieved by a few small islands dotted around in strategic positions that provide shelter and nesting accommodation for the resident waterfowl, mainly mallard, pochard, and tufted duck, which today bobbed around on the windblown wavelets like a fleet of buoyant corks. The water varies enormously in depth, from shallow bars where mallard and coot upend to dibble among patches of weed, to seemingly bottomless holes where the level drops sheer to almost 30 feet in places. Having been established for a number of years, there are a good many sizeable pike in the lake. One taken last summer in an eel net was reputed to have weighed on the heavy side of 30 lb (13½ kg), and after being photographed and weighed was duly returned unharmed to provide some lucky future angler with the fish of a lifetime. But it was not to be mine today. Although I persisted with the wobbled smelt at various depths and all manner of retrieves, it was not until I was about to call it a day that I felt a slight resistance on the rod. Thinking it to be the bottom or just another patch of weed, I eased the rod back slowly until a fierce kick told me I had attracted a fish at last. Giving it another few seconds to get a good grip on the bait, I felt rather gingerly for the fish and then struck hard as the line tightened. The pike ran out for a few yards just below the surface of the water, though being only of about 5 lb (2 kg) in weight, after a few short runs it was soon played out and brought quite easily over the net, the dead smelt still hanging from the corner of its mouth. I released it immediately, and after lying in the water at my feet for a few seconds, it suddenly kicked its tail and disappeared like a grey-green torpedo back to the cold depths of its murky winter world.

JANUARY 19TH

Arrived at the ponds in the afternoon for a dual-purpose visit, initially to gas some of the remaining rat-holes and then to round off the day by waiting for the wild duck to flight at dusk. Three teal rose from the furthest pond, the shrill piping notes of a drake echoed by my resident pair. The trio rose vertically into the wind and then curled back over me like winged bullets. Several mallard joined them from the adjacent stretch of the river, and conditions began to look promising for the evening flight.

It took far longer than anticipated to deal with the rats, for I discovered a maze of holes along the banks just above water level and each had to be cleared, opened up, gassed, and blocked carefully with a divot of earth. One rat did bolt prematurely, but luckily the fourten lay within reach and it did not travel far. By the time I had finished, the light was failing fast, and already I could hear the first muted chatterings of mallard circling the ponds ready to drop in for the night.

The first to arrive—a fine drake—dropped vertically over the ash clump to the water, but on spying me crouched beside an alder stump, it tried frantically to swerve away through the trees. The shot brought it splashing down in the centre of the pond, hitting the water like a brick and causing utter pandemonium for a few seconds among the resident fowl. By the time they had settled down, three more mallard had begun their approach, dropping down on set pinions before levelling out above the water. One seemed to hang on the wind, and I sent it spinning into a clump of dead bracken, narrowly missing the wire of the perimeter fence.

A flight of nine gadwall passed over high, easily recognized by their characteristically comical quacking, which always reminds me of a badly tuned duck call, showing no inclination to join us as they were swept over with the strong wind in their tails.

The light was failing fast, as threatening clouds were building in the southern sky. I decided to leave before dusk, thus allowing a few birds to drop in to feed in the last of the light, which would encourage others to return. As I walked away I could hear the chatter of more mallard arriving over the ponds, but I was content with my brace and by leaving early fostered hopes of their numbers building up to allow another evening's sport before the season draws to a close at the end of the month.

JANUARY 20TH

For some reason best known to herself, the female snowy owl was giving the little male a good telling off early this morning as I collected a bag of duck food from the brooder house adjoining their aviary. He stood quietly in the far corner of the pen looking suitably admonished by her remonstrations, his huge yellow eyes narrowed to mere slits as she pranced and paraded up and down before him, wings arched threateningly, booing, hissing, and shrieking in obvious disapproval. Perhaps he has been a little too forward in his attentions of late, possibly feeling the approach of spring when his thoughts should turn towards mating. I could only sympathize with the poor little fellow, obviously put back firmly in his place. Such a response would certainly have dampened my ardour, particularly in relation to such a large and potentially aggressive female.

JANUARY 22ND

The earth was even whiter than yesterday's hoar frost when I looked out of the window at first light, for the heavy rains of last evening had turned to snow in the early hours and at least two inches carpeted the ground. The migrant fieldfares and redwings have suddenly returned after a long absence and are now busy in the orchard searching for the remains of last autumn's fallen apples.

Although busy all day and getting literally soaked to the skin, I was unable to resist the chance of an evening flight on Spring Marsh. The first covering of snow is always something of a novelty and adds a real touch of wintry atmosphere to the place, sometimes bringing in a few more fowl than usual to spend the night sheltering along the deepest ditches.

At the edge of Marsh Wood two herons stood motionless against a backcloth of rushes, but as I neared they rose to the air and flapped gracefully across the river, their wild calls echoing from the nearby pine woods. Everywhere tracks bisected the snow; pheasant, moorhen, heron, and gull, and the unmistakable catlike pads of fox following the path of the old bullock trail. As I neared the river a wisp of snipe exploded from an open patch of mud, showing plainly against the whiteness of the snow, and a single dabchick, diving for its supper in the murky water, skittered upriver at my approach.

Heavy snow clouds were again building on the horizon. Moving in from the west, they blotted out the amber glow of the setting sun and brought a sudden chilled feeling to the marsh.

A few scattered bunches of wood pigeon were making their way to roost in the warmth of the fir woods, and by crouching at the edge of the boundary ditch, my four shots sent two tumbling into the depths of Marsh Wood. I found their crops tightly packed with hundreds of ivy berries, which I removed as they can quickly taint the flesh if left intact.

Strangely enough, there were very few duck to be seen at dusk, my only chance being at a wedge of five mallard that passed over very high. The first shot was to no avail, but the second barrel caught up with the leader and brought it crashing down behind me sending a flurry of snow high in the air. A couple of tufted duck went winging fast upriver, and just before the light faded I heard a loud swishing noise high above. I looked up to see a bunch of twenty or so teal whizz over like miniature rockets, showing no intention of stopping.

And that was it. The temperature gradually crept lower until my feet were numb and my nose began to tingle with the cold. I left the marsh in peace and not reluctantly made my way back home.

JANUARY 23RD

Having drawn a complete blank with the geese at dawn, I took Whisper, our German short-haired pointer bitch, a little further afield for her morning exercise to see if she could find a cock pheasant for the pot. She is still quite young and I have used her only rarely for hunting game, so an end-of-season foray would perhaps give her a taste of things to come. Whisper was as usual full of energy, though by the time we reached the hedge bordering the maize field she had settled down to work, her sensitive nose doing overtime as she tasted the exciting scents of the hedgerow. Cock pheasants are notoriously cunning at this time of the year, and when she finally came up with one it whirred out noisily to cross my path too far away for a shot, having judged the effective range of a twelve-bore to a nicety. Whisper watched the departing bird out of sight and glanced back at me with a look of disgust, but when I encouraged her forward she resumed hunting. The next bird flushed was unfortunately a hen, again leaving Whisper completely mystified when I allowed it to depart unscathed, preferring to leave all late hen birds as potential breeding stock for the coming season.

In the midst of the Grove we disturbed a woodcock. It clapped up from a tangle of brambles just in front of me, flitting skilfully back and forth between the trees like a giant moth before circling around behind us and dropping back to the wood, where its heavily mottled plumage blended perfectly with the dead fronds of last year's bracken.

By this time I was beginning to despair of ever getting a shot, but suddenly Whisper went into a classic point towards a clump of bracken, her body stiff as a board, one leg raised, and tail stuck out straight as a ramrod. There was obviously something in hiding. And so it proved. As I hurried forward to get within comfortable range, Whisper suddenly dived forward into the bracken to eject a noisy cock pheasant only inches from her nose. The bird whirred away to offer an easy crossing shot over the open meadow, spinning down to leave a little puff of feathers hanging in the air. Whisper was soon on the scene, her tail wagging with renewed vigour as she carefully made in towards it, whimpering with excitement. She would certainly recognize the next pheasant we encountered.

JANUARY 27TH

The recent floodwater on the marshes has lowered but marginally, leaving only the tallest of the ditch vegetation standing above the vast sheet of water to mark where the deep drainage channels divide the land. Having noted a number of duck present at midday I arrived in good time for the evening flight, on the way cutting a stout length of ash from the hedge to probe a path across the quagmire of mud and water. In places the marsh can be quite dangerous in times of flood, where rafts of floating vegetation conceal deep and seemingly bottomless pools of muddy water and potent bubbles of rank marsh-gas gurgle up at almost every step.

21

I reached the riverbank safely, finding sanctuary and concealment against an old fence post garnished with an armful of dead stalks and rushes that would provide sufficient cover to break up my outline by the time the light had faded.

It was a magnificent sunset, the flaming ball of the sun lowering to the western horizon creating a palette of colour no artist's brush could hope to emulate: a mixture of reds, oranges, purples, and pinks that blended together perfectly to be reflected accurately in the mirrorlike surface of the water. My eyes had wandered to follow a dabchick diving in the swirling flow of the river, when my thoughts were interrupted by the far-off bugling cries of a flight of wild Bewick's swans—hounds of heaven baying like a pack in full cry, the majestic sight and sound of the eight birds adding a real winter magic to the scene. They are the first I have seen this year and their appearance was timed to perfection.

The light dropped dramatically as the red orb of the sun was finally extinguished in the distant waters, and suddenly the evening sky became full of the sound of wild duck—small, chattering parties of mallard etched black against the blood-red sunset, carefully searching the wide area of floodwater for a suitable place to feed. Round and round they circled, joining ranks, at times passing almost within range but eventually arching their wings in a long downward glide and alighting in the very centre of the marsh. While I was bemoaning my choice of position, I was surprised by a bunch arriving from the rear, the swish of wings heard just in time to mount the gun and fire twice at the departing shapes, detaching two of their number to splash heavily in the floodwater a few yards away. One fell safely within reach and was gathered immediately, but the second bird was carried by its own momentum to hit the water beyond the wide boundary ditch, at that moment far too deep to cross. I would have to return for it tomorrow when the water should be down.

After the sound of the shots had faded into the distance all was quiet, with the first winking stars appearing in the east and a three-quarters moon beginning to cast faint shadows on the ground. It was time to leave, while enough light still remained to light my path across the treacherous marsh.

I had travelled only a few yards when the faint cackle of greylag geese sounded high in the night sky, their distant clamour gradually increasing as a large squadron flew towards the marsh. They seemed almost in the heavens, although the sound of their voices was deafening as they moved directly overhead, each and every bird totally invisible against the inky blackness, beating across a vast western sky that hid their journey's end. A more fitting end to the wildfowl season would be difficult to imagine.

JANUARY 29TH

I saw the first clump of snowdrops in full flower this morning, hanging their dew-soaked heads as the gentle warmth of the sun was beginning to melt an overnight rime from the foliage. The flowers seem to have appeared over-night, thrusting boldly through the cold earth to brighten the day and bringing with them one of the first real hints of spring to follow, when all life starts anew after its long rest during the cold, dreary days of midwinter. It was one of the many clumps I planted two years ago at the duckponds, together with clusters of wild bluebells, primroses, and daffodils, the latter already beginning to push their first tender green shoots through the stubborn earth.

I was relieved to find the floodwaters on Spring Marsh had dropped greatly during the night, allowing me to cross the drain without filling my boots, to where the mallard lay safely tucked among the rushes. Two carrion crows were busy beside the riverbank, reluctantly taking to the air and cawing in disapproval as I squelched across the sticky marsh to inspect their find. It was a small jack pike, undoubtedly stranded high and dry when the waters receded, but by now there were few remains except a cleaned-out backbone, a tattered leathery skin, and the hard bony structure of the skull. It was fortunate that the pair had not discovered my mallard.

Parts of the marsh remain covered with a skin of shimmering mud, where countless tracks and signs betray the presence of nocturnal visitors during the long hours of darkness. The criss-crossing prints of plover, gull, moorhen, and coot, and the broad, widely-spaced toe-prints of a heron showed where it had hunted for its breakfast in the dim early hours. There was a honeycomb of tiny holes around the remaining pools of water where snipe had been busy, probing their long stiletto beaks deep into the mud for worms and other delicacies, and here and there the neat little tracks of water voles showed along the ditch, the evicted animals already returning to inspect the damage to their flooded habitations along the steep banks.

It was apparently a good day for first sightings, for while returning home by way of West Lake I spotted a pair of shelduck resting on the gravel causeway—the first tired arrivals of perhaps a dozen pairs that spend the warmer months with us to rear their young on the warm shallow waters of the lake.

February

As today was the last of the game-shooting season, in the late morning I grasped the opportunity of taking Whisper for a final search of the hedgerows to see what we could find. There are always far too many cock pheasants left at the end of the season. Being polygamous, an ideal ratio of breeding stock is about three or four hens to every cock, but these numbers are seldom achieved and there are never enough hens to go round. An abundance of cock birds can lead to problems, the lonely and frustrated birds without a mate always spoiling for a fight and even attempting to copulate with females in late spring while they are incubating a nest of eggs, with the inevitable result of broken eggs and a string of deserted nests. It is therefore essential that their numbers are reduced as much as possible, though cock pheasants grow extremely cunning by the end of the season and are notoriously difficult to find, seldom allowing themselves to be flushed from cover for shooting.

The river had burst its banks again during the night, and while hunting out a line of bushes on a steep riverside bank, the water surged past us downstream in a swirling flood, the soupy brown liquid carrying a mass of debris washed from the water meadows and riverside copses.

There seemed to be little scent to encourage Whisper, but eventually she checked in mid-stride to point amongst an unlikely looking pile of sawn tree-trunks, a tangled heap interwoven with the remains of last summer's bracken and brambles. Preparing for a shot I encouraged her to enter in the hope of flushing something out. For several minutes she hunted back and forth around the woodpile, stopping frequently to thrust her inquisitive nose into the thickest parts, but still there was no indication of what was hiding. Even after moving some of the logs there was still no sign, and I began to suspect she had literally smelt a rat, for I uncovered a dark hole disappearing beneath the largest of the logs. Calling Whisper to follow I wandered off along the bank. After reluctantly obeying she suddenly dived back into the brambles to flush a very lively cock pheasant. Taken by surprise I swung and fired at the fleeing form, doubling it up as the old bird cunningly curled around a thicket of blackthorn scrub. Whisper soon found it lying in a clump of willow-herb stalks but without her help another old cock would have lived to fight another spring. I am really pleased with the way she is making progress, being still a young dog and having had only the very minimum of training and experience.

A successful conclusion to the morning. Whisper with our
last pheasant of the season.

FEBRUARY 2ND

As if rejoicing in the knowledge that they have survived the dangers of yet another shooting season, two cock pheasants were strutting boldly along the edge of the garden this morning, apparently completely unconcerned at my presence only a few yards away. The birds seem to possess some kind of uncanny built-in mental calendar and from now on will gradually reappear in all the old familiar haunts from which they absconded during the winter months when their presence was desired on shooting days.

Although sunny and bright the day was very windy. I was delighted to count no less than eighteen herons sheltering in a line beneath the dark alders of Marsh Wood, their identical upright postures reminding me of a parade of soldiers on guard duty, though they were probably simply resting after a hectic period of early-morning nest-building activities. Normally fond of their own company, the heron turns more gregarious as the time for nesting approaches, though squabbles are frequent during nest-building and later, at dawn and dusk, as the pairs swap over incubation duties, both male and female fulfilling their obligations in the month-long task. Most of the herons were adults, with bright yellow, dagger-like bills and a smarter overall appearance distinguishing them from the duller grey-blue plumaged juveniles—the latter standing in a close bachelor group at one end of the line and remaining at a respectable distance from their elders. The refurbishing of nests must now be well under way, for the first eggs are often laid in late February irrespective of what conditions the weather may bring, the first youngsters appearing on the scene as the trees begin to burst their buds in Marsh Wood at the beginning of April.

FEBRUARY 4TH

It was such a beautiful day that I could not resist the urge to fly Spectre, despite having a lot of work to get through before dark. At least the days are now showing some sign of lengthening. By mid-morning the sun was peeping gently through a layer of rising mist and after an hour or so there was hardly a cloud to be seen. Spectre appeared to be in one of her better moods, so I allowed her to follow me the half mile or so to the far side of Rabbit Hill, not really caring if we caught or chased anything, and totally bemused with the satisfaction of watching her soaring around in a cloudless sky, the welcome warmth of the sun on my back, and a feeling inside of complete contentment.

High above Chapel Field a female kestrel was obviously in the same frame of mind, and while I watched she soared still higher in ever-decreasing circles, spiralling round and round and getting lift from the warm air currents until she was just a faint speck in the sky, a tiny black arrowhead starkly outlined against the heavens. Below her Spectre glided overhead, finally coming to rest in a tall ash at the bottom of Rabbit Hill where it joins the marsh, scanning the rushes along the boundary ditch where we often find a moorhen. I decided to play along, not really expecting to see anything, but as soon as I started beating among the rushes a moorhen flapped out awkwardly from the far end of the tree belt, though much too far away. Spectre gained on it well from her treetop start, but despite flying hard, before she could get to grips the moorhen dropped gratefully into a tangle of dead willow-herb stems 200 yards away beside the river. Spectre followed it into the rough and by the time I reached them the pair were playing a deadly game of follow-my-leader around the bole of an alder, first one way and then the other, the moorhen somehow managing to keep Spectre at a respectable distance among the thick undergrowth and eventually emerging the winner by disappearing as if into thin air. Spectre flapped up to a branch of the alder while I searched their playground until the vegetation was almost flat. There was no trace of the elusive bird and certainly no sign of its hiding place. In the end we had to give it best, but though I did not begrudge the bird the freedom it had earned, Spectre was in an absolutely foul mood all the way home.

It was while feeding her later in the mews that I noticed a small growth on the roof of Spectre's mouth. It looks quite nasty although she shows no sign of pain or distress when gulping down her food. I rushed her off to the vet, who after a thorough examination, needs to carry out some research and to consult his partner, who is quite knowledgeable of bird complaints. I hope it is nothing sinister, for I have grown very fond of the bird. I will just have to await the outcome.

FEBRUARY 6TH

Spent the latter part of a wet and windy afternoon in Farm Wood, where there has recently been a fair number of pigeon dropping in to roost late in the day. It was still raining hard when I arrived, but I was encouraged to see a few early pigeon clatter reluctantly out of a stand of tall ash trees to wheel and circle in confusion before being swept away downwind towards the centre of the wood. I hoped they would return later.

The wood itself is an interesting little place on the eastern boundary of the farm—an undisturbed tangle of old ash and alder trees and rotten trunks felled long ago by storms, and covered with clumps of trailing ivy. Beneath the trees the ground is boggy, where thick patches of brambles provide daytime hiding places for woodcock before they venture out at dusk to forage for worms on the adjacent water meadows, and the elusive water rail skulks along the banks of a small drainage ditch carrying the overflow from the nearby lake.

I found a comparatively sheltered spot beside a small clearing just to one side of the favoured clump of ash trees, and erecting a branch or two to act as a screen, settled down as comfortably as the prevailing conditions would allow with my back propped against a wide alder trunk that offered some protection from the weather.

Eventually a few pigeons began to battle over the treetops against the heavy squall, though none showed any intention of stopping of their own accord. I was finally tempted to try a shot and was surprised to see the bird spin down from an almost impossible height, the sound of the shot carrying downwind to disturb more pigeon sheltering deep in the wood. For a few minutes a steady trickle of birds came overhead, blown like autumn leaves by the strong wind, and although it was extremely difficult shooting through the thick tracery of branches, a few shots began to connect and by the time all was quiet again I had seven birds down in the wood.

The last hour was not pleasant, with the steady drip-drip of water from the treetops and the wind beginning to penetrate my clothing. Being something of a masochist I continued to stick it out until the light had almost gone, adding an occasional pigeon to the bag until I had a good bundle, quite sufficient to carry across the rain-lashed pasture to where the truck stood waiting.

FEBRUARY 8TH

A severe wind-frost that iced over the puddles and chilled to the bone did nothing to cool the enthusiasm of the Hawaiian gander in the orchard this morning. Obviously regarding me as a potential rival for his mate, he

27

somehow managed to sneak up behind me without arousing suspicion while I was filling the food trough, grabbing my rear end with his beak and hanging on painfully with a vicelike grip until I eventually shook him off. He then proceeded to thrash his wings against my shin, the velocity of the blows bringing up red weals where his bony shoulder connected. Having emphasized ownership of the female in this enthusiastic fashion, he trotted back to where she stood, totally unimpressed by his aggressive behaviour and nonchalantly preening her feathers at the far end of the orchard, pausing now and then to pluck a tender morsel of grass. The species are normally very early nesters, though they have no chance this year as the female is far too young. At least they seem to have struck up a promising relationship, for he guards her constantly against anything intruding on their territory.

FEBRUARY 10TH

Collected an antibiotic solution from the veterinary surgeon last night, as the lump on the roof of Spectre's mouth could apparently be caused by one of many types of disorder and we are hoping that a course of the antibiotic might do the trick. I have to administer a daily dose injected into her food for a week, but if there is no improvement during this time surgical removal may be the only course of action. Unfortunately, surgery can only be carried out by putting her under a general anaesthetic, which is not without its risks, but if the growth remains there would seem to be no other alternative.

Spent a rather sleepless night pondering on the problem and worrying about the waterfowl enclosures. Heavy gales had built up through the evening and widespread damage had been forecast overnight. There are a number of tall ash trees situated around the pond enclosures, any one of which could be blown over to demolish a section of the perimeter fence. Luckily, an inspection at daybreak revealed no serious damage apart from a few small branches torn off and blown against the wire. It is fortunate that the trees are not in leaf, when the damage would have been far greater.

The strong winds continued throughout the day, and I was glad to be able to spend the afternoon inside making a start on my taxidermy work. I have rather neglected it of late and the list of work awaiting attention is certainly not getting smaller.

It was a pleasure to examine the subject in detail, a fine old case containing a red squirrel mounted originally in 1896 by Thomas Gunn of Norwich, one of the best known of all Victorian taxidermists whose work is of a consistently high standard. The case needed a thorough cleaning, and while this entails careful and rather delicate work to restore it to its original condition, I was pleased to find the mount and its surrounding vegetation had survived well, free from the depredations of moth or mite, despite the front glass being missing for some time. Much of Gunn's work remains to this day in pristine condition—a lasting tribute to his painstaking skills. I learned the trade from one of his latter-day pupils, an old character by the name of Fred Ashton, who served his apprenticeship with Gunn before eventually branching out alone to earn his living from the ancient craft he loved in a small bungalow on the outskirts of Norwich.

The task progressed according to plan and after resetting some loose vegetation and giving the animal and its surroundings a thorough cleaning, the piece looked almost as fresh as the day it was completed and, with any luck, all set for another ninety years to pass.

FEBRUARY 11TH

Rather tied up with work today, but as Spectre seemed keen I just had to take her out for exercise at midday, when a stiffish breeze had risen from the south-west. A good breeze is ideal for flying a buzzard, as she is able to take full advantage of her broad wings to get the necessary lift that allows her to soar high above me in obvious enjoyment, before closing her wings to drop like a stone to the glove as I call her back for food. She followed me for fully half a mile before I called her down, and then trailed along flying from post to post until we reached the limit of our excursion at the far side of the hill. Here we were promptly joined by a pair of blackheaded gulls, which set up such a shrieking and squawking on seeing Spectre that the noise attracted a vast flock of rooks that had been passing over at a great height. Spectre sat minding her own business on top of a telegraph pole, but very soon her peace was interrupted as the entire colony of rooks tumbled from high above her to swear and curse at one of their sworn enemies. This is the normal reaction from members of the Corvidae family, who can seldom resist the opportunity of mobbing any large bird of prey, especially in flight, and as Spectre followed me back along the road towards home, the rooks tumbled and fell in her wake, a huge column that stretched from just above the ground level to fully 500 feet. We crossed the open field towards the house, but still they followed. Despite my presence the attention of the entire flock seemed concentrated on the huge bird just in front of them, and the noise of their swearing voices was tremendous. Spectre seemed a bit bewildered by all the fuss and was forced to land on the field as if to get her bearings, totally ignoring my calls to get her back to the glove. I need not have worried, for directly I entered the garden I saw her alight safely on the house roof, waiting for me to call her down for her midday meal.

FEBRUARY 12TH

A beautiful sunny day following a sharp hoar frost, though a gentle breeze brought a chill to the air in exposed places. I watched a pair of treecreepers at the duckponds, the tiny birds busily engaged in searching out the tree-trunks for small insects and larvae that are probed from cracks and crevices in the bark with their tiny curved bills. They were moving up the trees in a series of short, mouselike hops, stopping once in a while as some dainty morsel of food was discovered encased in the bark. Once at the top of the main trunk, the little birds dropped down to the base of the next suitable tree, progressing in this fashion until all the best sites had been fully investigated. Being of a confiding nature, at one point I was able to observe one bird from only a few feet away as it scaled a wide ash trunk, the tiny bundle of feathers progressing up the gnarled bark using its stiff tail feathers as a prop against the tree. Six feet above the ground it discovered a minute spider, which it winkled out with its delicate little beak and swallowed with obvious relish. With such insignificant prey it must spend all of its waking hours in a never-ending quest for food, particularly during the cold and lean winter months when invertebrate prey is in short supply.

FEBRUARY 13TH

I spent another afternoon in Farm Wood waiting for the pigeons to come to roost. The day had started calm, with a sharp frost, but gradually the wind increased and by mid-afternoon was quite strong, which forces the pigeons to fly lower and also keeps them on the move. I was not too optimistic about the prospects of sport, but having seen several pigeons moving out of the wood in the early mornings at least it seemed worth a try, as several of the surrounding woods on adjoining farms would also be manned by roost shooters, thus helping to keep the flocks on the move.

Although there was no sign of a pigeon for quite some time, it was pleasant just to be there in the wood, tucked away among a cosy clump of fallen boughs arranged as a rough hide while the wind rattled the tops of the ash trees high above me and rays of late sunshine filtered warmly through the trees. A cock blackbird was singing at the edge of the wood, its beautiful liquid notes resounding through the trees and a great fountain of early gnats danced dizzily in a sunny clearing, having been tempted to take wing by the sudden rise in temperature.

The blackbird had finished his mellow song by the time the first pigeon appeared over the trees, closing its wings and dropping towards a sheltered clump of ivy. At the single shot it folded up and crashed through the thick canopy to the wood floor leaving a trail of feathers floating in the air.

A sudden barrage of shots announced the arrival of the first pigeons to the woods further up the valley, and a few minutes later a large bunch of about two hundred passed quickly overhead, the swish of their wings clearly audible as they searched for a quieter resting place. A few peeled away from the main bunch and set their wings to come in, but before they could alight, two of their number came crashing through the boughs above the hide, the remainder milling around in confusion before passing out of sight. This set the pattern for the rest of the afternoon, each distant volley of shooting followed a few minutes later by the arrival of more pigeons to Farm Wood, where I gradually accumulated a bird or two from each bunch that came in. The flight lasted well into the evening, by which time I had gathered almost a score of pigeons, plump of breast, sleek of feather, and well worth powder and shot.

FEBRUARY 14TH

Took my pike rod along to Wood Lake in the middle of the morning, hoping to make the best of a reasonably pleasant day. A stiff breeze rippled the water but the air was mild with an odd spit of rain from fast-moving banks of high cloud.

The lake, as its name implies, lies along the edge of Farm Wood. It is a comparatively small water, barely 250 yards long by 100 yards at its widest point, but it contains some very deep holes that are refuge for several large pike. In summer the fish can often be stalked as they lie basking in the sun below the steep banks, to glide lazily into the depths once one's presence is suspected.

A large flock of siskins were feeding at the edge of the wood, a constant twittering emanating from a stand of alder trees where the little acrobats were busily searching for seeds, the trees themselves already hung with masses of catkins that added a deep purple tint to the woods.

I worked my bait steadily along the lake, fishing a dead smelt by casting out and retrieving slowly, trying the water at all depths and at times almost brushing the bottom where I thought the pike would be. But it was all to no avail, and by the time I had covered the entire length of the lake I had caught nothing, the only indication of a fish being a very small jack pike of about 1 lb (0.5 kg) in weight that followed the bait almost to my feet. At the extreme end of the lake an arm of the river Wensum curls around through willow-lined banks, separated from the stillwater by barely 30 yards of marsh. This stretch of river is normally quiet and undisturbed. A heron rose croaking with annoyance at my intrusion, a mass of tracks imprinted in the mud showing it to be his favourite resting place.

In summer the riverbank is choked with vegetation and casting is difficult, but now it had all died down I decided to try a few casts downstream where the water runs deep, following a bend in the river, and a thick bed of phragmite reeds jut out into the water's flow. By casting out as far as possible and allowing the current to carry my bait until it was at least 80 yards downstream, I was able to draw it slowly back against the flow only a few feet from the reeds where the bottom runs deep. On the second retrieve there was a sharp bang on the line and I struck hard, the fish immediately running fast downstream stripping several feet of line from the reel. Hauling it back against the current was no easy task, but gradually I was able to work it towards me and after a few frantic runs as it saw me I was able to slip the net under a nice-looking fish, rather smaller than expected after such a hard tussle, though much of the strain was due to the stiff current. It went a shade under 7 lb (3 kg) on the scales, a beautiful bright-looking winter fish.

FEBRUARY 16TH

A very warm, spring-like day, with the clear skies remaining into the late afternoon to bring the promise of a sharp frost. While working in my study just before dusk, I counted eight wrens disappearing one by one into the disused house-martin's nest above the window, having followed one another in a little procession by hopping along the dry tendrils of the Virginia creeper that clings to the back wall of the house. An old martin's nest makes an ideal communal roosting place and this one in particular is used frequently through the colder months, the tiny bundles of life huddling together to share their mutual warmth during the long winter nights. One rough, snowy night I counted eleven tenants, the last bird appearing to have some difficulty in forcing itself through the small entrance hole, the nest so full that its occupants must have been packed like sardines in a can. The wren population suffers greatly in severe weather, but by roosting communally the birds can at least preserve a modicum of precious body heat.

I heard a vixen crossing the field at the top of the garden in the late evening, its blood-curdling screams sounding really sinister in the darkness and as usual making the hair rise on the back of my neck. Fearing for the safety of the orchard geese, I grabbed the gun and drove the truck across the field just in time to see her slinking away across the skyline, a shadowy figure that paused every few steps to look back towards me, the glint of her eyes reflecting brightly in the headlights. Unable to follow across the field of young corn, I watched her out of sight, hopefully discouraged from any idea she may have had of disturbing the orchard geese.

FEBRUARY 18TH

A severe overnight frost left a thick coating of ice on the puddles and glassed over a large area of the nearby lake, but as so often follows, the sun came up to give another really beautiful day, though it remained cold. The waterfowl were hungry at the ponds, their appetites heightened by cold weather and some, notably the hooded mergansers, practically took bread from my fingers as I floated it on the surface of the water. I tend to over-feed the birds slightly during cold spells to keep them in good condition in preparation for the coming months, when the breeding cycle commences with the increased hours of daylight. As the days already show some sign of lengthening, it will not be many weeks now before their instincts turn to reproduction.

As there was scarcely a ripple on the water, I searched part of the river adjacent to the ponds where there are often good chub to be found, though more so during the hot summer months when they spend most of the day beneath the shade of a stand of overhanging ash trees. There was little movement to be seen today apart from a couple of fish of about 1½ lb (0.7 kg) in weight, but at times there are far larger fish gliding lazily around the trailing patches of weed. I must spend an hour or two trying to catch one of these specimen fish. I have taken the odd chub on a pike spinner during the winter months, and a couple of seasons ago landed one of just over 3 lb (1.4 kg) on a very large spoon bait while working out some of the deeper areas for pike. I thought at first I was into a small jack pike, but when the fish allowed me to retrieve it to the shallower water, it rolled on the surface and then shot away downstream, showing itself to be a good strong chub. It gave a very good account of itself before I was able to draw it over the landing-net, a really bright-looking fish, scale perfect, and in the absolute peak of condition.

FEBRUARY 20TH

Early this morning I spotted what looked like a promising flight of pigeons moving across the far end of a barley drill that joins the garden and, as they were still passing along the edge of Bluebell Copse when I had completed most of my chores, I decided to try to get a few for the freezer. The wind was gusting hard from the south towards their roosting woods, and while the birds moved to feed on a field of young rape over the boundary, they appeared to be creating a strong flightline that passed between the copse and a large ash tree 30 yards along the hedge.

After collecting the gun and a bag of cartridges, I made my way to a point midway between the two and hurriedly erected a temporary hide from a couple of fallen branches interwoven with armfuls of dead grass. I was not kept waiting long. Within a matter of minutes the first birds began passing over, at a good height, and it took no less than eleven shots to put the first half a dozen in the bag. The field to my front was almost bare, so I set up the six birds with their heads propped on short sticks to act as decoys, their light-blue plumage standing out prominently against the bare earth. This had the desired effect, for although few birds actually came fully into the decoys, the majority dropped lower for a closer inspection and improved my chances of getting on terms. For a while shooting was fast and furious, with a steady stream of pigeon arriving in front of the hide from the valley fir woods, and a fair amount rocketing over from behind, the latter pushed by a following wind and offering only split-second chances as they whizzed over and were gone. Each time there was a lull in the proceedings, I added the shot birds to the decoy pattern, thus enticing a greater proportion of incoming pigeon to drop down and join them. For the next couple of hours there was a steady trickle from the woods. I was provided with some good shooting, taking one or two from each bunch that arrived as they battled against the wind, but gradually the flight seemed to slacken and very soon there was only an occasional bird to be seen. As I still had a number of tasks to be completed before dark and the pigeons stili had to be humped across almost half a mile of sticky ground, I decided to call it a day. The pick-up was completed within minutes, for despite a few long-range shots dropping birds deep in the copse, the undergrowth beneath the trees is thin in winter and they were easily found. I collected almost forty before beginning the long trudge home.

FEBRUARY 21ST

I put in a good afternoon's work at the duckponds, cutting up, clearing, and burning some of the boughs and branches left after the ravages of the winter gales. The constant rough winds have caused havoc among the trees, uproot-ing some of the taller specimens and snapping off branches in exposed areas, and there is a great deal of work to be carried out if all is to be tidied up by the spring, when major disturbance must be avoided for fear of upsetting the fowl during the critical nesting period. I got a good fire going and then set to work repairing some of the wooden nestboxes situated around the water. The boxes are about 15 inches square, with lift-off lids and a short tunnel concealing each entrance hole. The tunnels help to discourage winged vermin from entering, especially when garnished with a few small conifer sprigs fixed to overhang the entrance. I lined the boxes with a couple of inches of loose soil covered with straw to enable the ducks to hollow out a comfortable dish-like depression in which to lay their eggs. Besides the boxes, I use long, pear-shaped wicker baskets that have a small entrance hole at the narrow end, and these were relined with a handful of straw to encourage use. A large variety of nest sites are needed, and I must also dig a series of deep tunnels in the steep bank sloping up from the water, thus attempting to cater for the varied needs of each species in the collection, for few can be induced to breed unless conditions are exactly to their liking.

While I was busily working away, I heard the sudden harsh chattering of a pair of magpies from the tree belt adjoining the ponds, the excited tone of their voices telling me they had discovered something of great interest. Luckily the gun was close to hand, and concealing myself behind a small holly clump, I gave a few tentative squeaks with my lips pursed in the hope of attracting the birds and ridding the area of a pair of fervent nest-robbers. This deception usually arouses sufficient curiosity to warrant closer inspection and, sure enough, with a renewal of excited muttering the birds approached along the belt of trees, the first coming boldly towards me but its mate, as yet not fully convinced, alighting in a thick hawthorn bush 30 yards away from where it gave vent to a stream of high-pitched chatter. I dropped the flying bird with a snapshot as it veered off through the trees, the second just managing to sneak away behind the thorns before I could fire the second barrel. It will be some time before it falls for that particular trick again. The magpie was in good condition for mounting, and after picking it up I went to see what all the fuss had been about. Sure enough, a quick search of the bank below the trees revealed a partly eaten hedgehog, a fair proportion of its skin and bones already picked clean by the pair of pied scavengers. Presumably the animal had ventured out after being awakened from its winter sleep by the recent high temperatures, but with little or no food on offer to maintain its reserves of fat, it was almost certain to perish.

FEBRUARY 23RD

No rain for almost a week now—quite an event in itself during such a monotonously wet winter. With the help of the sun and wind, the land has now dried out sufficiently to enable the plough to be put to use. My cousin, John, was busy on one of the outlying fallows as I walked across to feed the ducks. He was travelling steadily back and forth along the shining furrow followed by a living snowstorm of black-headed gulls searching the freshly

Sparrowhawk kill at the duckponds—a female blackbird partially eaten.

turned soil for earthworms and grubs disturbed by the plough—rich pickings after a winter spent scavenging a meagre living from the local rubbish tips. As they circled, hovered, and dived in its wake, each vying with the other for the most succulent morsels, their high-pitched shrieking was distinctly audible above the heavy roar of the tractor.

I found a sparrowhawk kill on a rotten elm stump at the edge of the ponds —a female blackbird with its breast picked almost clean of flesh. My eye was attracted to the spot as the breeze ruffled a little patch of dark-brown feathers surrounding the remains, and as the body was still limp and warm I suspected the assassin would not be far away. This proved to be the case, for returning home by way of Rabbit Hill, I suddenly surprised a large female from a line of blackthorn scrub, where she had been secretly awaiting my departure before returning to finish her meal. The little hawk made off like an arrow across the open ground, her stubby rounded wingtips almost brushing the surface of the pasture until she reached the bottom of Rabbit Hill to gain sanctuary among the thick bushes. Not so many years ago the very sight of a sparrowhawk was something of a novelty, but now sightings are almost daily, if not prolonged— the little striped bandit with a bold yellow eye much preferring the pleasure of

35

its own company. I have often toyed with the idea of training one of these plucky little hawks, for its skill of flight and obvious courage would make it an ideal candidate for a hunting companion.

FEBRUARY 25TH

More by way of an experiment than with any serious expectations of catching a fish, I took my fly rod to the river for an airing and to see if I could provoke a reaction from the chub that lie beneath the row of ash trees. I have never flyfished for winter chub before, indeed, my total experience of the sport has been limited to half a season, but since landing my very first trout on the light fly rod last summer I have become addicted to this fascinating sport. I thought a little casting practice would not come amiss as the trout season starts at the beginning of next month.

I tied a white 'dog-nobbler' to the leader on a sinking line, a large fluffy lure made from turkey marabou feathers. When dry it resembles almost nothing except a bunch of turkey feathers, but in the water it assumes the lifelike actions and sinuous movements of a small fish fry. Chub are quite fond of taking fry, so I hoped it might do the trick.

It was good to feel the action of the rod in my hand again after the winter break, the line swishing back and forth until the required length was payed out in the air and then released to deposit the lure on the water at the far end of the swim. Allowing a few moments for it to sink, I worked it carefully back against the current by a series of jerky movements to give life to the lure, but several casts later I had still aroused no response from the fish, my only 'catch' being one of the lower branches of the nearest ash tree. Following a careful retrieve so as not to alarm the fish, I changed the lure repeatedly, trying the merits of all manner of colours and patterns and covering the entire swim thoroughly but still there was no interest from the steely water. Dog-nobblers, missionaries, polystickles, and damsel-fly larvae, each followed the other with renewed hope of success. Each cast was rewarded by the same frustrating result—absolutely nothing. Now and then the herons scolded from the depths of Marsh Wood, a suitably derisory comment on the feeble efforts that hardly matched their inborn fishing skills. For over an hour I flogged away, my fingers gradually losing all sense of feeling from handling the wet line each time the cast was retrieved. Very soon I had had enough, deciding to return another day to try to outwit the fish by more conventional methods.

As I was preparing to leave I spotted a slight movement beside a raft of floating weed in the mouth of the drainage channel beside me—a thin grey bar that materialized into a small jack pike, its pectoral fins fanning gently to hold position in the current. I tied a large polystickle to the leader and cast it carefully six feet past where the pike lay, waiting for it to sink almost to the bottom before twitching it back across its line of vision in the clear water. The polystickle resembles a small fish quite accurately, and although the first cast aroused no visible response, on the second attempt I thought I sensed something of a sideways glance as the lure twitched tantalizingly past, only a couple of inches from the long, tapered snout. It proved to be third time lucky, for this time my cast fell short and dropped almost beside the pike, which snapped it up immediately with a quick sideways dart as I began a hasty retrieve. It gave a good scrap on the light tackle, splashing back and forth among the shallows and stirring the mud from the bottom before I could draw it close enough to use the net. It seemed to fix me with its cold, glassy stare as I released it back to the freedom of the steely waters.

FEBRUARY 27TH

Winter seems to have returned again, with half an inch of snow falling overnight, and a chilling wind that brought dark grey banks of cloud rolling up from the north throughout the day from time to time adding their contribution to the white carpet already on the ground.

I took Spectre to the vet for an operation to remove the unsightly growth in her mouth, as the dose of antibiotic appears to have had no real effect. After an injection of general anaesthetic she was soon wobbling around sleepily on the glove, and finally collapsed in my arms before being taken into the surgery. The vet managed to remove the growth cleanly following some delicate work with the scalpel, and I was able to bring her home wrapped in my jacket in a comatose state, having decided to keep her in the warmth of the sitting room until the effect of the anaesthetic has completely worn off. Spectre took a while to regain her senses, wobbling around as if in a drunken stupor and falling over each time she tried to move. Just before I retired to bed she suddenly roused her feathers, stood up firmly on her stone block, and screamed to be fed, looking around at her unfamiliar surroundings as if wondering what all the fuss had been about. I can only hope she continues to make such good progress.

Alexanders.

37

March

MARCH 1ST

If there is any truth in the old proverb, 'When March comes in like a lion, it will go out like a lamb', the weather must surely improve by the end of the month, for the lion was certainly roaring in full fury when I awoke early this morning. A terrible gale was lashing sheets of hail and snow against the bedroom window, giving a timely reminder that winter has not yet passed and that all of nature is getting out of hand—the trees, plants, and other wildlife having been deceived into premature action by the early spell of unseasonably warm weather. While I lay in bed wondering just how I could avoid getting out, I could hardly believe my ears when a song thrush began pouring out his chirpy song from the top of a garden conifer, a particularly masochistic individual that greets the dawn from the same spot each morning—come sun, rain, high winds, sleet—and apparently snow!

I had nurtured hopes of putting in an hour or two at the Valley Lakes to see in the first day of the new trout season, but less suitable weather for a flyfishing session would be difficult to imagine, with banks of slushy sleet and snow pushed in continual waves by a blistering gale.

The garden bluetits were busy on the lump of fat suspended outside the kitchen window, gusts of wind at times threatening to loosen their grip, but although being spun in dizzy spirals as the lump of fat revolved on its string, the tiny acrobats clung on defiantly, eager to gorge themselves on their only source of available food.

As I drove to work through whitened fields, a black mass of rooks were digging for corn on a newly sown drilling, relentlessly shoving their heavy beaks deep into the soft, snow-covered earth and appearing starkly outlined against the huge white expanse. In marked contrast, a wedge of five mute swans battled bravely up the valley directly into the teeth of the gale, seeming almost at a standstill and shining pure white against the blackness of snow-clouds again building in the northern sky.

All thoughts of a flyfishing expedition were obviously soon dispelled. Instead, in anticipation of better days to come, I went to Norwich in the late afternoon to set myself up with the equipment needed for tying trout flies. Following a visit to my friend John's fishing-tackle shop, I returned home laden with all manner of weird and wonderful instruments and materials on which to practise my skills, together with a book designed to set one on the right path towards becoming proficient in this fascinating craft. At least it will be a comfortable and interesting way of spending the remainder of the long, cold winter evenings, with visions of calmer summer days ahead and the anticipated electrifying jolt of a taking trout.

MARCH 3RD

Spectre's mouth seems to have almost healed and, as she appears to have recovered from the effects of her recent operation, I took her out for flying exercise during a brief spell of afternoon sunshine. Despite a rapid thaw much snow still remains in the areas shaded from the sun. She seemed fascinated by the patches of stark whiteness, landing repeatedly in them as I tried to get her flying, and appearing somewhat mystified by the sensation of the cold feel of snow on her feet. She eventually tried to bathe in the stuff, erecting her body feathers while lowering herself to the ground, and shuffling her legs in a vain attempt to wet her plumage. It made me shiver just to watch her.

I carried on walking and by the time I reached the bottom of Rabbit Hill, Spectre had tired of her attempted ablutions and had flown to the top of a telegraph pole, spreading her broad wings as if to dry while she had a good look around, obviously enjoying her regained freedom. A cock blackbird was scratching for food among a pile of dead leaves in a nearby hedge bottom, but its search was rudely interrupted as Spectre swooped from the post and glided towards it—at the last moment diving deep into the bushes with talons outstretched with thoughts of a blackbird supper. She missed, and the blackbird scuttled out of the far side in alarm, and stood scolding her from the depths of a blackthorn bush, its tail flicking in annoyance as it directed a string of obscenities towards her. Spectre was unperturbed, returning to her lookout post and fluffing up her feathers to make the most of the afternoon sun, glad of the chance of being at last in the fresh air after her recent period of convalescence in the mews.

MARCH 5TH

Set up the fly-tying equipment in my study, for I am planning to visit the Valley trout lakes over the weekend and would like to start the season by attempting to catch a fish on a fly of my own tying. I decided to make up a batch of dog-nobblers, the main material of which is dyed turkey feathers. The nobbler is not a true imitation fly, but a lure commonly used at this time of the year when there are as yet few natural flies for the trout to feed upon, the fish themselves remaining well down in the water. The lures are normally weighted and fished on a sinking line, which is allowed to descend almost to the bottom of the water, and although sometimes frowned upon by the purist flyfisher, they are a good choice for the novice to use, besides being a relatively easy pattern for tying. I clamped a long shanked hook into the vice and selected the materials—turkey marabou feathers, chenille, and tinsel— and, by following step-by-step instructions in the manual, the 'fly' gradually began to take shape, though at times an extra pair of hands would have been something of an advantage. Ten minutes later, the first specimen emerged from the vice, neatly tied and looking reasonably convincing, although its resemblance to the finished article in the book left something to the imagination. I appeared to have invented a new pattern. No matter, for under certain conditions trout will snap at almost anything, whether or not it bears a resemblance to any living form. I pressed on regardless, completing an hour-long session with half-a-dozen lures of varying standard and colour—yellow, white, blue, and black, the latter with a pinch of green tied in below the tail, in some ways resembling a type that brought success in the murky waters at the back-end of last season.

I can hardly wait to try them out, and come hell or high water, I intend to christen them sometime over the coming weekend, though the weather forecast of snow and high winds leaves much to be desired.

A selection of dog-nobblers.

MARCH 6TH

Despite almost an inch of snow and several degrees of frost, I made my way along treacherously icy roads to the Valley Lakes, on the way collecting my partner, Ray, with whom I have shared many an adventure with rod and gun. It was cold—bitterly cold—with a stiff westerly breeze that had an edge like a knife, but as the sun was shining and we were both brimming with enthusiasm on the first trip of the year it hardly seemed to matter.

On arrival, Ray elected to try the furthest of the three lakes, which is stocked with large fish, leaving me to try a favourite corner of the nearest water, Home Lake, where I have previously contrived to take a fish or two on most of my visits last season. The lake is of a few acres and roughly rectangular, just over 200 yards long and flanked on its western edge by a copse of scrub alders, although rather open and exposed along the opposite

40

boundary. The wind was cutting down the valley, creating high waves that lapped against the downwind bank and on which a small party of tufted ducks bobbed wearily, the bright black-and-white drakes shining conspicuously against their soberly dressed partners.

I tied one of my nobblers to the leader and cast it well out: a bright-yellow version with a long streamer-tail that wriggled tantalizingly through the water with an action that looked most attractive. But it failed to attract the fish, for half an hour later I was still flogging the water without so much as a tentative pull to reward my efforts. Now that the initial enthusiasm had worn off, the wind began to penetrate my clothing, my fingers already so numb that it was difficult to handle the line. I searched for a more sheltered spot, noting that the waves were far less pronounced at the top end of the lake, where a casting platform was installed under the protection of a steep earth bank. This was far more comfortable, though the tall bank restricted the backward sweep of the line and reduced the distance of casting. Yet again there was no response from the fish, although an occasional roll on the surface was evidence enough of their existence in the swim. All the time I had been fishing deep to where the trout apparently congregate in such cold conditions, but even repeated changes of fly did nothing to stimulate enthusiasm, apart from an occasional bump on the line as I made contact with a patch of dead weed on the bottom. A heavy splash a few yards in front prompted me to change tactics, trying a few retrieves with the fly skimming just below the surface. This did the trick. On the third cast there was that sudden, long-awaited thump on the line, and I was into a fish, the pull on the rod immediately dispelling all thoughts of the cold as the line raced away into the depths. Following the initial run I was able to draw the fish gradually towards the bank, but on seeing the landing net waiting, it shot off along the bank with renewed vigour, ending its run by burrowing deep among a bed of phragmite reeds. Allowing a fish to get among weeds is the surest way of losing it, but I kept the pressure on and gently teased it out. Moments later, I landed a beautiful silver trout of just under 2½ lb (1 kg), the first ever taken on a homemade fly. I found the catch particularly satisfying.

A few casts later, this was followed by a second, a slightly larger and much darker fish that glowed deep bronze along its flanks, which were suffused with a subtle shade of pink that appeared to have been added by a single bold brushstroke in a line from gill to tail.

Ray returned along the bank soon after, having also taken two fish before the cold began to penetrate: one a large hen that tipped the scales at 5¾ lb (2.6 kg), an ideal fish for smoking. We were both well content with a brace apiece on our first outing, my day being all the more rewarding for catching the fish on flies of my own tying.

MARCH 9TH

How fickle our weather can be. A few days ago the wind was carrying bitter flurries of sleet and snow, but today a gentle breeze brought beautiful spring-

The female hooded mergansers were beginning to take an interest in
the boldly marked drakes as they displayed.

like weather, with a multitude of larks trilling in the heavens and the first
peacock butterflies tempted out of winter hibernation by the balmy air. The
first pike are running up the marsh drains in readiness for spawning, and
pairs of mallard skulk among the withered vegetation, some even now having
laid their first eggs.

As I made my way across the field of winter barley to the duckponds with
the sun warm on my back, I could hear the quaint frog-like vibrations of the
hooded merganser drakes as they displayed, their alluring notes carried some
distance on the still morning air. The two drakes were obviously attempting to
surpass each other in volume, and as they reared up on the water in unison
with crests erected, the females began to gather round and take an interest,
one even lying flat on the water in readiness for mating, but eventually moving
off as the drakes continued to show a preference for their own company. I
suppose they will learn! At the far end of the pond, a Barrow's goldeneye was
performing his rather comical bouncing ritual to a responding female,
although I have grave doubts regarding his sexual prowess—in previous
years I have frequently observed him attempting to mount a willing female
from the wrong way round. I suspect this has a bearing on their complete lack

of success as a breeding pair to date. Its close relative, the European golden-eye, was going through a similar routine, an involved display of head-throwing, leg-kicking, and wing-stretching, the entire performance taking anything up to fifteen minutes to complete before any actual physical contact takes place, and following a very precise and exacting procedure. Not so with my old pintail drake, who has little regard for such niceties towards victims of his promiscuous activities. He merely pursues, catches, and rapes anything even remotely female, be it shoveler drake, a half-submerged log of wood or—rather less frequently—his actual mate, who normally spends half the morning waddling seductively up and down the enclosure awaiting his advances, and quacking vociferously in sex-starved tones in the rather forlorn hope of attracting his indiscriminate attentions.

MARCH 11TH

The snowy owls are at last definitely beginning to show an interest in one another, for early this morning I observed them sitting side by side on a perch in the far corner of their aviary, apparently gazing with rapt attention into one another's eyes, the male cooing softly while gently bowing up and down and flicking his tail in his most alluring manner. Later in the day I kept watch from my study window just after feeding, when the female was prancing up an down in a kind of outrageous war dance, tearing great divots of earth from the aviary floor with her beak and talons, and pursuing the male around the enclosure as he carried a dead chick in his beak with which to tempt her. These are definitely steps in the right direction, for although the nesting season is still a matter of weeks hence, the female will not generally allow her mate within six feet, seeming to regard him as well beneath her dignity and arching her wings and hissing threateningly if he dares to approach too closely.

Encouraged by their actions, I gave their nesting-boxes a thorough spring cleaning, replacing the lining of earth in the bottom and adding an armful of pine needles and moss raked up from beneath a clump of Scots pines that shelters their enclosure. My handiwork was given a thorough inspection a few minutes after I left, the female peering intently into each box for several minutes, although glancing around suspiciously in case I should be watching.

MARCH 13TH

Gave Spectre some light exercise at midday, as she has seemed off-colour of late, despite the apparent full recovery from her operation. She seems to lack much of the fire and enthusiasm she possessed only a few weeks ago, and no longer seems to revel in the joys of flight. When spending a great deal of time with a bird in its training, flying, and hunting, a deep rapport develops between man and bird and it is usually easy to sense that something is amiss, no matter how trivial. Today I had an ominous feeling that all was not well.

As if to prove me wrong, Spectre suddenly took it into her head to clear off on her own, gliding down from the house roof where she had been waiting and, totally ignoring my calling, followed the path of the road until she reached the hedge that runs at right angles towards West Lake. She banked sharply around the corner and was lost from sight. Moments later, a small flock of blackheaded gulls took wing from the adjoining field, wheeling and diving in disarray and protesting loudly at being disturbed. The cause of the trouble was not difficult to find: by the time I reached the corner, Spectre was crouching on the ground, wings mantled widely over a ragged white object she held in her talons. Somehow she had contrived to take one of the gulls. It was already still by the time I reached her side, and she covered it with spread wings and glared at me with a look that defied me to try to take away her prize. I eventually separated the two, substituting her kill for her normal meal of chicks. It had been a relatively short flight and I was surprised to find her panting with exertion.

Despite the successful flight, I took Spectre to the vet later in the afternoon. He was pleased with the way the operation has healed, but feared the growth may have been a visible indication of something far more sinister, possibly avian tuberculosis. If this is the case, the writing is already on the wall, for there is little or nothing that can be done to overcome such a serious condition. I will get a sample of her mutes sent off for analysis, but it remains to be seen whether anything can be done.

An unexpected capture. Spectre mantled possessively over the gull.

MARCH 16TH

Spectre appears to have taken a downhill turn over the past couple of days, for despite feeding well, she is nothing like her old self and I suspect my worst fears may have been realized. I have sent mute samples for analysis, and although it may not prove to be of any use, it may at least confirm what is causing the trouble.

I took her on my fist for a stroll around West Lake, stopping *en route* at the ponds to feed the ducks. The female red-crested pochard was hanging around rather sheepishly near one of the nesting baskets, eyeing me with suspicion as I did my rounds with the feed bucket. She is usually the first bird to lay eggs and, sure enough, when I risked a quick peep under the lid while she was away feeding, I found a single egg in a scraped depression, partly covered by a few beakfuls of straw. Another busy season has started and from now on much of my spare time will be occupied in the breeding, hatching, and rearing of this year's fowl.

We continued on our journey to the lake, Spectre content to remain on the glove instead of flying off ahead of me as is her usual habit. Four goldeneye took wing as we reached the edge of the water, two ducks and two drakes in immaculate full colour, moving swiftly towards the river closely followed by a flight of seven cormorants that beat past in a ragged line, most displaying the prominent white throat-patch denoting adult birds. Through the binoculars I counted a further fourteen congregated on the centre of the gravel causeway that crosses West Lake, several standing with wings outstretched to dry after fishing, their identical poses reminding me of a row of animated church lecterns as they viewed our approach with suspicion. The shelduck have again turned up in numbers for their summer stay, and while bobbing about in well-spaced pairs, the quarrelsome males chased off any other bird that strayed too close to their spouses, the drakes themselves displaying the prominent red knob on the top of the bill that is typical of breeding condition.

Signs of the first flush of spring are all around. The countryside is alive with joyous birdsong. The trees are beginning to burst their buds, bringing the first hint of colour to the hedgerows and woods, and the first daffodils of spring are nodding their heads in the breeze around the boles of the apple trees in the orchard. Spring is my favourite time of the year.

As we turned for home the first gulls were beginning to glide back to the roosting sands on tired wings, having an hour or so of daylight still remaining in which to carry out their ablutions before settling for the night.

MARCH 18TH

An early-morning shower of sleet had turned to a heavy drizzle when I set out from home just after eight o'clock, and I began to wonder if I had made the right decision to attempt a flyfishing session in such appalling conditions. Luckily, the sky had brightened a little by the time I arrived at the Valley Lakes, and I opted to try Rainbow Lake—a large water containing good trout from about 3 lb (1.4 kg) in weight. The lake is the furthest from the fishing hut but I was encouraged on my way by an odd fish or two that broke the grey rippled surface of the water.

Rainbow Lake has a small grassy island almost in its centre, where a pair of mute swans have already taken up residence, the large cob proudly standing guard over the future nesting site while his lady dibbled for weed in the adjoining shallows. A small bunch of coot bickered noisily amongst themselves close by, the more argumentative among them rushing around with heads lowered, displacing rivals with a sudden splashing charge across the water. They moved away across the lake as I began fishing on a narrow peninsula that juts out towards the island, trying a white nobbler from my own vice fished well down in the deepest water, until a heavy swirl on the surface just in front inspired me to try the top, dropping the fly well past the rise and working it back through the widening ripples in a series of short jerks. There was a sudden bang on the line and, as I tightened to the take, the trout took a gigantic leap completely clear of the water. It looked a powerful fish, a fact

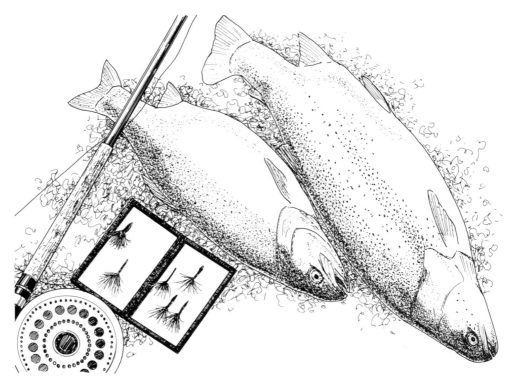

Before the rains came. A superb brace of rainbow trout on the bank.

confirmed a few moments later by the heavy pull on the rod as it surged away. I gave it as much line as it wanted on the initial run, and it raced away boring deep and making the line sing as it cut great arcs back and forth across the water. The fish was a long time weakening, playing about in the deep water for several minutes before I was able to steer it towards the bank. It took even longer to get near the net, for several times—even though I thought I had at last gained the upper hand—it surged away yet again to continue the struggle. My arm was aching by the time I eventually got the fish on its side, and gratefully slid it over the net: a superb fish of wide girth that pulled down the balance to 7¼ lb (3.3 kg).

It seemed almost pointless to continue fishing, for anything else caught could only prove something of an anti-climax after such a fierce and rewarding tussle. Nevertheless, I worked my way along the bank until I reached a sheltered corner at the extreme tip of the lake where the water was protected from the wind by a thick copse on its upwind side. My first cast with the white nobbler produced a savage take, the fish hooking itself before I could strike, and streaking away tearing line through my fingers, its frantic run culminating in a massive head-shaking leap from the water as it tried to throw the hook. Luckily it was firmly hooked and another long battle ensued, the trout full of fight and tearing away with a new burst of energy each time I drew it near the net. It finally allowed me to lift it clear of the water—a fine companion for the first fish and just 1 lb (0.5 kg) lighter in weight.

The rain came on again and the cold wind increased, although after landing a brace like that I really couldn't have cared if it had rained for the rest of the day. As a matter of fact, it did!

MARCH 20TH

Watched eleven wild Bewick's swans passing along the valley early this morning in a straggling V formation, their bugling cries ringing loudly on the still air as they said a last farewell to their winter quarters. The travellers were moving at a great height along the spring migration route, once again leaving British shores for the vast, barren tundra regions of northern Russia and Siberia where they will spend the summer rearing a brood of youngsters. They will return late in the year when their northern home is again in the terrible clutches of an arctic winter. My companion, Ken, also heard the voices of wild swans in the early morning a couple of days ago, and straining his eyes skywards could just make out a large flock of almost fifty travelling north, the beckoning of their distant lands compelling them to make the journey along the time-worn path used by generations before them. In March there is a mass exodus of many birds towards the north, and I have recently observed travelling flocks of fieldfares passing over with their smaller cousins, the redwings, setting out on the relatively short journey to Scandinavia until another autumn gale brings them back. To breach the gap, many birds from southern climes will soon be here, and it will not be long before the woods and copses echo to the songs of willow and wood warbler, the unmistakable notes of the chiffchaff, and the unsurpassable mellow song of the nightingale on warm summer evenings. The marsh reedbeds will come alive with the incessant grating churr of uncountable reed warblers as they skulk among the swaying stems with their tiny relation, the sedge warbler, who together make the long and perilous journey from the heat of Africa to turn up exhausted on British shores. Cuckoos, turtledoves, the swallow tribe, and many others, soon will arrive again in their old haunts to nest and rear their young, until once again called south as the days begin to shorten.

There was a new arrival at West Lake—an exquisitely dressed oyster-catcher that has moved inland from its coastal wintering ground. I heard its loud 'peep-peep' long before spotting the bird circling at the far end of the lake in typical stiff-winged flight, its bold black-and-white plumage flashing conspicuously in the bright morning sun. It alighted delicately on the central causeway, its brilliant orange beak and pink legs highly visible even at 100 yards. It was in an excitable mood, running up and down and calling loudly. I watched its antics for several minutes, but there was no sign of its mate.

MARCH 22ND

Watched a pair of wild Egyptian geese practising their courting routine near Spring Marsh, cackling hoarsely to one another while the gander pranced around his mate with wings hunched aggressively, showing off his strength and flaunting the fineness of his feathers. The geese are feral descendants of birds kept in waterfowl collections many years ago, and have colonized the area and increased their numbers dramatically, joining ranks in the winter to form flocks of up to fifty individuals, though at this time of year they are split into breeding pairs that take up residence on islands and in hollow trees to hatch and to rear their young.

The pair were displaying beneath an old gnarled oak where they have nested for many years, the nest site itself being a rather uncomfortable scrape where the first boughs at the top of the trunk spread outward to form a dish-like depression barely sufficient to conceal the bird on her best. But the union is usually successful and within hours of hatching the little pied bundles of fluff are encouraged by the anxious parents to drop several feet to the earth below before being gathered together to form a noisy little procession that quickly makes its way to the comparative safety of the river.

Despite the fact that there were as yet no eggs in the nest, some pairs breed very early in the year. In fact, I have often seen youngsters swimming on West Lake by the middle of March. The geese obviously have an extended breeding season.

48

MARCH 23RD

Crept quietly around Rabbit Hill with the gun in the late evening, making my way carefully towards an open area of short grass surrounded by thick bramble bushes, with hopes of getting the main ingredient for a fresh rabbit stew. Several new burrows have been scraped in the sandy earth and directly the days show signs of lengthening, a few rabbits often venture out to feed as the light begins to fail.

It was a mild evening, heavily overcast and with a hint of drizzle. An early pipistrelle bat hawked for insects above the crest of the hill, wheeling and dipping in skilful flight as it conducted a great slaughter among fountains of dancing gnats, and a jay screeched noisily from a prominent oak, warning all and sundry of my stealthy approach. Luckily, the rabbits had not heeded its warning, for I spotted two as I peered through the bushes, one standing bolt upright scanning its surroundings while its companion apparently dug for bluebell bulbs in the sandy earth. Sensing my presence, the lookout stamped his foot on the ground and they scampered back to their burrow, although I rolled over the slower of the two as it lingered on the margin of the brambles—a nice clean rabbit and luckily free from myxomatosis.

Having removed the paunch, I washed my hands in the nearby marsh drain, my presence greeted by a chorus of croaking toads busily engaged in their springtime breeding activities, each spawn-bloated female weighed down by a mass of clinging males all competing to pass on their own particular genes to the following generation. I always feel a certain sympathy for the hounded females, always heavily outnumbered and almost squeezed to death by the tenacious grip of their suitors. One solid croaking mass had grown almost to the size of a small football, a disjointed accumulation of heads, legs, and feet all bound together in a heaving tangle of desire. A large amount of spawn has already been deposited along the slower-flowing drains, primarily the solid, jelly-like mass produced by frogs, although a few long strings woven around the underwater reeds showed that the toads have also made a start. I left them to continue their orgy in private.

MARCH 25TH

Having been busy over the last few days organizing a new rearing system for the waterfowl, I convinced myself that I had earned the chance to slip away for a few hours to the Valley Lakes. It seems to have become a habit.

Rainbow Lake was very quiet, with no fish activity showing on the surface, although the trout had been rising earlier in the morning and I noticed a few nondescript flies skimming across the water. The female swan was beginning to get her nest together at one end of the island, shuffling a scrape in the hard earth and pulling grass around her to build up a thick nest, adjusting each beakful carefully until it was exactly to her liking. Above her a mallard drake pursued his mate in an aerial courtship chase, and in the boundary copse a sparrowhawk slipped unobtrusively through the leafless alders, causing a few moments of panic and confusion among the resident blackbirds.

I tried the top corner out of the stiffening wind. The water was strangely clear even after the recent heavy rains, and toads croaked their love songs deep among the reedy margins, already heavily garnished with patches of newlaid spawn. It will soon be time for tying lures to imitate the tadpoles, for trout apparently take many of the creatures as they begin to venture into the open water from the comparative safety of the reedy shallows.

I had worked the water for some time with a blue nobbler before there was any suggestion of an offer, but when it came the take was fast and furious, the trout immediately leaping well clear of the water and shaking its head like a terrier with a rat as it tried to discard the fly. It was a very fit fish, which at one time tore all the spare line through my fingers and made the reel scream as it stripped off several yards of backing and took off towards the centre of the lake. Each time I tried to slow its progress, the resistance resulted in another splashing leap, but the rushing around finally took its toll and I brought it over the net totally exhausted—one of the finest rainbows I have seen, with beautiful colouring and immaculate tail and fins. It was exactly 4 lb (1.8 kg).

It proved to be my only fish of the day, for though I tried several other areas where the strengthening wind made casting hazardous, there was not so much as the merest twitch of the fly, and I saw no other fish caught despite the concerted efforts of half a dozen other anglers. By the time I had prepared to leave, angry clouds were building on the southern horizon and twice I heard the distant rumble of thunder preceded by a searing flash across the darkened sky.

My catch was rather too large to be eaten at one meal, so I decided to leave it at the fishing hut to be cured by smoking. I have yet to taste smoked trout and it will be interesting to see if it lives up to its delicious reputation.

MARCH 27TH

A bright and warm afternoon, for the sun is gaining real strength as the weeks of spring unfold. Recovering from the effects of a belated birthday party that lasted well into the early hours, I was content to take a leisurely stroll around Rabbit Hill, drinking in the warmth of the sun and observing the little hints and signs of an awakening year.

Wild primroses are in full flower along the sheltered banks, thrusting their exquisite yellow heads through the dead vegetation and, as I parted the brittle bracken fronds covering a large clump beneath a stand of dead elms, their delicate perfume filled the air, the scent so evocative of early childhood days and reeking fragrantly with nostalgia of many springtimes past. Almost overshadowing the colour of the primroses, a male brimstone butterfly fluttered daintily past, a flash of vivid yellow that paused briefly on a moss-covered log with wings outstretched to absorb the power of the sun. It is always one of the first butterfly species to put in an appearance and one of the most beautiful.

A dog fox has excavated the old earth deep among the bramble patch as an emergency retreat for his vixen and cubs. A pair of foxes normally has several such holes on their territory, spring cleaned and reused each year when moving their cubs from one hole to another if danger threatens the nursery in use, the animals ferrying the young in their mouths to a new home during the hours of darkness.

A sudden raucous chatter betrayed the presence of a pair of unwelcome visitors in Bluebell Wood. Magpies wreak havoc among nesting birds, being equally fond of both eggs and nestlings, and a pair normally build their huge, domed nest of sticks and roots among the thickest thorn bushes at the top end of the wood, from where they search out the nearby hedgerows and bushes for nests. Sadly, very little activity escapes their vigilant eye, and if left alone many broods will be destroyed, both game and songbirds alike. I made a mental note to return later with the gun.

MARCH 29TH

Collected a load of bantams this afternoon, ten neat little broody types plus a lordly cockerel to rule the roost and keep them in order. Normally all my waterfowl eggs are hatched in an incubator, but a few delicate species have proved extremely difficult to hatch by this method and need the more natural attentions of a real foster mother. The whole process of incubating ornamental waterfowl eggs is a complex subject, for although the ubiquitous mallard hatches with ease, many types require constant attention if a successful hatch is to be achieved. It is far from being a case of simply switching on the incubator and hoping for the best, for eggs must be kept in exactly the right condition throughout their development—neither too hot, too cold, nor too wet or too dry—and even minor changes in the weather regarding temperature and humidity can have a detrimental effect.

Some of the bantams are still in lay, a fact proved when I discovered an egg in the crate by the time I reached home, but with luck a few will have turned broody as soon as the weather warms up and the ducks begin to lay. I already have a red-crested pochard incubating a clutch of eggs in one of the nesting baskets beside the water, though this particular bird invariably starts laying long before any other species apart from the mallard, which can make a start at any time after Christmas has past according to the weather conditions. It is usually mid-April before I start to pick up any real quantity of eggs.

During the last couple of weeks much of my spare time has been employed in designing a new and, I hope, better method of rearing my young waterfowl, and my carpenter friend, Ronnie, has been working overtime constructing a system of huts and enclosures. The new pens all have raised wire floors that will allow all waste matter to fall through the mesh and should keep the birds much cleaner than the previous method of rearing them in strawed pens: a system requiring constant attention in order to keep the ducklings in a clean and healthy environment.

51

MARCH 31ST

I have noticed an encouraging amount of pheasants about the farm these past few days, their high numbers due indirectly to the fierce gales of last autumn, which felled countless trees in the coverts and provided a maze of hiding places where the birds could easily conceal themselves to avoid the beaters on shooting days. Now the danger of shooting has past, the pheasants have become almost as tame as farmyard fowl and it is difficult to believe that they are the same birds that proved so elusive in winter. As many as forty regularly feed on a field of spring corn near the farmyard in the early morning, the chainmail-plumaged cocks easily outnumbered by the drabber hens, though this is always desirable and augurs well for the breeding season. One particular old character has a regular harem of eleven hens, and he struts around as proud as a peacock and challenges his rivals with gusto, though such a surfeit of ladies must eventually take their toll on the strength of their lord and master. He will not crow with such alacrity once his spring duties have been performed.

The partridge coveys have divided into territorial pairs. Most are red-legged, but there is a scattering of the indigenous greys, a far more desirable and much revered sporting bird that flies fast and well on shooting days, providing testing shots as they are sent skimming over the guns. Partridge numbers depend greatly on the survival rate of the newly hatched chicks. Being hardly bigger than bumble bees, they are highly sensitive to adverse weather conditions, and during a cold and wet spell many will perish soon after hatching.

April

APRIL 1ST

'Oh, to be in England, now that April's there ...'. A few lines of the well-known verse came back to me as I ventured out to feed the geese in the orchard this morning. It must surely have been on a day such as this that Browning was inspired to pen his immortal poem, for the cock chaffinch was certainly pouring his heart out from the orchard bough as a strengthening sun climbed ever higher in the purest azure sky, the first really warm day of the year sufficient to entice the first ragged tortoiseshell butterflies from their long winter sleep to enjoy a few, last, short days of life.

It was just the day for wandering around the lakes, and an ideal opportunity to observe how the mallard were faring with their nests. When I parked the truck on the bank of Bulrush Lake, a carrion crow rather ominously took to its wings and sneaked towards the wood, disturbed in the act of robbing a nest rather foolishly placed on an exposed bank beside the water. The ground foliage has not yet grown sufficiently to afford protection from its evil eye and I was too late to save the nest, the bird already having made a breakfast of the contents, the remains of which were scattered untidily around the soft, down-lined scrape in the almost bare earth.

Following a search of the lake margins, I discovered only two nests with the eggs still intact, though in several places more empty shells littered the banks where the crow had digested his ill-gotten gains. My cousin, John, has picked up a few early broods for his incubator, and it is hoped by the time the ducks lay a replacement clutch the vegetation will have grown enough to offer some concealment.

In the centre of an open sheet of water, a pair of great-crested grebes were involved in mutual display, both birds garbed in the nuptial headgear of plumes, ruffs, and frills, and totally absorbed by the intricacies of the complicated courting routine. As I stood watching, the pair reared up on the water, breasts touching, in the so-called 'penguin dance', presenting beakfuls of fresh weed to one another gathered from the bottom of the lake, the first step towards building a floating nest of the same material on the edge of an island or reedbed. Canada geese hung around the islands in pairs, and a pied wagtail with a spring in its step skipped daintily with bobbing tail among the washed stones at the water's edge, at intervals darting sideways to pick a stranded fly from the surface of the shallows.

It was a peaceful scene, but one can feel an underlying sense of urgency in the air as all of nature prepares to burst forth into the full glory of its richest season.

APRIL 4TH

One of our more distinguished visitors turned up at West Lake early this morning. My neighbour, Ron, who lives at the far end of the lake, rang early to inform me that an osprey had arrived and was hunting for its breakfast over the shallow water. An odd bird or two normally passes along the valley at this time of year and often makes a brief stop to rest and feed. This breaks their long annual pilgrimage from the fierce heat of Africa to the more temperate air of breeding grounds in Scotland or the Lake District, where they will remain for the summer to attempt to nest and rear their young. The magnificent raptor was heavily persecuted towards the end of the nineteenth century by skin- and egg-collectors and over-zealous protectors of game. It was finally exterminated in the early 1900s, but returned in small numbers in the 1950s and has now recolonized several of its former haunts where it is received with a more enlightened attitude and rigidly protected by the Royal Society for the Protection of Birds, who maintain a regular watch on most of its nesting sites.

The new arrival caused quite a stir among the local bird-watching fraternity, for although an occasional osprey moves through the valley in spring and again on the return journey in September, it is still a rare and impressive sight as it quarters the open water on huge, sharply angled wings and pauses to hover like a giant kestrel searching for signs of a fish far below.

Having spent some time hunting above West Lake, the osprey moved towards the farmhouse, though returned a few minutes later following an unsuccessful search of the deeper Bulrush Lake. West Lake is for the most part comparatively shallow, and resuming its search it suddenly checked and plunged headlong into the water on half closed wings and emerged clutching a fish of about 2 lb (0.9 kg) in its powerful talons. The sky was heavily overcast, and there was quite a swell on the water from a cold north-easterly wind, demonstrating the bird's incredible eyesight in being capable of discerning the movement of the fish many yards below. With its catch held firmly head to wind, it was last seen heading towards the open fields, passing directly over my house as it sought a quieter place to consume its meal. I carried out a quick search of the surrounding countryside with the binoculars but saw no indication of where it had gone. Being spring, it will be keen to reach its breeding grounds to establish a territory, though if conditions are to its liking and the fishing is good, it could grace the lakes with its presence for a further day or two. It would certainly be a most welcome guest.

APRIL 6TH

The weather forecast promised another calm and sunny day, so I gathered my gear together after work and slipped away for a few hours trouting. By way of a change I journeyed to the Mill Pools—a small fishery of a few acres consisting of five small lakes, the entrance to its waters guarded by a picturesque old flour mill standing above a clear, fast-flowing stream. The trout in these lakes are comparatively small, mainly around the 1 lb (0.5 kg) mark, but what they lack in size is more than compensated for by a fiery fighting spirit worthy of fish more than double their size.

Chiffchaffs were chanting monotonous double notes from a bed of tall poplars as I walked the length of the fishery, and from deeper in the wood I heard the far more melodious trillings of a willow warbler, the two species almost indistinguishable by sight and recently arrived from warmer regions. The willow trees situated tastefully around the water are beginning to burst into fresh green leaf, and their boles are ringed by clumps of golden daffodils that nodded a polite welcome on the gentle breeze as I passed them by.

At the extreme end of the lakes lies the deepest water. Seeing an odd fish or two dimpling the surface a few yards from the bank, I decided to fish a shallow fly at first and gradually deepen if there was no response. There was little time to ponder. True to form, the first fish snapped up the lure with a lightning take on the third cast, putting a bow in the rod and leaping high as the line pulled tight. It fought like a demon, kiting sideways across the water and arching clear each time I applied a little pressure with the rod. It ran fast and hard many times before it was fully played, coming to the net fully exhausted—a small, silver fish, barely 1 lb (0.5 kg) in weight.

The trout were obviously in a taking mood, for during the next hour four more of a similar size followed the path of the first before I decided to stop for a late lunch break. The sun had broken through the layer of light cloud and added a sparkle to the clear water. I lazed on the grassy bank and shared my sandwiches with a pair of tame Canada geese, the distended rear end of the female showing she was on the point of laying her eggs in a scrape on the nearby island. A green woodpecker laughed from the woods and at intervals drummed on a dead bough with a machine-gun rapidity, and all around the air was filled with birdsong, the vocalists rejoicing that winter has at last lost its cruel grip and we have suddenly been transported into more agreeable days.

I resumed casting with the same blue lure in an adjoining water, locating another trout almost immediately—a bar of silver that snatched my offering almost beside the bank with a sudden sideways lunge and streaked off like a torpedo towards the deeper water. If anything, the fishing was rather too easy and all too soon I had reached a self-imposed limit, a somewhat excessive bag of ten fish. None the less, it provided an ideal opportunity of fulfilling promises of fresh trout to a few non-fishing friends.

APRIL 8TH

It looks as though the osprey has left us, for though I kept an eye cast in the direction of the lakes all through the day there was no sign of it, and the bird has almost certainly resumed the last leg of its journey northwards. Luckily I have been treated to some memorable sightings over the past couple of days, watching while it scoured the lakes for unwary fish, its progress hampered by a persistent following of gulls, lapwings, and rooks that mobbed unmercifully and distracted it from fishing.

Most of the osprey's time was spent alternately soaring and hovering high above the steely water, but early yesterday morning it plummeted to snatch a small jack pike from the shallow end of West Lake, shrugging its broad wings visibly to shake the water from its plumage while climbing forcefully with its burden to clear a bank of spoil. After a laboured journey, the bird finally gained the top of an oak behind my house, where it alighted delicately on a dead bough to consume the fish, the lifeless corpse clenched firmly in its powerful talons. It provided me with an unforgettable sight.

APRIL 11TH

Ray called in the afternoon, having received a plea for help from a farmer friend who is being plagued by rabbits. The damage to his growing corn is apparently severe, and the rabbits will need to be thinned out by whatever means possible to avoid losing large areas of the crop.

Such a desperate situation calls for desperate measures, and I arranged to collect Ray well after dark when the rabbits would have strayed well away from their burrows to forage on the open fields, where we planned to account for as many as possible in the lights of the truck. To the uninitiated this method of control may appear heavily one sided, but shooting from the back of a moving vehicle at rabbits bolting for their burrows requires a keen sense of balance coupled with split-second timing if shooting is to be successful. The only other option in such a situation at this time of year is to gas the holes, just as effective from the point of view of rabbit control, but highly wasteful as those destroyed can only be left to rot in their burrows.

I collected Ray just before nine in the evening. It was already pitch dark, and with no sign of the moon conditions were ideal. When we turned into the field gateway it was all too easy to appreciate the farmer's concern. The damage had to be seen to be believed, for acres of growing corn had been nibbled to ground level and a crop of wheat that should by now have been several inches in height had been reduced almost to the bare earth over a large portion of the field.

Ray climbed on the back of the truck for the first session. While I drove around the headland he accounted for several rabbits bolting for their holes along the bordering hedge, and I disturbed a few others by quartering the centre of the field where they had squatted on the open ground. I covered the adjoining field in the same manner, where the damage was if anything worse—the land absolutely devoid of greenery where the wheat had been nibbled to the root. By the time we had completed the search we had picked up a dozen rabbits, good clean animals all free from myxomatosis.

We changed positions before moving to a nearby unploughed stubble running beside a railway embankment honeycombed with fresh holes, and once again rabbit numbers called for rapid shooting as we bumped along the edge of the field. I took them as they reached the high bank, and on two occasions managed a left and right. When this last field had been fully covered we had collected exactly thirty rabbits in just under an hour, enough to alleviate the farmer's immediate concern although it will take several such forays to make a real inroad into such a high population. We intend to return providing the weather remains dry enough to allow access to the fields.

APRIL 14TH

A long-awaited spell of fine weather and a strong drying wind has at last rendered the farmland workable following one of the wettest seasons on record. The countryside now vibrates to the roar of many tractors as the rush to complete the last of the ploughing and spring sowing gets under way. In more benign years, most of the fallow land is turned by the plough in autumn and left exposed to the elements throughout the winter, allowing the action of snow and frost to crumble the earth to a fine tilth for spring seedbeds, but last autumn many fields—particularly the heavy land—were drenched to the point of saturation, which prevented the work from being carried out.

Two small fields near the house have been drilled with spring barley, and a few pigeons have discovered areas of spilt grain, a far more attractive alternative to the rape and other greenstuff that has been the mainstay of their diet through the winter months. It may be worth keeping an eye on the crops in case pigeon numbers build up sufficiently to allow a few hours shooting, although with so many fields sown at the same time the birds are rather spoiled for choice. Crops of peas have also been sown in the area, but although these were formerly a certain draw for pigeons, nowadays the seed is heavily coated with an unpalatable dressing of fungicide that acts as an effective repellent unless washed off by the rain. It is seldom until the first tender green shoots push through the earth that the pigeons begin to take a real interest, when great damage can be caused to the emerging plants at their most tender and vulnerable stage.

The autumn-sown corn is growing fast as the weather improves. Coupled with the lush pastures, it is rapidly transforming the countryside into a patchwork of fresh spring green after the long period of dormancy. Soon the trees will add their verdant mantle of leaves and the distant winter horizons will contract as the entire countryside is enveloped in a vernal cloak of green.

APRIL 15TH

Spectre looked much brighter when I went to feed her in the mews this morning, appearing so keen that I decided to take her with me to the duckponds. I have rested her completely for the past month and built up her food supply accordingly, in the rather forlorn hope of restoring her condition. She certainly seemed full of life as she jumped to the glove, her eye bright and sharp and lacking the ominous sunken look so typical of a sick hawk.

I held her aloft as we walked out of the garden, and to my delight she stretched her wings and allowed the stiff breeze to lift her into the sky, beating purposefully across the field of wind-waved grass to alight in a hedgerow ash beside the road. This was certainly a welcome change from her former weak and lethargic state when she declined even to fly, remaining hunched on the glove and displaying little or no interest in the things around her. This time she followed me all the way to the duckponds, where she gained the top of an alder and stood preening the month-long dust from her feathers.

While I was filling the feed bucket, I heard the tinkle of bells and looking up was just in time to see her dive almost vertically to the ground, the short flight ending somewhat abruptly as she performed a rather clumsy landing on a freshly excavated molehill. She peered inquisitively between her feet and stooped to pick up a huge earthworm, teasing its full length rather gingerly from the soil before swallowing it in a couple of quick gulps. Appearing well pleased with the success, she wiped her beak, roused her feathers into shape, and stood looking for another game to play. This was more like Spectre.

Encouraged by her actions, I continued our walk along the drain bordering Spring Marsh, and while I carried out a search for spawning pike, Spectre followed me closely, flying from tree to tree. By the time we reached the river we had heard the cuckoo's call in the far distance and encountered our first swallow of the spring, the latter vigorously hawking flies disturbed by a herd of bullocks on the marshy ground, to replace some of the energy expended on the arduous journey home.

I counted no less than seven pike lying like mottled steel bars along the 400-yard stretch of water, mainly small fish 2–3 lb (0.9–1.4 kg) in weight, though one female of at least 8 lb (3.6 kg) lay partly concealed beneath an outcrop of sedge, her marbled grey-green body heavily distended with spawn. Soon she will be free of her burden and will make the return journey downstream to the river, there to lurk among the weedbeds and gorge herself during the summer months on shoals of fat roach, dace, and chub.

APRIL 17TH

The incubator has now been warming up for almost a week, and as the temperature is remaining at a constant level I am planning to collect the first batch of duck eggs within the next few days.

The pond residents have become a regular source of interest as the drakes go to great lengths in exhibiting their spring attire to their partners, and the business of mating and laying eggs gets under way. One of the more endearing sights is provided by the tiny male ruddy duck, who in the course of his so-called 'bubble' display inflates his neck to huge proportions prior to beating his bright-blue bill rapidly against his chest, a process that produces a curious rattling sound and causes a ring of tiny bubbles to form on the surface of the water. The mergansers have already laid their first eggs and a golden-eye has the beginnings of a clutch in a nest-box propped above the water— two beautiful deep green eggs that appear far too large to have been produced by so small a bird.

The day began bright and warm, though by late afternoon a chilling east wind was blowing in from the coast. It had turned bitterly cold by the time I collected Ray for another session at the rabbits. There were far less abroad than on our previous visit, but as we had then taken thirty of their number this was only to be expected. Those remaining were very shy, having learned a lesson from our last visit and heading for their burrows directly they were outlined in the lights.

It was a cold task crouching on the back of the truck and driving against the wind, but we were soon forced to restore some heat after managing to get the vehicle embedded in a deceptively boggy area lying adjacent to a water meadow. Having broken through the dried-out crust, the earth was a morass of mud, and it was only after a great deal of pushing and shoving that the truck was eventually extricated. We were grateful to be on our way with a further fifteen rabbits on the back.

APRIL 19TH

It seemed that I had just drifted off to sleep when the alarm clock jerked me from my slumbers. Having just turned four-thirty, it was still dark outside, but already the first hesitant twitterings of the dawn chorus were warming up as the pale flush of dawn crept across the eastern sky.

I was feeling rather less chirpy—though hopes of an early-morning pigeon shoot soon shook off all thoughts of tiredness. Yesterday afternoon an hour had been spent watching a large flock of wood pigeons feeding on a peafield adjoining the farm boundary, and although the desired spot was well out of bounds, one of the main flightlines to the feast had passed within range of an accessible belt of trees where I had hurriedly built a hide. With any luck there seemed a good chance of tempting a few birds off course to the fresh-drilled ground, particularly at first light when they would pass it on their initial journey to the peafield.

Having revived myself with a welcome mug of tea I was on my way, and following a short drive, was soon trudging towards the belt of trees in the half-light of dawn. The air was mild beneath low grey cloud, but as so often happens at dawn, a fresh breeze had suddenly begun to feather the tops of the trees and appeared to be steadily increasing in power. Beside me the woods were alive with an orchestra of birds, the principal musicians an uncountable number of blackbirds that poured forth their long, sweet, liquid notes to welcome the day. The sound alone seemed reward enough for rising at such an unearthly hour.

I froze in my tracks as two roe deer emerged silently from the hedge before me, ears twitching and nostrils flaring as they sensed my nearness, their lithe bodies still as statues until a betraying breeze carried my scent towards them and sent them bounding up the hill, white scuts flashing, to disappear from view over the far skyline.

My hide was a rough screen of elder branches interwoven with dead grass at the bole of a towering ash, and as the first flood of daylight began to bathe the moistened earth, I placed the decoys in a well-spaced group several yards upwind, in the hope of inducing incoming pigeon to cross the front of the hide and give the best possible chance of offering sport.

59

The first customer sneaked up on me from behind the trees, but spotting the decoys flipped over the ash to join them, gliding down on curved wings to present an easy crossing shot. The following pair were less co-operative, beginning their approach boldly but veering off in panic just before I fired. The first shot passed well wide, but a second barrel, as the birds hurtled back over with the wind in their tails, caught up with it, sending it crashing through the trees far behind. The cause of their alarm became apparent when I spotted the first bird laying flat on its back, wings outstretched, and pale breast uppermost, a warning that all was not well.

Propping both birds among the decoys I regained the hide just as the dawn move really got under way—a continuous stream of pigeons all bound for the centre of the peafield. A few amongst their ranks set their wings and glided back to the decoys, curling around wide and pitching towards the wind across my front to provide steady sport. A spell of reasonably accurate shooting added several to the bag, and these I propped on short sticks to supplement the decoy pattern that now showed conspicuously against the bare earth and was proving more attractive as it grew in size. In a relatively short space of time I had well over thirty set out, but then the flight stopped as suddenly as it had begun and nothing moved for almost half an hour.

During this quiet spell a hare came loping over the brow of the hill, stopping abruptly as it reached the decoys where, completely mystified by their lack of movement, it reared up on its hind legs while cautiously pondering which way to go. Its mind was soon made up when the pigeon returned. At the first shot, it pelted hell for leather back the way it had come, not even bothering for a backward glance until the long back legs had carried it safely over the top of the hill.

For the next two hours the pigeons arrived in a steady trickle of ones and twos, the majority appearing over the trees behind me and flinging themselves into the decoys without a moment's hesitation, providing excellent sport. The tally mounted steadily but all too soon the flight slackened and eventually ceased, the flock evidently having discovered a less hostile place to feed. After the pick-up, I sacked seventy-two pigeons at the hide, and following a long haul back to the truck returned home for a late breakfast well satisfied with such an eventful start to the day.

APRIL 21ST

My old pintail drake was up to his tricks again when I went to collect the first clutches of eggs for the incubator. His perpetual sexual perversions are becoming something of a nuisance, for this time his attentions were directed towards a mandarin drake—a garishly plumaged bird of the wrong sex that under no circumstances could be confused with the sombre drabness of the pintail's true mate. However, he is not in the least bit fussy and continued to pursue it relentlessly, on and off the water, at one point cornering the hapless bird against the fence and hanging on grimly to its long orange mane. He has chosen a most unwilling partner.

I left them to sort out their differences and the feathers were already beginning to fly as I collected a clutch of nine eggs from the red-crested pochard, the sitting female puffing up her feathers in warning but allowing me to remove the eggs gently from beneath the warmth of her breast. She will now be free to lay another clutch. A tiny ringed teal was far less obliging. Ensconced deep in a nesting tunnel, she hissed and swore as I tried to part her from her eggs, stabbing me with her bill and defecating over the entire clutch before reluctantly taking her leave. This last act caused a slight problem, for I normally carry all partially incubated eggs home inside my shirt to conserve their heat, but with the help of a handful of dry grass I managed to restore them to a near pristine condition.

I examined the eggs before transferring them to the incubator, inspecting the contents with the aid of a strong torch held behind each egg, which allows the fertility to be confirmed and reveals the stage of its development. The pochard eggs are almost on the point of hatching, but the teal are far less advanced, a 'spider' of blood vessels radiating from a tiny heartbeat easily visible against the light. It is fascinating to inspect the eggs, as one can observe the various stages of growth from the first beat of the heart to the full-grown ducklings' eventual emergence from the shell.

APRIL 23RD

Spectre's steadiness was put to the test this morning, as my friend, John Wiison, was being filmed for another programme in his 'Go Fishing' television series and wanted Spectre to put in an appearance. The programme will show John fishing at several locations along the river Wensum, and a few of the sights he encounters on his travels.

While Spectre is completely fearless and confident in my presence, we normally hunt alone and I was unsure of how she would react when confronted with the cameras and a group of complete strangers.

John duly arrived with the six crew and together we stumbled along to Spring Marsh laden with cameras, tripods, sound equipment, and the extraordinary amount of other paraphernalia required for such a venture. When the team had set up the cameras and taken the first shots of John fly-fishing in the river, I collected Spectre from the mews for the next sequence. Despite not being handled much since her illness, she seemed in a reasonably keen mood, taking little notice of the cameras that had been set up at long range to film her flying to my fist. After a couple of long flights, the producer seemed satisfied and re-arranged the cameras for some close-up shots. With both cameras bearing down on us from a few yards, this was rather more claustrophobic, but Spectre's reactions were somewhat better than mine, although in fairness she had the advantage of having no lines to remember, remaining patiently on the glove while John and I chatted and enduring take after take before the scene was completed to the producer's satisfaction. Spectre's only slight lapse was when she pecked the finger of the female assistant as she tried to stroke her, but luckily she was wearing gloves and no

Spectre's steadiness put to the test. The bird comes readily to the
glove while being filmed for television.

blood was drawn. I finally managed to convince her that the misdemeanour
was just a sign of Spectre's affection.

We then humped all the equipment to the ponds to get some footage of the
ducks in their spring attire. They were not bothered in the least by all the fuss,
carrying on with their displaying as though nothing was happening and giving
the camera some nice shots as they dived for food thrown in the water.

The producer seemed well pleased with the way filming had gone, and was
particularly impressed by Spectre. I look forward to seeing how it all turns out
in the next series. It was certainly an interesting experience to see just how
much time and effort goes into producing a mere few minutes of film.

APRIL 24TH

The clutch of red-crested pochard eggs were in the process of hatching yesterday. When I peeped into the incubator last thing at night I found all nine had emerged safely, although they were still wet and exhausted following the task of chipping their way from the tough shells. I left them in the hatcher overnight to dry and when I peered beneath the lid early this morning, I was greeted by nine tiny, chirping bundles of fluff. The ducklings were transferred to a brooder, where they will spend their first days under a heating lamp that fulfils the role of foster mother. Within only a few minutes they had all settled down to sleep beneath its comforting warmth, huddled together in a soft, contented bundle of down.

We were able to go rabbiting again in the evening, for the night was dark and the weather has remained dry over the past couple of days. On the first wheatfield we accounted for several rabbits along the headlands, but the adjoining field was strangely devoid of them despite widespread damage to the growing corn. This remained a mystery until we spotted a hunting vixen in the headlights, working her way along the hedge but streaking towards the cover of the woods as the lights picked up her outline, her long, white-tipped brush streaming out behind. As Ray steered the truck back towards the centre of the field, I glimpsed another pair of glowing eyes at the far end, possibly the vixen's mate, though he too quickly slinked away among the trees of a nearby copse. It appears we have some competition for the rabbits, but although the foxes are aiding us in reducing the population, they scare many underground. If the pair are hunting the fields regularly, I suspect this is the reason we are seeing rather fewer than expected each time we shoot. However, we did manage to collect just over a score of rabbits by the end of the evening.

APRIL 27TH

Ray rang last night with the news that he had discovered a large flock of pigeons causing trouble on a field of recently drilled beans, so without further ado we arranged to make an early start this morning.

The ground was white with frost when I collected him just before dawn, but although very cold the hoped-for wind had not materialized to raise our hopes of a busy day. The field itself was no stranger to us, for despite not having shot over it for a considerable time, the last session had produced a total of 210 pigeons, though present weather conditions did not bode well for a repeat performance.

I dropped Ray off at the top end of the field to make his way to a small clump of trees that jutted well into the field, an ideal spot on high ground where his decoys would show up from a considerable distance, and after parking the truck, continued to the bottom-field boundary, where an acre of ground had been re-drilled with wheat and was covered with pigeons on the previous afternoon.

At the end of an adjoining wood I reached the area of wheat, where heavy

It took almost half an hour to gather the bag together in front of the hide.

land had formed into large clods of dry earth that made drilling difficult and left a fair amount of grain uncovered to attract the feeding flock. Erecting the netting hide at the junction of two hedges that met at right angles and projected into the field, I assembled the decoys to cover both sides of the corner in the hope of attracting birds from either direction.

My first visitor was a female kestrel. She came flickering towards the hide as the sun peeped above the horizon, sweeping up to a tall oak above me where her barred underparts immediately became as part of the tree. After eyeing me suspiciously for several seconds, she suddenly panicked and streaked away out of sight along the hedge.

The few pigeon that moved at first light drifted aimlessly overhead, but eventually one came down and the first easy shot found its mark. The report put others on the wing and for the best part of the next hour several bunches arrived over the field, a number of which dropped for a closer inspection and enabled me to add to the decoy pattern with a spell of accurate shooting.

As the strengthening rays of the sun burned the frost from the adjoining

64

meadow and brought the hawthorn bushes into full colour, a rising wind began to ruffle the feathers of the decoys and stirred the smaller branches of the oak above. Our prayers were being answered. Pigeon now started arriving in greater numbers and much lower as the wind increased. Regular bunches appeared over the skyline every few minutes following the same path to the hide, where I was beginning to accumulate the makings of a respectable bag. As the wind grew stronger the shooting improved accordingly, and by mid-morning I had pigeon lying all around the hide, with little chance of setting them up for there were birds constantly in the air all beating a steady line towards the decoys. During a short lull I did manage a quick tidy up, simply rolling most birds onto their breasts where they had fallen to create a wide, enticing patch of blue that in turn attracted more, the incoming pigeon taking little notice of those lying at all angles as they dropped to join them. Ray was now shooting steadily at the top of the hill, and what had started rather quietly was rapidly becoming a day to remember. I did a rough count that amounted to well over eighty birds, and then the pigeon really went to town, arriving from all points of the compass and hurtling down among the decoys without a second thought. I had long since emptied my cartridge bag of seventy-five, and was making inroads into a further hundred box always carried in the decoy sack. By the time I was almost halfway through them I had taken well over a hundred pigeon. I began to choose my shots more carefully in the hope of making the cartridges last until the flight was over.

Eventually the flow subsided, but with a few bunches still turning up at intervals it was not long before I had slipped the last cartridge into the breech and taken a high-crossing pigeon jinking away from the decoys. It had to be the last shot of the day.

But what a day. It took almost half an hour to gather them all together, with fallen pigeon along the hedgerows and a few towered well across the field. The prospect of humping them the half mile to the truck was rather daunting, but luckily I was able to drive right up to the front of the hide. After loading 152 pigeons with my gear, I collected Ray on the way back, who added over eighty birds to give our highest bag for some time, a total of 236 wood pigeons, more than enough to satisfy our host's concern for his crop of beans.

APRIL 30TH

Ken accompanied me on the raft this morning, and together we explored the islands on Bulrush Lake to see how the wildfowl were faring with their nests. It was bright and very mild, with the sun sparkling on the water and picking out the clumps of marsh marigolds, whose fresh blooms added splashes of golden colour to the beds of greening sedge. The raft was tied at the far end of the lake, and while walking to collect it we disturbed myriads of winged insects from the reedy margins, some of which rose high in the air to be snapped up by a busy team of swallows foraging in our wake.

There was a sudden commotion of wings ahead of us when a greylag erupted from a tangle of low bramble at the water's edge, her anxious cackling

65

immediately summoning the gander from the open water. The pair scolded us noisily as I inspected their nest. Strangely, it contained only a single egg, although the smoothness of its shell and the thick layer of down lining the nest showed it was already being incubated. Twenty yards further along the bank another greylag crouched flat on her nest among the rushes, but she too took to the water as we neared, vacating a clutch of six white eggs set cosily in a down-lined hollow.

Once afloat we searched the lake margins before crossing the open water to the islands, discovering two coot nests of seven and eight eggs, one sited rather precariously in a gorse clump overhanging the water and the second, a floating raft of sedges placed deep among a bed of dry phragmite reeds.

Considering the number of mallard bobbing around us on the water, our search of the islands revealed very few nests, the majority of early clutches having fallen victim to the local pair of carrion crows, one of whom croaked from the top of an alder in Farm Wood, eager to return to his plundering. Only one mallard was seen with youngsters—a diminutive brood of two that, having survived the crows' attentions, will now have to run the gauntlet of the many pike in the water, most of which are extremely partial to a meal of young duckling. Were it not for hand-rearing, very few would grow to maturity to provide a shootable surplus for the autumn.

The prospects for the geese seem brighter. Among the half-a-dozen nests we found, one belonging to a Canada contained no less than eleven eggs. A few geese have already hatched, and on our return a family party of greylags slipped from the bank to paddle across the lake in single file, the proud goose leading her little flotilla of downy goslings to safety with her faithful gander bringing up the rear.

May

MAY 1ST

Having got my work forward enough to allow a fishing trip to the Valley Lakes today, it seemed an ideal time to set up the vice to tie some imitation tadpoles to try on the trout: there were masses of developing spawn on my last visit.

I used a couple of long-shanked hooks, building up a thick body of chenille around a large split-shot pinched to the shank and tying in a generous amount of black marabou plume, which would act as a tail and reproduce the enticing squiggling action of a swimming tadpole. It would be interesting to test the trouts' reactions.

The bulk of the tadpoles had already disappeared along the weedy margins of Rainbow Lake, only a few remaining to wriggle around the bankside reeds like little animated black commas. The trout have become addicted to the easy pickings and are snapping them up directly they stray into the open water.

I reached my favourite spot at the top corner of the lake where the water was gin-clear beneath the bright sun, allowing me to scan the depths clearly to some distance from the bank. At first nothing happened. There was no sign of a follow as the lure was retrieved, and somehow my tadpole did not look entirely convincing. I tried a few slower retrieves, tugging a few inches of line and then pausing, causing the weighted lure to rise and fall in the water and giving a far more realistic action as the tail of marabou wriggled behind it each time the tadpole dived. Totally absorbed in my experiments, I was suddenly surprised by a huge white mouth that snapped the tadpole almost beside the bank, the fish surging away with a swish of its tail as it saw me and almost breaking free when forced to an abrupt halt as the line snagged around my boot. Fortunately, the hook held and, following a short and rather uninspired tussle, I landed a fish of just over 4 lb (1.8 kg). A few more casts across the same spot produced a second to the slowly worked lure, this time a far livelier and more energetic fish, which put up a good fight before being banked, churning the bottom silt to a muddy soup before tiring. This one went exactly 5½ lb (2.5 kg).

By the time it was beached the sun had climbed higher across an almost cloudless sky. For a while nothing moved on the surface. It was an ideal time to break for lunch.

The resident pair of mute swans slumbered quietly on the island, the pen tight on her eggs only a matter of yards from an incubating Canada goose, the pair separated by a coot with her rush nest set in a dividing hollow. The little group were surrounded by a party of tufted duck resting peacefully in the sun, creating an idyllic island scene, the very picture of peace and contentment on a beautiful warm spring day.

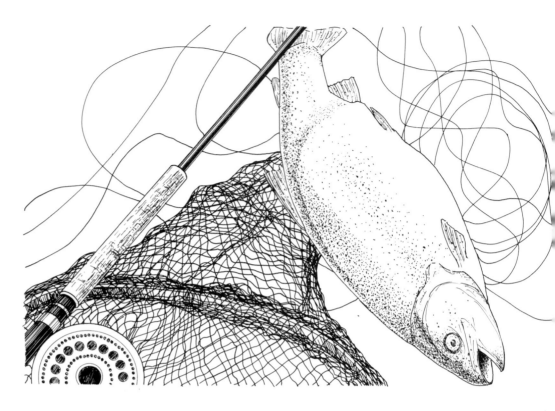

The second fish was far livelier, a 5½-pounder (2.5 kg) which put up
a good fight before coming to the net.

Presently a cloud came across the sun. The tufted duck drifted off to
resume diving, the cob swan roused himself to feed, and the moment was
gone. I took my leave and wandered back along the smaller lake, intending to
try for a brace of smaller fish to provide a tasty supper, but in fact taking four
in barely half an hour for here the fish were rising eagerly on the surface. As I
prepared to leave, three exquisite oyster-catchers came fluting down the
valley engaged in stiff-winged pursuit, making two complete circuits of the
water before retiring, the sight and sound of their presence setting the seal on
a most perfect day.

MAY 3RD

While watching the orchard geese from the study window this morning, a tiny
male sparrowhawk came winging his way along the edge of the garden,
alighting daintily on the corner fence-post and sending a blackbird scuttling
for cover among the shrubbery. The binoculars lay close at hand on the desk
and I was able to give him a close, though all too brief, inspection. The sun

picked out the rich rufous shades of the barred breast and flanks, glinting dangerously in his brilliant yellow eye as he scanned the garden for any indication of prey. Finally spying something in the distance, he bobbed his head and was away, the short flickering wings rapidly picking up speed as he flashed past the study window and swept along the row of conifers towards the front of the house. Rushing to the front bedroom, I was just in time to see him disappear around the corner of the nearby spinney, the hastening brown blur of what appeared to be a dunnock only feet in front and being easily overhauled by a burst of sheer speed. I watched for several minutes but he did not reappear, being almost certainly engrossed in taking a late breakfast at the far end of the copse.

A sparrowhawk would certainly be an exciting bird to fly and to hunt, and with this in mind I have already begun enquiries towards obtaining one for the late summer—there being quite a few being bred now and hand-reared in captivity. With a maximum weight of little over 10 oz (285 g) the birds are notoriously difficult to keep in optimum condition for flying, though I think it would be well worth the effort if a suitable candidate can be found. A good female lacks nothing in courage and boldness and is capable of tackling prey up to moorhen size. Indeed, in winter I have frequently come across the remains of wood pigeons taken by the hawks around the farm, although the majority of prey undoubtedly consists of far smaller birds.

MAY 4TH

The colony of terns are back with us again for the summer and, lying on the grassy bank amid clumps of seeding coltsfoot overlooking West Lake, I spied two birds resting on an island below, in company with a bunch of dozing lapwings and an industrious little ringed plover that searched the perimeter of the island for titbits among the shallows. Above them three more terns were quartering the lake like huge white swallows, occasionally plunging headlong into the water as a fish was spotted, but appearing to catch very little, until one bird plummeted into the water below me and emerged with a tiny silver fish clasped firmly in its beak. It was immediately joined by a watchful black-headed gull, the larger bird pursuing it closely in the air and shrieking loudly to intimidate the tern into dropping its catch. The chase continued until its harassment achieved the desired effect, causing the tern to drop the fish to where it was recovered from the water and swallowed in one gulp by the greedy gull, which then retired to a partly submerged tree-trunk to preen itself and await further developments.

A dizzy flock of sand martins were busy excavating their nesting holes in the sheer south bank—the beginnings of a honeycomb of tunnels placed row upon row like a miniature block of flats. A swarm of birds hovered around the bank while a few of their number tunnelled into the soft sand, stopping now and then to kick little puffs of spoil from the entrance holes. There is much to be done before they can deposit their clutches of tiny white eggs at the end of the tunnels, which can sometimes extend a full yard into the bank.

A female shelduck came gliding in for her daily wash and brush-up, having spent another long vigil on her brood of eggs. I have already discovered the nest hidden deep in a strawstack in the nearby Dutch barn, the site betrayed by a wisp of white down left rather carelessly at the mouth of the entrance hole between a row of bales. She was soon joined by her mate who had been resting on the causeway with his head tucked beneath his wing, and after a noisy welcome, she fed quickly, eager to eat her fill and return to brooding duties before the eggs cooled. It should not be long before she leads a pretty little brood of pied ducklings to the shallow waters of the lake.

MAY 7TH

Climbed the hollow oak overhanging the river just downstream of the duckponds to search for trout, for beneath the tree a shallow swim holds a few wild brownies during the summer months and I usually contrive to take a fish or two in the heat of the day as they shelter in the leaf-dappled waters. Being rather early in the year, there were only a couple of small fish taking refuge beside a patch of weed, their supple tails fanning gently to hold position against the strong current and outlined plainly against the gravelly bed. Previously the fish have been taken on a maggot or minnow while perching precariously on a horizontal bough above the water, for casting from the bank is impossible due to the mass of overhanging branches. However, having acquired all the necessary equipment since my last attempt, I will probably try the rather more sporting approach of dapping a dry fly on the surface.

While scanning the river a kingfisher came upstream, passing almost beneath me to perch on a dead branch of the neighbouring oak, a living jewel of cobalt and vermilion that joined me briefly in the search for fish. Seeing nothing to its liking, it resumed the journey upstream in direct flight, calling loudly as it flew and banking sharply across the meadow to continue the search at the mouth of a drainage channel.

Beneath the oak the bluebells are a picture on the sloping bank, the earth cloaked by massed ranks of multi-flowered stems almost bright enough to confuse the eye, the brilliant carpet of blue enhanced by the delicate pink and white flowers of the taller campions. It seems but a moment ago that the earth was barren and bare, but now everywhere there are new wonders springing up to delight the eye every day as spring marches steadily towards summer.

MAY 9TH

Brian, the gamekeeper, rang to arrange an evening search of the woods near his house, as a fox has been causing trouble on the estate that borders the farm. A number of hen pheasants have been taken from their nests, his neighbour has lost quite a few chickens, and a nearby farmer has suffered the loss of several newborn lambs. It seems high time to try to put an end to the slaughter.

We planned to drive out two of the nearby woods where the fox was

The swim holds a few wild brownies during the summer months.

believed to be lying up during the daylight hours, ready to resume his slaying under the cover of darkness. The large tracks of a dog fox were much in evidence as we crossed a muddy corn drill adjoining the first fir wood, although nothing emerged when the cover was hunted out towards where three of us crouched concealed along its downwind edge, except a stream of wood pigeons that clattered out of the thickest stand of firs and an odd rabbit or two that was started from the brambles. The second drive also proved fruitless. After another steady stream of pigeons had beat tantalizingly past where I crouched at the corner of the wood among a hostile bed of nettles, all was quiet apart from the drumming of a great spotted woodpecker on a huge dead elm, the sound echoing among the trees in the stillness. My interest was momentarily aroused as a large brown animal came loping through the bushes, but it proved to be a hare, the first of many that picked their way stealthily towards us as the beaters advanced from the far end of the wood. It stood bolt upright on its back legs looking for a safe exit, peering around from only a few feet away until a pigeon suddenly clattered from its nest in a thick hawthorn above it, sending the animal scampering for safety across a field of growing wheat. The beaters made plenty of noise as the drive was completed but our quarry was obviously elsewhere, having chosen a safer spot to spend the day until darkness covers his movements.

It is possibly the same dog fox that has been hunting near the duckponds, where I found his fresh padmarks on my path. It came right up to the pond gate but luckily stopped short before attempting to climb the wire. Although high, the fence poses no problem to an agile fox, as I have already found to my cost. I suspect he may lie up in Marsh Wood, and I must try to spend an evening waiting for him before he pays another visit.

MAY 11TH

Went to see John again at his fishing-tackle shop in Norwich to set myself up with a carp rod, as he has promised me a day or two at the carp on his private lake. John had the lake excavated beside his bungalow a few years ago, among an attractive birch wood, and has landscaped and planted it in a most commendable fashion and stocked the water with a wide variety of fish. I was treated to a preview of the carp yesterday afternoon, when we attempted to catch some of the goldfish from the same lake for Barbara's garden pond— massive fish of anything up to 20 lb (9 kg) that cruised temptingly close on the surface and sucked up lumps of bread and trout pellets thrown in to attract the goldfish. I have never yet taken a carp, and can hardly wait to put their reputation of being solid, strong and tireless fighters to the test.

Sadly, my old glass-fibre rod, bought almost thirty years ago for the sum of three pounds, is scarcely man enough for the job, though it has served me well over the years and taken a wide variety of fish ranging from the diminutive gudgeon to pike well into double figures. Glass fibre is now a thing of the past, being replaced mainly by carbon fibre, of which John showed me a baffling diversity of rods that would serve my purpose. Needing a rod that would also double for catching pike narrowed down the choice, and I eventually settled for a 12 ft (3.7 m) rod of carbon fibre—very light in weight compared to my old faithful and with a good springy action that should give a nice 'feel' if and when I should be lucky enough to make contact with one of the double-figure fish. I look forward with mounting anticipation to the beginning of the open season on June 16th.

MAY 14TH

Finding myself with an hour or so to spare in the late evening, I decided the time might be well spent waiting on the meadow near Marsh Wood to see if the rogue dog fox might put in an appearance. I tried to avoid laying a trail of scent by keeping close to the boundary ditch on my approach, but on reaching its junction with a smaller channel I caused a commotion by disturbing a mallard duck with her family of downy young. It was a good brood of nine ducklings, not long hatched, and they skittered across the surface as the duck quacked a harsh warning, disappearing among a labyrinth of sedges growing from the water. She then caused an even greater disturbance by feigning injury in her 'broken-wing' display in an attempt to lead me away from her young, keeping this up until I had dutifully followed for 50 yards or more before suddenly taking wing and moving to the river. From there she watched my progress until I was well clear before sneaking back to re-group her ducklings. So much for a quiet approach.

There were a number of fox tracks in the mud beside the bridge, one leading to a patch of fresh earth nearby where a white object revealed one of his stores of food. It proved to be the tip of a chicken wing, rather carelessly buried, and I unearthed the remains of the well-ripened owner, killed and stored by the fox for a night when the hunting was poor.

Checking the wind was in my favour, I settled down in a large rushbed commanding a good view of the wood edge. A constant trickle of herons were trafficking to and fro with food for their youngsters in the huge stick nests, and high above a snipe was engaged in his aerial drumming flight: a swift, black arrowhead that rose and fell against the last of the light.

Half an hour later it was almost too dark to see, but suddenly out of the corner of my eye I caught a fleeting movement, a dark sneaking shape outlined against the lightness of the grass. The fox was out. Presently he stopped and stood listening, his nose raised to test the wind but then, his fears apparently allayed, trotted off in the direction of Rabbit Hill. The range was far too great, but directly I squeaked he stopped abruptly and altered course, his loping run ending barely 20 yards away. The report rolled around the marsh in the stillness of the evening, bouncing off the hill and echoing through the woods like the sound of distant thunder. A moorhen croaked a warning from its roost somewhere along the river, then all was quiet once more. The fox lay still, his career of killing over. The remaining hens could now roost untroubled by fear of his nocturnal attentions.

MAY 16TH

In a final effort at clearing the rabbits from the growing wheat, Ray and I had what will probably be our last session on the cornfields tonight, for the crop has grown fast and is almost too high to drive through without causing damage by our tracks. Coupled to this, the daylight remains much longer in the evening and it is now quite late by the time we can get under way. It had rained hard during the late afternoon, the swollen sky at one time releasing a torrential downpour that soaked the top few inches of soil. However, realizing that progress would be difficult, we decided to give it a try and risk the chance of getting bogged down on the heavy land.

It was almost a quarter to ten before it was fully dark, and although being a bright evening at first, when we eventually set out a thick bank of drizzly cloud had veiled the moon to give more favourable conditions. Being late, the rabbits had ventured well away from their holes and we discovered them in small groups clear of the hedges feeding among the growing corn, where they gave better opportunity than those just emerged and sitting almost beside the burrows.

A welcome sight to the farmer. Sorting the previous night's bag of rabbits.

Ray shot first while I drove over a couple of fields we had not covered before. Located beside a low water meadow, the going was very sticky, but as we slipped and slid around the field he missed very little and it was not long before we had accumulated quite a number, adding a few rabbits on each fresh sweep of the corn, which always seemed to produce another one or two. We encountered a healthy stock of hares on the higher ground, all of which were given a wide berth, and once I caught a fleeting glimpse of a little owl, disturbed in his search for earthworms among the short grass of a nearby pasture. We saw nothing of the pair of foxes, although I heard one barking in the distance as we exchanged places to finish with a search of the original fields. Here there were far fewer rabbits, except on a long strip of fresh drill beside the fir wood, where I was kept busy as they bolted in all directions at our approach. I held the gun straight and the bag mounted steadily. By the time the run was completed it was well past eleven o'clock, but in the hour and a half of shooting we had collected a total of well over fifty rabbits.

MAY 17TH

Rainbow Lake is reputed to hold trout of well over 10 lb (4.5 kg) in weight, though as yet this season none have been brought to the net. With our sights set on one of these specimen fish, we rowed out to a mooring buoy in the centre of the lake in the early morning sunshine, myself at the oars with Ray perched in the stern of a trim little fishing punt. We planned to cover the seldom-fished areas of the lake where these monsters were suspected to lie, the water undisturbed and well out of range of bankside casting. A rising wind from the east restricted accurate casting, though more so to myself than Ray, who delivers his fly with an ease and fluency that somehow eludes me, making my own efforts seem rather cumbersome by comparison.

In the vicinity of the first buoy the water was far shallower than expected. By fishing low our flies were repeatedly fouled by bottom weed and there was little reply from the fish apart from a couple of half-hearted tugs that failed to set the hook. After a long and fruitless hour, I rowed to the opposite end of the lake where the water is very deep. On the journey I disturbed a pair of little ringed plovers from the island, which circled the lake in typical butterfly-like flight before alighting back on the stony margin when we had passed. There could be a nesting scrape hidden among the gravel.

The wind was rather kinder beside a thick alder belt lined with a row of poplars in full leaf, and here Ray was soon into a fish: a good-looking trout of about 5 lb (2.3 kg) that strangely put up very little of a fight considering its condition, wallowing around on the surface for a few minutes and allowing itself to be lifted into the boat with hardly a struggle.

I again tried everything I could think of without result, stolidly wading my way through nobblers, nymphs, bugs, and a succession of likely and unlikely looking lures without success, my frustrations heightened as Ray's line once again took off, this time a far fitter fish of similar size that ran several times before allowing itself to be hauled on board.

We kept up the campaign for the next few hours, my efforts totally ignored, seeing no sign of another fish, much less the hoped for monster. Even Ray had no further luck. By this time I had become really frustrated, and returning to the bank decided to try my luck with the smaller and normally more co-operative fish in Home Lake, though even there they eluded me, another full hour passing uneventfully despite going through the contents of my fly box yet again. It was small consolation to note very little being taken by fellow anglers.

And so—for me—ended a fishless day. My right arm was stiff with incessant casting. My head was throbbing and my eyes ached with the constant glinting of the sun on the water, and to cap it all my left boot had sprung a leak. If this was not enough, I managed to capture the neck of my pullover with a poorly aimed dog-nobbler and the strap on my camera gave way. It was obviously not my day, but such are the joys of flyfishing.

It is the first time I have drawn a complete blank for many a day, though in fairness I have taken a good number of nice fish lately and a blank only serves to make me keener in the long run and dispells the rather blasé attitude that can set in if fishing is too successful. Within a few days I have no doubt that I will be looking forward to enduring the whole masochistic experience again, though the trout will need to be very careful on my next visit.

MAY 19TH

Returned from feeding the ducks by way of Charles's small carp pond situated 200 yards downriver on the edge of our northern boundary. The last few days have been sunny and warm, probably enough to raise the water temperature sufficiently to induce the carp to spawn, and sure enough, watching from a high bank overlooking the water, a few fish could be seen splashing beside the banks, depositing their tiny pinheads of transparent spawn among the marginal vegetation, while a great many others soaked up the sun in the clear water, great dorsal fins cleaving the surface and broad tails pulsating gently as they cruised lazily in the warmth of the day. A shoal of a dozen or more fish of a few pounds each drifted aimlessly around a bed of emerging lilies, the sun glinting on their metallic sides protected with huge bronze scales that shone like polished armour. As they continued their ceaseless driftings, a willow warbler poured his song continuously from an island willow, his descending verses answered by rivals from a dozen different bushes, and while the sun beat down to create a heat haze across the meadow, a procession of orange-tip butterflies fluttered along the bank, all freshly-minted specimens recently emerged from their pupal cases.

I glanced up briefly as a sharp-winged shadow passed over the pond and there, sweeping across my front at no more than 15 yards, I was delighted to see a most beautiful hobby, an unmistakable and very immaculate little falcon looking like a miniature peregrine, with its rusty-red 'trousers' and dark moustached face pattern, a most unusual visitor and only the second I have seen in almost thirty years of bird-watching on the farm. The bird was not

76

long in passing, but as I focused the binoculars on its fleeing form it breasted the wind to rise in an easy upward sweep towards a kestrel hovering beside West Lake, the pair coming together to swoop and dive in mock battle, each endeavouring to display its superiority of flight, though both masters of the air. The pair spiralled together for several minutes, gaining lift from the warm air currents and rising directly over my head towards the heavens, their colours gradually fading to blackness as they passed into silhouette. The last I saw of them was two tiny specks rising steadily into the glare of the sun, its very brightness obscuring all trace of their movements.

MAY 21ST

During the past week I have been organizing a selection of taxidermy specimens, for I had been invited to put on a display of my work today at the nearby village 'Country Day' as part of a small rural-crafts exhibition. The final selection included birds awaiting my attention in various stages of completion, endeavouring to show the treatment each specimen receives before its eventual housing in a glass case. Most visitors were surprised to discover just how complicated the process becomes, many thinking the task merely entailed removing the subjects entrails and stuffing the remains with cottonwool! If only it were that simple.

During previous displays I have often worked on a specimen to explain the procedure further, but as this usually receives a mixed response this time I declined, realizing only too well that watching the skinning and dismemberment of a dead bird before their very eyes is not everyone's idea of a good day out, however enlightening the demonstration may be.

There was a regular stream of visitors to my tent throughout the afternoon, many displaying a genuine interest in the craft. The past few years have definitely seen a marked revival in the popularity of taxidermy as an art, following a decline when much priceless and irreplaceable work was literally thrown out or burned when the collecting of specimens went out of fashion. Many people, especially among the older generation, had a story to tell of a case discarded at a time when they were regarded as unwanted and rather quaint relics of an age when almost every country village had its own taxidermist, and most households owned a case or two of stuffed birds or animals. As proof of the renewed interest I could have sold most of my exhibits, but being part of a collection of British birds I have been adding to over many years, much of the work is irreplaceable. Unfortunately, I have found little time for taxidermy work so far this year, although having carried out quite a lot of casework and renovation at odd times when a spare hour or two has allowed. Actual skinning, preservation, and mounting requires far longer periods of time, the best part of a day's work being needed on a specimen before it can be set aside to dry for completion later. I have a growing number of specimens awaiting attention in the deep freeze for which I must soon make time, but at the moment the call of the gun, rod, and hawk and the wide open spaces seem far too strong to concentrate on indoor work.

MAY 22ND

When feeding the ducks this afternoon, I was honoured by a visit from a lesser-spotted woodpecker. On arrival, the little bird clung limpet-like to a vertical branch of a decayed elm beside the river and began to work in haste, methodically stripping the dried bark from the branch in an effort to uncover any insects hidden beneath. It was a strikingly attractive bird with a boldly striped back, a black facial stripe, and a glowing scarlet crown, the latter feature showing it to be a male. It appeared not to be finding much in the way of food, and while I stood watching, its search was interrupted by one of its larger cousins, a great-spotted, which suddenly appeared in dipping flight along the belt of trees. As if to emphasize its higher station, the newcomer chose to alight at the very same spot on the tree, displacing the smaller bird, which retreated to the topmost branches to resume its tapping. It gave me an ideal opportunity to compare the two species in detail as they are seldom seen together, the lesser-spotted being hardly bigger than a tree sparrow and its relative comparable to a thrush. The pair continued to work industriously until the lower bird suddenly spotted me below the tree. It made off across the river in its weak undulating flight, uttering a loud 'chick-chick' as it returned to its nearby nesting wood.

MAY 25TH

Carried out a thorough search for duck nests, for most species are now well under way and I have noticed several females missing at the regular feeding time—a sure sign that incubation has begun. The earlier nests are normally made in the baskets and boxes provided for the purpose, but as the natural cover develops, more birds show a preference to choose their own nesting site. As there is the best part of an acre of rough vegetation inside the enclosures, finding them all before they hatch is no easy task. It is amazing just how quickly the ground cover develops, and in a few short weeks the place has been transformed into a veritable jungle, with hostile beds of stinging nettles, thick clumps of hogweed, and tall stands of flowering cow parsley, now well above head height.

A few nests can usually be discovered by following the duck's little secret trails through the foliage, though the majority are far more careful, only approaching the nest by a roundabout route and leaving little indication of their movements.

The European pochard posed no problem, for as usual she had raked together all the surrounding foliage within reach of her nest, piling it up high to form a great mass of wilting vegetation on which she was prominently perched, arching her neck and hissing loudly when I stumbled across her. Others were not so easy to find, but a systematic and painful search of the nettlebeds revealed many more nests, and by the time the entire area was covered, I had enough eggs to fill the incubator, their removal thus encouraging the birds to lay a replacement clutch.

78

It is interesting to note that certain species always show a preference for a particular type of vegetation when siting their nests. Wigeon invariably prefer tall nettles, garganey choose the shorter areas of grass, while the green-winged teal can always be found in the very centre of a thick clump of dog's mercury.

I left the pair of barnacle geese to carry on with their own hatching. Finishing her clutch last week, the goose is now tight on her five eggs at the summit of the high bank rising from the water, the site jealously guarded by her gander, who, although small, will attack and drive off almost anything that approaches too closely—myself included. The eggs should come to no harm under his watchful eye.

MAY 27TH

The house martins are now busy beneath the eaves above my study window, with a constant twittering and an untiring procession flying to and fro with tiny beakfuls of mud to add to the cup-like structures of their nests that are rapidly taking shape. There has been very little rain of late to provide them with mud, but despite having to collect each precious cargo from the shores of West Lake almost a quarter of a mile distant, they carry on determined in their task, travelling countless miles in the course of a day's toil. It is surprising just how quickly the work progresses. Those birds taking a break from building were shadowing the reaper as it roared around felling wide swathes of lush grass on the field beside the garden, snapping up a host of winged insects disturbed by the machine, while high above them a team of black, sickle-winged swifts screamed lustily as they revelled in their powers of flight.

The mown grass will lay for a day or two to fill the air with its agreeable scent before being collected, chopped up and compacted into a silage clamp, where it will mature for the rest of the summer to be used eventually for cattle feed once winter is upon us. Other farm crops are growing apace. The fields of wind-waved winter barley have sprouted their tender ears of grain, the rape fields are glowing with acres of lemon flowers, and the hay grows tall and fragrant on the meadows, soon to be ripe for cutting. In the orchard, where a blackbird is feeding her brood of four fully fledged young, the fruit trees are beginning to shed their blossom, and soon the boughs will begin to groan and sag as they become burdened with slowly swelling fruits. How quickly the year seems to be passing.

MAY 28TH

Collected a clutch of hooded merganser eggs from beneath a mallard in one of the pond nest-boxes last night, where they have spent the last thirty days being incubated naturally. Merganser eggs are extremely difficult to hatch in an incubator, so when the mallard had completed her clutch, I removed the eggs and replaced them with those collected from the merganser, thus giving the latter the best possible chance of hatching. The mallard appeared not to notice the deception, but I was only just in time as some of the ducklings had already chipped a hole in the tough shells. I ferried them home in my shirt to conserve their heat, and by the time they were safely in the hatcher one bird had almost broken free of its shell.

The trick appears to have worked, for this morning all seven fertile eggs had hatched, the remaining four proving infertile when tested with the light. However, my problems are only just beginning. Besides being difficult to hatch, the ducklings are also very difficult to rear, requiring specialized treatment and care if they are to survive. The normal diet of chick crumbs given to other species has to be ground to a fine powder to avoid it compacting in their gizzards, and to this a regular supply of chopped mealworms and a sprinkling of finely grated egg has to be added to ensure a high intake of protein.

I moved the ducklings to a brooder as soon as they had dried, adding a small youngster from a previous brood of teal, which would encourage them to begin feeding by copying its actions. After a couple of days they should have been taught where their food and water is and the 'teacher' can be removed and returned to its rightful family.

To further complicate matters, wild mergansers normally nest in disused woodpecker holes, from which their young instinctively climb soon after hatching. This instinct to vacate the nest remains very strong for the first couple of days, the young birds being very adept at escape by scaling the wire sides of the brooder, which has to be covered to prevent them getting out. All in all, it is certainly a challenge to breed and rear such an unobliging species successfully.

MAY 30TH

The rain has come at last. Following almost three weeks of dry and sunny weather that has dried the earth to dust, one could almost feel the land breathing a sigh of relief as soothing rain fell on parched ground to gurgle away in the wide cracks that have appeared across much of the surface of the heavy lands.

On Spring Marsh a scattering of this year's young herons stood huddled dejectedly in the downpour, wet and bedraggled bundles of little more than skin and bone, with snake-like heads withdrawn between hunched shoulders waiting for the rain to ease. In a drain outlet near the river four birds had gathered in a delinquent huddle, to watch and wait motionlessly in a tight coven as if conspiring some foul deed or mischief. Murder was on their minds, for the heavy rains would bring out frogs and other delicacies from the thick protection of the reedbeds. Spring Marsh is now a dangerous place to venture, with many pairs of eyes on constant alert for anything edible. Nothing moves unnoticed, particularly if live and capable of being swallowed. Fish, amphibians, young birds, or small mammals—all are grist to the heron's mill if foolish enough to stray too close to the stabbing stiletto of this far from fastidious bird. Even the moles that occupy the underground colony beside Marsh Wood are not safe, for if one surfaces for anything but the briefest of moments it is snapped up and swallowed whole, its remains ejected later below the roosting trees in the form of a regurgitated pellet after the edible parts have been digested. The Marsh Wood heronry is now strangely silent after many weeks of activity and no longer echoes to the begging cries of ravenous youngsters when parents had returned from countless fishing trips with cargoes of food. The young have been abandoned to fend for themselves, the huge white-washed nests lying deserted until another spring, except for an odd youngster or two that returns to its platform to while away the short hours of darkness.

Eventually the rain ceased. The strong rays of the sun peeped between the clouds to transform the marsh, emphasizing the first sprouting heads of the yellow flag-irises and casting a rich rainbow over Marsh Wood. The earth was refreshed, blankets of mist rising gently as the marsh steamed, accentuating the warm and earthy vapour laden with the rich scent of the vegetation.

One by one the herons roused and shook themselves. Three of the murderous group wandered their separate ways, leaving one bird to remain immobile on a broken fence-post as though carved from stone. Its patience was swiftly rewarded, for soon the heavy bill stabbed among the rushes at his feet with the speed of a striking snake, a quick, neck-stretching swallow and the prey was gone. It was as if nothing had happened, the bird immediately resuming its vigilant stance to await the coming of its next victim.

Wild gooseberry.

June

There is no doubt that of all the months, June is the most bountiful, when all of nature surpasses itself by an unrivalled wealth of beauty and colour almost bewildering in its variety. The delicate spring flowers are now but a memory, but replaced with such a profusion that one is confused by its richness. Everything strives towards reproduction. Wild flowers struggle to set their seeds before being overwhelmed by the luxuriance of vegetation that forges ever higher, their alluring petals attracting butterflies of many-coloured wings and buzzing bees that are busy with the search for life-giving nectar.

The still-hatching mayflies are joined by a host of other insects to provide a rich glut of food for nesting birds, the former often snapped up in beakfuls by yellow wagtails, bright as canaries, that return to youngsters tucked away under tussocks of grass or among the upturned roots of a fallen tree beside the water, where swarms of metallic damsel-flies of every hue dance together in heart-shaped loveknots. Along every pond and lake the marginal reedbeds are alive with the churring of countless members of the warbler tribe, and between the stiff stalks, moorhen and coot lead little parties of sooty young-sters, pausing now and again to offer delicate morsels of weed gleaned from the bottom.

On the higher ground, fox cubs are beginning to venture further afield from secret earths, still supplied with food by their parents but becoming steadily more independent as each day passes and beginning to assume much of the rusty redness of the true fox coat. The rabbit warren supplies much of their food, its occupants multiplying at an alarming rate as only the rabbit knows how.

Hedges are full of nests and fledgeling birds, the younger of which gape hungrily as one examines the nest, expecting yet another beakful of food. The more advanced birds are practising their unsteady flight, still weak of wing and providing easy meat for the wily sparrowhawk that hunts silently with stealth and cunning, its approach announced by harsh parental warnings as anxious birds fear for the safety of their charges.

Over all there is still the song of the birds, who even though labouring endlessly still find time to usher in the dawn with a musical chorus, the nightingale alone continuing his unequalled song in Bluebell Copse well into the darker hours, when a host of moths and other night-flying insects emerge to conduct their secret lives under cover of the decreasing hours of darkness as we hurry towards what will soon be the shortest night of the year.

JUNE 3RD

Scaled the hollow oak again that hangs over the river to search for trout, but the water level has dropped dramatically since my last visit and even the two small ones, seen previously, have disappeared. This was rather a disappointment as I had prepared my fly rod to give them a try.

Climbing down the gnarled trunk I heard a strange hissing sound emanating from below my foot, but it was several minutes before I discovered its source, a shelduck sitting on her nest deep in the hollow heart of the tree. She was tucked away almost at ground level, her entrance hole nothing more than a tiny crack in the rotting wood and the nest virtually impossible to see.

I left her to it and continued the search upstream, where another gravelly bed lies sheltered beneath a row of overhanging ash trees—also a spot favoured by the occasional wild brown trout. A fish of some size was rising regularly beneath the branches, and considering the heavy splashes was a good deal larger than the normal ¾ lb (0.35 kg). Try as I might, I could not reach it with a fly. Even by wading into the river my casting was restricted by a thick hawthorn bush, the fly snagging each time on the backward cast as I payed out enough line to put it over the fish. The rising increased and I noticed a massive hatch of olive duns floating past me on the surface, their large lace-like wings fluttering enticingly as they fought to rise clear of the water, providing a tempting target and disappearing every so often as a heavy boil on the surface marked their passing.

There seemed to be only one way of reaching the fish. Picking my way carefully through a solid wall of head-high brambles, I eventually widened a hole beneath the ash branches to allow just enough room to poke the rod through to try dapping a fly at the upstream end of the trout's lie. A search of my fly box produced nothing even remotely resembling the natural insect, so in desperation I tied on a tiny pheasant-tailed nymph, lowering it gently on the surface and allowing the current to carry it towards the fish, still unseen but now lying only a couple of rod lengths downstream. After several minutes there was still no sign of an offer. Presently one of the duns alighted on a nettle beside me, sparking an idea. I attached it lightly to the nymph and lowered it gently to the water, watching closely and twitching the rod as the current carried it along the lie, giving the insect the appearance of trying to take off. As it reached the spot, a huge bow wave approached. There was a heart-stopping glimpse of a wide mouth and an almighty splash as the brownie tore away. A classic take! The line tightened instantly to the run, the rod jerking wildly as the fish surged downstream when the hook went home, stripping several yards of line from a screaming reel. Back and forth it went up and down the river, causing anxious moments as time and time again it dragged the line towards a tangle of overhanging brambles. I dared not try to hurry it for I could hardly move the rod and could only pray the tiny size-14 hook would hold. At this point I remembered having left the landing-net several yards downriver. There was no hope of reaching it. The bank where I stood was four feet above the water, leaving no choice but to join the fish in the river and hope that I could snatch it out by hand. Luckily I was wearing waders. Beating through the remaining brambles I dropped into 18 inches of water, the splash prompting the fish to run again. I thought it would never tire, but luckily it was firmly hooked in the scissors of the jaw and I finally saw the gold of its belly as, completely beaten, it turned on its side and allowed me to lift it from the water.

Such had been the tension and excitement, I was shaking like a leaf. Totally drained, I lay on the bank admiring my catch for several minutes, 2 lb 9 oz (1.16 kg) of solid streamlined muscle, its bronzed sides speckled black and flecked with vivid scarlet spots—a beautiful and truly wild brown trout and certainly one of my best from the Wensum.

JUNE 6TH

I have virtually given up hope of the snowy owls breeding this year, for although both birds have been displaying lustily and going through their paces, as yet nothing has come of it and the time is quickly slipping away with no sign of any further developments. The racket they make in the late evenings is tremendous. The male begins the proceedings by emitting a string of harsh barking hoots, flaunting himself proudly from a high perch as though he really means business. Soon his mate is responding eagerly, but unwittingly cuts him down to size by chasing him from branch to branch around the aviary until, his ego entirely deflated, he retires to conceal himself in the corner of the enclosure, all the time keeping a fearful eye on her movements. I must admit that when she fluffs up her feathers and rears to full height she looks an immense and rather daunting prospect, her feathered talons armed with black, inch-long spikes, and gaping beak—a powerful weapon that tears prey to shreds with intimidating ease. Sadly, it will not be long before the owls begin to moult and by then it will be far too late for them to start a family.

On the other hand, Whisper, our German short-haired pointer bitch, is looking far more promising. Following a visit to her estranged boyfriend in the middle of April, her formerly sleek and shapely figure is rounding up nicely and the litter should be due in about a week hence. At the moment she slouches her portly frame around the garden in a semi-lethargic state, her normally boisterous temperament much calmed by the delicate condition. I can only hope she retains some measure of this highly agreeable placidity in the future.

JUNE 7TH

On my way to deal with a nest-robbing crow at dusk, I came across a barn owl hunting Spring Marsh, systematically quartering the thick drain banks and areas of low vegetation for unwary voles and shrews. The bird ghosted around the marsh in buoyant, bouncing flight, its head pivoting visibly from side to side, eyes and ears alert for betraying movements of prey. It came to within a few yards at the end of its beat, appearing not to notice me standing quietly among the rushes. Its wings were silent, the wraith-like apparition flitting soundlessly above the marsh like a huge white moth, at times merging into the heavy blue-grey mist that hung like a blanket a few feet above the dampened earth. At the end of a sweep beside the river, it unexpectedly switched course, hovered briefly, and plunged with outstretched talons among a patch of knee-high willow-herb, where it was completely lost from sight. The whole manoeuvre took hardly a second, but was evidently successful, for a full minute elapsed before it reappeared to continue scouring the marsh, finally melting into the mist around the far corner of the background wood.

Not a breath of wind stirred the rushes and a deep stillness hung over the marsh. A few duck were talking higher up the river and the occasional shriek of a heron rung from Marsh Wood, but presently I heard the sound I had been waiting for—the first husky croak of the crow returning to its nightly roost in the tall ash clump. Its movements did not pass unnoticed. A pair of protesting lapwings shadowed it across the meadow, mobbing, diving, and wailing until the larger bird gained sanctuary among the trees at the far end of the ash belt. For a few tense minutes I crouched motionless as the bird, cautious to the last, surveyed the area carefully before flying to roost. It finally committed itself and the single shot shattered the silence, putting an oyster-catcher on wing to circle noisily but unseen among the misty loneliness in the failing light. There would be few to mourn the crow's passing.

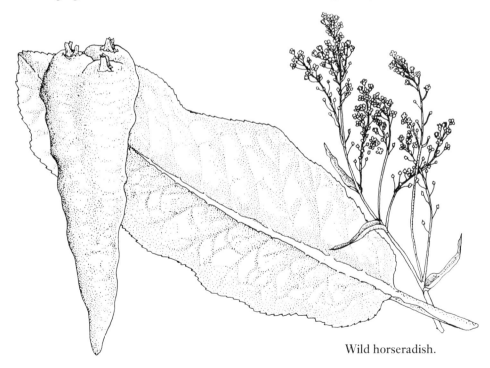

Wild horseradish.

85

JUNE 9TH

The day was glorious, clear blue sky and fleecy clouds announcing the fact that summer has arrived at last. Taking a welcome break from a mound of boring paperwork at lunchtime, I sneaked off to West Lake to see how the terns were progressing with their nesting duties on the small island lying parallel to the causeway. Last year the island, barely 20 feet in diameter, was completely overgrown with dense vegetation. As terns favour open ground with little or no cover for nesting, they eventually deposited their eggs on the open causeway, where they were all too easily discovered by a foraging fox. Earlier this spring the island was cleared in the hope of tempting them back. The effort has proved worth while, for using binoculars I was just able to make out five nests, each containing three eggs, the actual nests little more than a spartan scrape among the gravel, lined with a few roots and bits of grass raked up from local materials. The eggs varied greatly in colour from deep olive green to rich khaki, heavily overlaid with blotches of darker brown. While I scanned the island the terns hovered uneasily above, a few braver birds swooping vigorously to miss my head by a matter of inches.

A great crested grebe shuffling down on her eggs after returning to the nest.

86

One by one they returned to the island as I wandered to the far end of the gravel causeway, where a great-crested grebe slipped unobtrusively from her floating nest anchored to the edge of a phragmite bed, having first covered her eggs with weed to conceal them from hostile eyes. She surfaced 20 yards from the reeds, an immaculate bird that surveyed me with an eye of brilliant glaring red before submerging quietly beneath the surface again, leaving hardly a ripple on the water. Wearing thigh boots I was just able to wade to the nest—a mass of rotted marsh plants pulled carelessly together to form a moist raft just above water level. Grebe eggs are a curious oval shape, and the three it contained were badly stained and obviously close to hatching. A reed warbler hissed a warning as I picked my way back through the reedbed, taking care not to disturb its neat little cup-like nest woven carefully around the stiff phragmite stems.

The steep sandbank on the southern edge of the lake is now a honeycomb of sand-martin nesting-tunnels, with literally hundreds of birds milling around the entrances like a swarm of angry bees. I counted well over four hundred nests before giving up. As most birds lay a clutch of four or five eggs and often attempt a second or even a third brood, the breeding potential of such a colony is obviously colossal, possibly amounting to thousands of youngsters in a favourable year, although vast numbers succumb during the long and perilous autumn migration to winter quarters in Africa, and on their return journey in the spring—thus keeping numbers relatively stable from year to year.

JUNE 11TH

Arranged to meet Andy Davison at the Valley Lakes for a few hours trouting, although the weather outlook was not very encouraging: a low sky the colour of lead and promising heavy rain.

Andy has recently returned from a fishing trip to India, where he and John Wilson experienced some exciting times in pursuit of the massive mahseer, a huge and powerful fish frequenting the turbulent waters of fast-flowing, boulder-strewn torrents, where they took fish up to 88 lb (40 kg) in weight.

Andy joined me soon after lunch, electing to try for a specimen fish in Rainbow Lake while I settled for something nearer frying-pan size, for a number of small fish were rising in Home Lake.

I tackled up with a new floating line to allow presentation very close to the surface, using a tiny black-and-peacock spider attached to a 4 lb (1.8 kg) leader. On the floating line, trout 'takes' are less easily recognized, for while the sinking line is kept tight and a sudden thump on the line denotes a fish, the slackness of the leader when practising the former method disallows such close contact, and one has to watch carefully for a sudden twitching of the line on the surface to signify the fly has been taken.

I worked long and hard for my first fish, slowly covering the rise with the spider by a pattern of tiny jerks and draws until a sharp kick suddenly straightened the kinks from the line. Striking instantly, I was into a small rainbow of about 1 lb, which in spite of its size put up a spirited fight. Continuing with the same fly, I managed to deceive two more in rapid succession before the rain began, a steady, drenching downpour that soon discovered the weak spots in my fishing jacket. The sky had assumed a general gloomy grey, so I decided to see how Andy was faring, meeting him halfway returning with a trout of a good 5 lb (2.3 kg). Beneath the shelter of a leafy oak we debated whether to carry on, but by the time the rain eased we were both soaked to the skin and it seemed pointless to worry about getting wet. Returning to Rainbow Lake we resumed fishing.

For almost an hour I repeatedly moved a good fish at the top corner that, although following the fly almost to the bank, simply refused to commit itself, until I changed to a homemade black-and-yellow nobbler that was snapped up instantly. Unfortunately it pulled free after a short tussle: a disappointing conclusion to a battle of wits, for it would certainly not try again.

Andy was even more dispirited, having hooked and played out a really big fish before it spat out the hook just before reaching the net—a really sizeable trout, or possibly even one of the longed-for freshwater salmon that frustrate almost all attempts to catch them.

The rain came on again, even harder and more persistent. It was time to call it a day. Absolutely drenched, we decided to finish the job off properly by getting wet on the inside too, and with this in mind gratefully retired to the local public house to drown our sorrows. An hour later our spirits were considerably higher—literally in fact—and although it had been a rather trying day very soon the day's fish begun fighting harder and longer and increased in size, particularly the one that got away.

JUNE 12TH

The spell of wet weather continues, an unrelenting deluge that has now saturated the land, postponing the hay harvest and making life difficult for the young pheasants and partridges now reaching their peak time of hatching. The tiny chicks have enough to contend with in the form of stoats, weasels, foxes, feral cats, and the many winged predators, without the weather taking its toll. Many will surely perish if the period of cold wet weather is prolonged. The newly hatched chicks are extremely sensitive to the vagaries of our summer climate during their first few days of life, and it is little wonder that few can stand the endless trailing through the tall, wet, and inhospitable vegetation that forms their natural nursery. The availability of insect food is also a major factor in their survival rate, good weather being essential to ensure prolific hatches of their main food supply.

I flushed a good brood of eight pheasant chicks from a field of winter barley a couple of evenings ago—the birds able, although unsteady fliers, of a few days old—accompanied by the mother hen who dropped back into the barley after flying a few yards ready to muster her offspring together again when I had gone. With the arrival of such hostile conditions, I fear there are now not many of the brood remaining.

JUNE 14TH

Arrived home from work in the middle of the morning to find Barbara in a state of great excitement. Whisper was in the process of giving birth to her pups, having already produced six animated velvety bundles and making it quite clear that more were on the way. Whisper had been very restless last night, pacing interminably up and down and seeming unable to settle comfortably. The arrival of the pups looked imminent. She had even dug a couple of holes in the garden shrubbery, presumably with the intention of using them as a nursery. When we went to bed she was confined safely in one end of the goat hut together with a roomy, straw-lined box.

Although Barbara checked through the early hours there were no further developments overnight, and when released in the garden first thing this morning Whisper immediately excavated another large hole beneath the low, sheltering branches of a conifer. When returned, she resigned herself to the box and starting given birth half an hour later, at least choosing a reasonably sociable hour to produce her pups.

By lunchtime her labours had finished—the final count a large litter of ten endearing little puppies, six dogs and four bitches, licking each one clean as it arrived with a tender and patient gentleness so unlike her normal energetic and boisterous self. When it was all over she emerged to stretch her legs rather shakily around the garden, but was soon back with her offspring, allowing them to suckle until they lay in a contented huddle. In the meantime, Barbara, who was far less calm about the whole affair, continued to fuss around like an old mother hen with her brood.

When I peeped in last thing at night the pack were sleeping in a velvety bundle nuzzled against their mother below the warmth of an infra-red heater, a chorus of little contented grunts and sighs emanating from the nursery box. Whisper looked thoroughly exhausted, hardly bothering to raise her head as I entered but wagging her tail gently as I stroked her head. She has had an extremely tiring day.

JUNE 16TH

I have just returned home from an exciting first night of the season spent on John Wilson's private carp lake, where I was placed in the capable hands of Michael Saunt—known to his friends as 'Dickie'—and his wife, Dawn, both ardent carp fishers of considerable experience. It was an overcast but tolerably warm night, with just a hint of drizzle that failed to dampen our enthusiasm for the night that lay ahead.

The coarse-fishing season began at midnight, but at this time of the year the sky seldom completely darkens and it was easy to keep an eye on the bobbins of silver paper attached to our lines that acted as bite indicators to the bait of cubed luncheon-meat weighted lightly on the bottom.

I had a couple of tentative early runs though failed to connect. It was left to Dawn to provide an early lesson when one of her pair of rods bent alarmingly to a very strong fish that raced away to give her a particularly trying time among the lily pads. It was eventually persuaded back into the open water and in due course a magnificent carp of 16 lb 9 oz (7.5 kg) lay gasping on the bank.

As it was my first carping expedition, Dickie thoughtfully nursed me through the night, supplying mosquito repellent, sound advice, and a helping hand when my spool of new line became frequently entangled around the reel, which provided a convenient excuse for missing a few more half-hearted bites. What the line really needed was a good strong fish to straighten out the kinks. Dickie also took a carp on each of his two rods, one a lively, hard-fighting silver metallic of about 4 lb (1.8 kg).

Almost mesmerized by the slip of silver paper, I kept a constant vigil until the drizzly grey dawn returned some colour to the bankside rushes; the lake again bloomed with clumps of yellow iris and the pink and yellow flowers of the waterlilies spangled the floating rafts of leaves. High above us, a wood-cock croaked back and forth in its roding flight and an early heron back-pedalled over the surrounding pine trees as he glimpsed us fishing beside his favourite spot. A chiffchaff had just begun his chirpings from a group of silver birches when I was roused from dozing by the bite indicator lifting steadily towards the bottom rod ring. This time I hit the run quickly and the hook held fast. It proved to be another of the small metallic 'ghost' carp, and very lively for its size. I eventually got it to the bank, a handsomely marked little fish that streaked away with a powerful thrust of its tail when returned to the water.

As the sky slowly lightened a few fish began to stir the surface calm. We lobbed a few bread crusts on the water to attract their attention, but a particularly stubborn mallard duck continually frustrated our efforts, return-ing instantly to gobble up the crusts each time we threw out a fresh batch to entice the fish.

Determined to see me catch what could be considered a real carp, at 8 a.m. Dickie wandered along the bank with half a loaf of bread, eventually finding a good-sized mirror gliding around one corner of the lake below a stand of silver birches. It began to take the floating crusts.

Finding a position well above it, I cast a sizeable chunk of crust from the high bank as it lazily cruised the clear water, hardly daring to breathe as the blue-black monster slowly turned to glide for a closer inspection. Following a cautious study, a huge white mouth appeared below my offering and gently sucked it in. It all seemed to happen in slow motion. Forcing myself to wait until the fish had turned away, I struck, feeling a strong kick as the hook went home. The carp instantly came to life and surged off towards the nearest bed of lilies. Even after a thorough briefing, I was still not prepared for what followed, the fish was so strong it put an alarming bend in the rod and ripped off yards of line before disappearing among the lily pads without a chance of heading it off. My hopes plummeted when I felt a solid resistance as the line wrapped around the stems, but by relaxing pressure on the rod I managed to coax it out, though no further than the next patch of weed. The fish obviously knew its way around, taking a very long time before co-operating enough to enable me to steer it towards the bank, and even then causing anxious moments among the marginal reeds before I could guide it over the landing-net—my first mirror carp, an impressive fish that scaled in at 12 lb 1 oz (5.7 kg).

It was more than I had hoped for, although much of the credit for its capture was due to a patient tutor who, to cap it all, then served up a delicious breakfast of bacon and eggs cooked on a portable stove beside the lake. What a splendid way to round off an exciting opening night, but having not slept for well over twenty-four hours, the entire episode possessed a strangely unreal, dream-like quality.

JUNE 19TH

There was a great cackling commotion among the orchard geese this morning, for one of the female red-breasted geese has at last started excavating a nesting scrape, her distended rear end bearing testimony to the fact that she is on the very point of laying an egg. In common with all nesting geese, the birds have become extremely territorial, fiercely attacking anything foolish enough to approach the nest site. With the assistance of her gander, Snuffles, the cat, was sent packing in no uncertain terms while taking his morning stroll around

The scrape completed and lined to her satisfaction with dry grass and
roots, the redbreasted goose settles down on her nest.

91

the orchard and even the pair of collared doves that are normally allowed to raid the nearby food trough were set upon with zeal.

Besides being the smallest and rarest European goose, the red-breasted is also the most colourful: a striking blend of black-and-white markings and the characteristic rich chestnut-red breast that make the bird a most handsome, expensive, and much sought-after species among collectors of ornamental fowl.

On their native breeding grounds in northern Siberia, red-breasted geese invariably choose to breed in company with a large bird of prey, notably peregrine falcons or rough-legged buzzards, where some measure of protection is afforded to the nests from the attentions of Arctic foxes and egg-eating skuas by the raptors' defending the surrounding countryside from unwelcome intruders. Possibly for this same reason the goose has again chosen to place her nest tight against the wire of the snowy-owl enclosure, some latent instinct prompting her to select a site beneath the protection of these large birds of prey.

By noon the scrape had been completed and lined to her satisfaction with beakfuls of dry grass and roots, and I am now awaiting the arrival of the first egg. I think there will be one by the morning.

JUNE 21ST

The peafield on the farm boundary has taken a recent hammering from a flock of two or three hundred wood pigeon, now returning to pilfer the crop as it flowers after leaving it virtually untouched for several weeks.

The afternoon was bright and windy, and if there was an accessible flightline it seemed an ideal situation for a few hours flighting. With the help of binoculars I discovered a small but regular passage of birds along the boundary hedge, their approach against the wind at one point passing between two clumps of tall ash trees where 6 acres (2.6 ha) of growing barley ended at a strip of sugar beet. It took only a few moments to create a hide among the ample undergrowth of shoulder-high nettles and bracken fronds, a roomy if somewhat uncomfortable spot concealing me from the pigeons' main approach. The wind was increasing, whipping up fierce waves across the green sea of undulating barley and straining the creaking ash boughs above me, now heavy with leaf in the full flush of summer growth.

Despite a powerful headwind the pigeon were passing over very high, appearing as distant grey specks from the background woods to provide difficult shooting by side-slipping deceptively on the wind gusting along the spinney. I shot rather indifferently at first, wasting several cartridges before connecting with the first really high bird that planed down like a falling sycamore leaf a long way behind. With some measure of confidence restored, I began to fare better, though was frequently outsmarted by birds that hovered almost suicidally overhead until spotting the glint of sunlight from the barrels when the gun was raised. A flip of a wing on the wind whisked them hastily out of range. Fortunately I improved with practice, only mounting the gun at the very last moment to take almost vertical shots, dropping several among the field of sugar beet where they could be easily gathered.

The result of one shot plunged into the nettles beside the hide, and while searching for it during a quiet spell I came across a most exquisite creature, a beautiful eyed hawkmoth newly emerged from its pupal shell, its expanding wings quivering gently while it sunned itself on a sheltered log. It was a perfect specimen, the camouflaged forewings partially concealing under-wings of a deep salmon pink, bordering the bluish tinted 'eyes' rimmed with mascara black that winked boldly as it flexed its wings.

A frantic rustle of pinions overhead sent me scuttling back to the hide as half-a-dozen pigeon scattered back over the trees. Safely hidden once more, I was allowed another full hour of difficult shooting by pigeon stirring from the downwind woods in small parties until the wind brought a belt of dark cloud racing from the west. The best of the day was gone, the clouds releasing the first cool spits of rain as I prepared to leave. Like the weather, my performance with the gun had been extremely variable, but I neglected to count the empty cartridge cases, and almost two dozen pigeon were enough to carry home to stock up the game larder.

JUNE 24TH

A delightful midsummer morning of the kind one remembers from child-hood days, when the summers were always endless and scorching, and trilling larks hung all day in skies of the purest unbroken blue. A heat haze shimmered across Spring Marsh, where neat rows of new-mown grass lie wilting in the sun to fill the air with one of the richest scents of summer. The drying action of sun and wind are preparing the hay to be turned and 'made' in advance of its being carted to the shelter of the barn before the weather has a chance to take a turn for the worse to spoil the harvest.

A cock kestrel rode the warm air currents high above the marsh, pausing occasionally to hover above the swathes of grass for unwary voles and shrews, their hitherto secret movements now exposed by the grass-cutter. Below him a cuckoo wheezed apologetically from Marsh Wood, but soon gave up. 'In June, he changes his tune', and his voice is now husky and broken, the poor bird giving the impression of suffering from a bad attack of hiccups. He will not be with us to know the first early bite of frost in autumn for, 'In July, away he must fly' to pass the winter in Africa, followed about a month later by the parasitic youngsters of his species, now growing out of all proportion to overworked foster parents in the nests of warbler, wagtail, and dunnock.

The adjacent water meadow is still a golden flood of buttercups. Here no chemical spray has as yet penetrated to eliminate the 'weeds', and the marsh is grazed only lightly by a motley crew of bullocks, at the moment gathered beneath the shade of scrub alders, tails swishing to keep the hordes of vicious stinging flies at bay. As of a few decades past, the marsh drains are lined with wild flowers of every hue, among them the ragged robin, water forget-me-not, lady's smock, and meadow cranesbill, while the drier regions still boast a few of the now-rare wild orchids that still survive and bloom, their rich purple flower spikes visited by a procession of nectar-seeking bees. Along boundary hedges the early snowstorm of mayflower has been replaced by the white inverted parasols of elder—its flowers held in high esteem by brewers of homemade wine for a delicious palate so reminiscent of champagne—while among its heady perfume the pastel pinks of the delicate dog rose unfurls to add a subtler and elusive fragrance to the balmy air.

JUNE 25TH

Fed the brooder-house ducklings well ahead of schedule this evening, for I had a rather important appointment to keep with a fellow falconer. Catering for the youngsters at this stage is a time-consuming task, but I arrived at his house well before the appointed hour for an introduction to what will hopefully be my constant companion in a few weeks time: a young female sparrowhawk I hope to train for hunting.

The nestling has been bred in captivity. Hatched only five days ago, she is being hand-reared and was brought out for a brief inspection in a cloth-lined box—a tiny chick weighing barely a couple of ounces and still nothing more than a plush, pink-skinned creature rather scantily clad in fluffy white down. Her long, gangling legs, at the moment flesh pink, are tipped with miniature claws that will one day mature into malevolent black talons as sharp as needles.

I have deliberately chosen a female that, when fully grown, should be capable of hunting prey of up to moorhen size, though at present she looks extremely vulnerable and is hardly able to raise her proportionately heavy head for anything but the briefest of moments—her resemblance to a swift, cunning, and deadly hunter leaving much to the imagination. Watching the frail and helpless form, it seemed strange to think that if all goes well I will be hunting her along the hedgerows in a few weeks' time. Sparrowhawks have a deserved reputation for being difficult birds to maintain in peak condition and she will need constant attention before this is achieved, particularly when she first comes to me in about a couple of weeks, although by then she should have assumed more hawk-like proportions.

Following an all-too-brief introduction, the chick was returned to the warmth of a brooder lamp under which she is being reared. Assuming all goes well, I look forward to our next meeting in a fortnight's time, though not without some trepidation.

JUNE 27TH

Plucked up sufficient courage to carry out a final assault on what is now an almost impenetrable jungle of undergrowth at the duckponds, hoping to discover what will probably be the last few clutches of eggs this year. The stinging nettles have now reached an unfriendly shoulder height and, tangled with brambles, thistles, and giant burdock plants, they make the task a

Among the prettiest of all young ducklings. A clutch of day-old shelduck.

difficult and painful operation. Most birds have reached the end of the egg-laying period and are beginning to moult, the drakes losing their brightly coloured plumes—together with their amorous feelings—to make the transition towards the sombre 'eclipse' plumage in which they resemble the females until another moult in autumn restores their gaudy attire. They have done well, for in spite of a later-than-normal start, I already have well over a hundred ducklings in the brooder house and many more eggs developing in the incubator. The pair of barnacles have hatched their quintet of goslings that gorge themselves continuously on the lush growth of grass, and in the orchard the red-breasted goose is well on the way to producing a sizeable clutch of eggs.

My search was a long, tedious, and painful experience, but at length I emerged from the undergrowth covered with scratches, nettle stings, and insect bites, and with a few extra eggs. I was sweating profusely and also attended by a disagreeable odour, for which a female Chiloe wigeon was to blame, following the discovery of her nest deep in a bankside tunnel. Aware of the dangers of a cornered bird, I encouraged her to vacate the tunnel by tapping the entrance, but she refused to budge, leaving me no option but to lay flat on the ground and force my arm into the passage to retrieve the eggs,

95

trusting she would remain calm. An incubating duck that has not been off the nest for several hours is not to be taken lightly. While allowing me to stretch my hand almost within reach of the eggs, she suddenly decided that enough was enough, evacuating both the nesting tunnel and her bowels simultaneously with dire results, the consequences of which were an unimaginably offensive mess distributed the complete length of my arm that lingered stubbornly despite copious ablutions in the duckpond.

The final batch of shelduck eggs had hatched during the night and, like myself, had almost dried out by the time I returned home, each of the nine eggs hatching within a few minutes of one another. They appear a strong and healthy lot and are among the prettiest of all the ducklings.

JUNE 30TH

Accompanied Barbara Wilson to the Royal Norfolk Show, where we spent a pleasant afternoon at the event held at Costessey on the outskirts of Norwich. The show is held annually, allowing town to meet country to gain a little more understanding of the country way of life, and an insight into where and how the real necessities of life are produced.

The agricultural show of old was one of the country dwellers' few days out during a busy year, allowing them to exhibit the best of their crops and animals against the best the county could produce. Fortunately, much of the rural atmosphere and competitive spirit still survives, although part of the show has become 'commercialized', and now includes trade stands and displays that are far removed from the original country theme. Many of the crafts and pastimes the country person takes for granted are on display, from farrowing to farriery, show-jumping to sheep shearing, plus shooting, fishing, falconry, dog training, archery, and taxidermy—the latter grouped together in a special section devoted to country sports.

Avoiding the massed trade stands, we spent a great deal of time in the field-sports section where, following a brief gundog demonstration, a variety of birds of prey were flown from the display ring. I was particularly impressed by a formidable-looking ferruginous hawk, a large North-American species that, when released, circled the ring on broad, buzzard-like wings, and despite clearing off for some time, returned to display an agility in the air that belied its rather cumbersome appearance. I think the hawk would make an ideal hunting companion. It was followed by an obviously fit lugger falcon that was flown to the lure, the bird ranging widely around the showground gaining height from the wind prior to stooping quite competently at the lure. In complete contrast was a young eagle owl that refused even to take to its wings, appearing put out by the large crowd that had gathered to watch, and it obstinately refused to budge even after much encouragement from an exasperated handler. I knew just how he felt. Barbara fell in love with a pretty little barn owl flown to the fist (obviously an imprinted bird hand-reared from an early age), for it would not allow its handler to walk away for more than a few yards before following.

96

And so on to the livestock section, where vast numbers of sheep, cattle, horses, pigs, goats, donkeys, and rabbits were penned or tethered, waiting for the most part patiently to be returned to quieter pastures at home, where they could rest from two days of continual disturbance. In the nearby cattle ring stockmen proudly paraded their charges, the animals turned out in pristine condition after what must have been hours of patient grooming, their coats sleek and well tended and many adorned with prizewinning rosettes. There were some impressive animals, many the best of their breeds.

As they were led away to their stalls one of the young bulls decided to play up, having fun and games with its handler as it frisked out of control, towing the unfortunate stockman along on his rear end in a undignified manner before eventually breaking free. Luckily the bull did not travel far before being recaptured, and a potentially dangerous situation was averted without serious injury.

After a welcome pint of beer to compensate for the warm weather, it was on to the cage-bird exhibition, where row upon row of budgerigars chirped, canaries sang, and a varied collection of foreign birds flaunted their colourful plumage. All too soon it was time to leave, although we stopped *en route* to catch the tail end of the final raptor display. As we left, workmen were already beginning the mammoth task of dismantling the exhibition stands and marquees, the two-day event over for another summer, though almost 100,000 visitors were to go away the richer for its experience, and with a more enlightened attitude towards the country way of life.

Pig-nut.

July

JULY 1ST

The longest day has passed, the sun having reached its zenith, and from now on all of nature begins the slow winding-down process towards mellower days when the fruits of her labours will become apparent. For the moment all nature seems out of hand, having squandered its wealth in almost wasteful profusion, the hedgerows, thickets, and wild places overwhelmed by the effort, some even now beginning to look tarnished and outgrown. Even the rivers and ponds are choked with plant life, although alive with the humming insects and countless tiny froglets that emerge from their watery homes in force, having lost their wriggling tadpole tails to form miniature replicas of their parents.

The slowly ripening cornfields, bright with poppies where the spray has missed, are beginning to transform the monotonous green swards into a patchwork of pale gold as the winter barley ripens, soon to be fit for harvesting. The first hungry broods of house sparrows have already discovered its bounty, congregating *en masse* to raid the ripening ears until put to flight by the hunting sparrowhawk that also finds rich pickings in the cornfields.

July is probably the busiest month of the year, though much of the activity is hidden beneath the luxuriance of vegetation that smothers the familiar well-worn paths around the countryside. Birds rush hither and thither in an endless search to find food for ever-hungry offspring, their songs subdued for now they have little time or energy for such pleasures. Luckily there is a great abundance of nourishment in the form of countless millions of caterpillars munching their way through the greenery, the birds laboriously collecting them from dawn till dusk after the all-too-brief respite of the short dark hours.

A heavy downpour throughout the night has almost stripped the dog roses of their fragile blooms, although their purpose of attracting the pollinating insects is complete and soon the blood-red hips will swell and form to provide yet more food in the leaner times that are to come as surely as autumn follows summer.

The heavy rains have also flattened a few patches of corn, and it will be worth keeping an eye on these 'laid' areas for they can provide good shooting when the wood pigeon begin to take an interest.

JULY 3RD

It was an oppressively humid afternoon, with banks of dark, ominous clouds that rolled around the valley to bring the threat of a thunderstorm, even though it never came. Strolling down the lane to see if the young terns had hatched on West Lake island, I was sidetracked by the sight of several carp rising in Charles's little lake, barely an acre of water surrounded by steeply shelving banks that enable one to look down upon fish gliding lazily around the blossoming lily pads. The terns could wait.

Twenty minutes later I was back with the rod. Tackling up with nothing more than a no. 4 hook, I cast a breadcrust to the main area of activity, where long dorsal fins were describing wide S-bends across the mirror-like surface. The result was immediate: a small common carp of just under 2 lb (0.9 kg) coming to the net after a short battle, to be followed the very next cast by a fish identical in size that shone even brighter, its armour of polished scales gleaming like layers of newly minted pennies. Both fought well for their size, for even small carp are deceptively strong, although they glide around giving the impression of being very slow and lethargic creatures.

Having taken the pair all surface activity ceased, but presently a better fish began dimpling the water at the far end of the lake. I cast my bait among a few crusts thrown out to tempt it, but the fish was extremely cautious, nosing it around for several minutes until a sudden swirl marked its disappearance. Although I struck instantly the fish was long gone, having furtively teased the bait from the hook.

I twitched out another offering, waiting for what seemed like hours while it toured the area, raising my blood pressure each time it returned for another cautious inspection of the crust. An azure-bodied damsel-fly hitched a lift as it drifted, taking to the air as a ring of approaching ripples gently rocked the crust. A sudden splash and the bait was gone. I straightened the rod to feel a satisfying pull as the fish bored away deep, powering relentlessly towards a bed of dead reedmace. Applying as much pressure as I dared, I managed to head it off, the line singing as it kited sideways to another patch, but again I stopped it short. A few more strength-sapping runs made it more amenable, but just short of the net it suddenly lunged sideways to yet another tangle of stems, where I was horrified to see it purposely wind the line irretrievably around a particularly stout root. Round and round it went in ever-decreasing circles until it was completely stuck fast. I had never seen a fish do it so blatantly, though luckily just within reach of the telescopic net. I eventually retrieved a nice mirror of 6¼ lb (2.8 kg), which erected its fins prominently as I removed the hook.

Upon its release it must have spread the word that all was not well, for the activity ceased until I was preparing to leave for a very late dinner, when a fish began cruising regularly beneath the far bank. My cast fell only inches short of an overhanging willow and, following a very long wait, the carp finally engulfed the bait, sucking it below the surface with a distinctly audible slurp. I somehow dragged it clear of the branches to the open water where,

The last fish of the day. An attractive common carp comes to the net.

unhindered by snags, it was simply a matter of stolidly hanging on until it tired itself out—this time an attractive common carp of about 5 lb (2.3 kg).

When I finally arrived home it was to an icy look and an equally cold dinner, but having enjoyed such an exciting afternoon I must admit it was quite easy to assume a brave smile as I consumed the remnants of what was now my supper.

JULY 5TH

Made another journey to see the island terns, this time managing to get past Charles's lake without succumbing to temptation, but it was touch and go when a very big mirror carp flaunted itself by rooting around a clump of reedmace stems.

As I gained the causeway a shelduck hustled her depleted brood of three ducklings to the water, disturbing a redshank that lifted noisily from a sheltered bay to trill around the lake before alighting daintily on the mud-flats—bright pillar-box red legs flashing conspicuously in the sun. A group of four tufted drakes drifted sleepily under the steep south bank, their partners presumably tucked away on secret nests among the marginal sedges. They are the latest of the duck species to nest and I have yet to see a mother with her brood of sooty-brown youngsters. Many will fall victim to the many pike that lurk in the deeper regions. An armada of fully fledged Egyptian geese have survived their depredations as usual, as for some reason the geese seem to escape the pikes' attentions, even though very small and vulnerable when first hatched.

Nearing the island two young terns paddled from its safety to the open water, the adults screaming overhead and diving boldly as I got to within a few yards. It took several minutes of careful searching with the binoculars before I could just make out two more groups of chicks crouched among the stones, their mottled sandy-coloured plumage a perfect match for the gravelly shoreline. However, most of the island now supports a light growth of vegetation and there were almost certainly others keeping out of sight.

The two adventurous chicks had by now travelled some distance from the shore, so I took my leave before I caused them to venture too far over the open water where the pike probably lay waiting. By the time I reached the lane both had paddled back to their island sanctuary to be greeted by anxious parents. Clearing the island has certainly proved a worthwhile venture, and if the young continue to thrive it should ensure a permanent breeding colony at the lake.

JULY 8TH

Whisper's puppies are making good progress, all ten having so far survived and beginning to acquire the first signs of their dappled adult coats. Until now they have been a peaceful and contented litter, their entire lives consisting of alternately feeding and sleeping, but with eyes now fully open and muscles

101

forming in tottery and unstable legs, they are swiftly learning how to scramble over the edge of the nursery box to explore the big outside world. It is most amusing to watch them. The problems will begin with this increased mobility, and a tendency to wander and explore, but at the moment Whisper is always on hand to cart them back to the box in her mouth. She is proving an excellent mother, the experience of parenthood having done her a wealth of good and calmed her previously boisterous character, though she is sometimes intolerant of their continual demands for milk and welcomes the chance to slink away to keep watch from a distance. She receives precious little peace as the pups immediately attach themselves to suckle directly she returns to the box. Instead of one good meal a day, Whisper now wades through at least four heaped bowlfuls, besides titbits scrounged from the kitchen and anything else she happens to come across on her travels. She still seems hungry. Always one for bizarre eating habits, she is forever an opportunist and consumes even the most unappetizing objects—as diverse as rubber gloves, toilet rolls, plastic clothes-pegs, and empty sweet-wrappers: in fact, anything that looks even remotely edible. If given the opportunity, she will sneak to the bathroom to pinch a bar of soap, which is considered a real treat and devoured with obvious relish. This craving for the unusual has remained since puppyhood, but despite gorging ravenously from dawn till dusk she still appears to suffer from perpetual starvation. At the moment I suppose this is fully justified, providing ten equally ravenous puppies with milk must be putting a great strain on her resources.

To help alleviate the demand, we are teaching the pups to lap milk from a bowl, albeit not too successfully. They are as yet totally lacking in table manners, getting far more milk distributed over themselves and the surrounding area than the trifling amount that actually ends up inside their bloated little tummies. Whisper probably benefits most of all when licking them clean, but following another bout of rough and tumble the whimpering pack are soon clambering over one another to fall fast asleep in an untidy-looking heap, their appetites fully appeased and causing no further trouble until the pangs of hunger once more return.

JULY 10TH

Started to clear up the rear lawn adjoining the orchard, where I finish off the job of raising each season's waterfowl. Containing a sizeable pond, the pen has housed my little flock of red-breasted geese during the breeding period, and being purposely left undisturbed, the grass has all but disappeared beneath a tangled confusion of tall docks and nettles.

I herded the geese into the orchard, replacing the dividing fence to avoid conflicts with the young fowl, for geese remain somewhat territorial and can be rather aggressive towards young birds unable to fend for themselves.

After a ten-minute argument with the strimmer, the starting rope finally parted company and I was faced with an hour of hard graft with billhook and slasher to put paid to the worst of the rubbish. When the task was done, I

Wild raspberry.

caught up the more advanced birds from the brooder house, releasing them near the pond. They seemed rather wary of the water at first, but a few bolder spirits began to venture closer and by early evening all were splashing and diving in obvious enjoyment, preening their feathers vigorously and rejoicing in their new-found freedom. Frequent bathing will do them a world of good, being essential to waterproof their plumage to acclimatize them to the worst of the weather.

The new brooder-house system of raised wire pens has worked extremely well, resulting in clean, well-feathered birds that have been reared with the minimum of fuss: a vast improvement on the previous straw-lined pens that needed constant attention to keep them in a clean and healthy condition. At this rate they will soon be ready for sale—the sooner the better—for my feed bills have soared astronomically over the past few weeks.

I called in to see my young sparrowhawk in the evening. I had intended to collect her, but as the weather has turned cold and wet, and she has only recently been removed from a brooder lamp, I thought it wiser to leave her for a few more days.

I am surprised at how much she has grown since our last meeting. The first stubby wing and tail feathers are now peeping through the thick layer of down, and her grey eyes are bright and sharp, taking an interest in all around her in typical, glaring fashion. At the moment she is being reared with her smaller brothers in a large cloth-lined box, fed at four-hourly intervals on a diet of minced rat—a disgusting mess that smells as good as it sounds, although far more nourishing than the day-old chicks rejected from hatcheries that provide the staple diet of most captive birds of prey. I think I will feed her on sparrows!

JULY 12TH

Had a rather nerve-wracking experience with Spectre this afternoon when, against my better judgement, I allowed her to take wing in what was approaching a gale. During the long summer moult a hunting bird is normally rested and gorged with food to promote good feather growth, and as over-feeding makes a hawk lethargic and unresponsive, it is not generally flown until the all-important flight feathers have re-grown, allowing food to be reduced sufficiently to make the bird keen enough to hunt and to return to the glove when called.

I have been flying Spectre occasionally during our regular walks around the farm, for a hawk totally rested during the moult needs extensive retraining and much exercise to tone the muscles before it will be of any use for hunting in the autumn. An occasional flight helps to keep her in trim.

We had just gained the top of Rabbit Hill when Spectre bated towards her favourite telegraph-pole beside the road. She seemed in a benevolent mood, so ignoring the windy conditions I let her go. She swept easily to the top of the pole and stood waiting to be offered a titbit when we were disturbed by the untimely arrival of an irate pair of oyster-catchers, the extroverts of the valley displaying a bold disposition by calling, swooping, and diving in an un-provoked attack. Possibly the pair have youngsters in the area and the presence of a large bird of prey was evidently not to be tolerated. Within seconds the noise summoned a pair of terns to join the fray, and soon there was complete pandemonium unleashed a few yards above my head, at the centre of which Spectre had begun to show signs of restlessness as the attackers gained courage, almost striking her as they swooped threateningly close. This was too much for the buzzard who suddenly took wing, beating stiffly into the wind until she had climbed well out of reach. During normal flight she rarely ventures above the tops of the trees, but this time she spiralled higher and higher, her broad wings fully spread and pushed aloft by the blustery updraught from the brow of the hill. Soon she was but a small speck in the sky at least 200 feet up and steadily drifting away over Bluebell Copse. By now I was really worried, for at such a rate she would soon be swept far out of sight behind the copse. She took no notice as I called and whistled from far below, revelling in the power of the wind while soaring into the distance, leaving me completely helpless to await the outcome.

I have always had complete confidence in Spectre, though this time it was sorely shaken. Fortunately my fears proved groundless. Eventually tiring of her game, she closed her wings and planed down to alight among the dead branches of a hilltop elm, from which—after a brief look round to get her bearings—she swooped back to the glove, receiving an unusually handsome reward for her loyalty. The complete performance had taken barely ten minutes, although it seemed many times longer waiting anxiously on the crest of the hill.

104

JULY 15TH

Took advantage of a calm evening to try out some new dry flies on the trout, reaching Valley Lakes with the scorching sun still high in the heavens and with some way to travel before the evening rise. The tranquil weather had enticed several other fishermen to the waterside, but very little disturbed the surface except a pair of great-crested grebes leading a single striped young-ster—the little Norfolk 'diedopper' begging to parents for food each time they surfaced. The air was still and sultry, full of the drowsy purr of turtledoves and the benign cooing of wood pigeon deep among the alder thicket where thick leaf gave dappled shade from the sun's harsh glare.

The water was warm to the touch, so I began with a sinking line and boldly dressed lure, concentrating on the bottom where the trout would probably remain in the cooler regions until the sun lowered. It was hard but enjoyable toil, and presently I felt a slow pull from very deep that indicated a heavy fish, its slow but powerful run taking the line to the backing before I turned it halfway across the lake. There are few fish above 3 lb (1.4 kg) in Home Lake, but as it wallowed and kicked on the surface, it showed itself to be far larger, quite long, and of a very wide girth—could it be a salmon? I was never to find out. After a few more good runs it contemptuously spat out the hook, leaving me with a slack line, and a feeling of acute frustration. There was no way I could tempt that one to take again.

As the air cooled the trout began rising regularly to a good hatch of mixed flies skating across the water, receiving some competition from the skimming swallows that snapped them up as they became airborne, and from a pair of willow warblers hunting along the bank that disappeared among the bramble patch to feed their youngsters.

I switched reels to a floating line, tipping the leader with a nondescript dry fly from a selection treated with flotant to keep them riding proudly on the surface. Advanced entomology is not one of my stronger subjects, but there were many flies on the wing to which it bore more than a passing resemblance and it seemed to fit the bill. One fish was rising enthusiastically only ten yards from the bank, and it was possible to follow the progress of the fly easily, leaving it motionless for a few seconds, then working it through the area with short pulls to create an attractive bow wave that imitated a fly trying to lift clear of the water. Twice the fish boiled close, but each time stopped just short of taking. At the next cast it took on the drop, a classic head and tail rise, obligingly hooking itself before I had the chance to strike—a lively one of 1½ lb (0.6 kg) that played around vigorously before coming safely to the net.

The light faded all too quickly as the sun sank below the level of the trees, but I remained until it was too dark to see the fly, taking a further two fish just over 1 lb (0.5 kg) apiece. With a brace and a half in the bag, it was a rewarding way of spending a warm July evening, but I would happily have exchanged all three for the one big fish lost earlier. Why must it be the big fish that always provide the story of the one that got away?

JULY 17TH

Collected my young sparrowhawk last night, for if I am to succeed in getting her imprinted on me it is essential to start feeding and tending her at the earliest possible opportunity, thereby assuming the role of foster parent and teaching the bird to accept me as the provider of her every meal.

She travelled home in a large cardboard box that, trusting she survives, will provide a portable home for several days until she gains enough strength in her legs to use a perch comfortably. As yet she seldom stands upright, her leg muscles insufficiently developed to support her for any length of time. She has certainly grown more hawk-like in appearance as her feathers develop, and the proportionately long legs are now equipped with the tools of her trade: an armament of slender grasping talons tipped with black claws for catching and dispatching prey.

Safely installed in her new home, she spent the remainder of the evening sprawled out on my lap in the armchair, adopting the folds of my pullover as a new nest, and appearing to ignore the hustle and bustle around her, which included continual visits from the children and frequent cautious inspections from Whisper's enquiring nose. This is all to the good, for if she is to be reared, trained, and flown successfully, she must become accustomed to all the sights and sounds likely to be encountered in everyday life. This process (called 'manning') is the first vital step in her management, for all fears and doubts of strange objects and places must be allayed before training proper can begin.

Finally deciding that we meant her no harm, she allowed her eyelids to flicker drowsily and to close, resting her head on my arm to fall fast asleep, where she remained until I gave her a feed before retiring to bed.

When I peeped into the box early this morning she was fully alert and waiting for her breakfast, taking the finely diced meat eagerly from a pair of tweezers until her crop was almost bursting. Unable to cram in any more food, she wiped her beak, roused her feathers, and nonchalantly ejected an accurate mute high over the side of the box—a suitably informative gesture that her appetite was for the moment fully appeased.

I have been pondering on a suitable name for the hawk. The answer came as I studied her defiant little face and deeply hooded eyes, where dark feathers are beginning to appear in the shape of a mask, likening her to a little, masked bandit. Besides appropriately describing her outlawish looks, it seems to sum up the fiery disposition of the species admirably—so Bandit she will be!

JULY 20TH

With so many mouths to feed, my summer rearing duties take up a considerable amount of time each morning, so finding a few hours to spare I took the opportunity to try for a pike at the lakes. Few anglers fish for pike much before the frosts of October, but being of necessity an opportunist, I tend to take my chances where and when they arise and have found the lakes far more productive during the summer months. This morning the weather was also kind: warm sun and scented breeze—a pleasant change from the chilling winds of my last excursion in mid-February.

Cousin John has now released most of his reared mallard on Bulrush Lake, the large raft of ducks following my progress along the bank being a welcome sight, for very few wild adults have produced more than an odd duckling or two. The resident greylag geese have met with more success, two broods of five fully feathered goslings launching clumsily from the causeway, still under the supervision of uneasy parents.

Crossing a sheltered corner of 'waste' ground beside the wood—where a high bank creates a sun trap and a wild garden now blooms—I was amazed at the number of butterflies attracted by the flowers. The familiar meadow browns, ringlets, and small skippers fluttered up at every step, and at last I discovered a good sprinkling of common blues, a butterfly that has up till now appeared only in small quantities this summer. A small copper flitted gaudily past, its burnished scales glinting metallically in the sunlight, to where a gorgeous peacock had paused to sample the flowering willow-herb spikes, adding a rich splash of unnecessary colour from its velvety wings.

I began fishing halfway along Wood Lake, using a favourite old spoon bait with which I have taken a great many pike over the years. It has now lost much of its original colouring and looks visually quite unattractive, but still deceives pike with deadly efficiency. Within minutes it had added another to its tally, a lean fish of 4 lb (1.8 kg) that snapped it up during the first few yards of a deep retrieve.

The following hour was uneventful, by which time I had worked the length of the water and crossed the causeway to Bulrush Lake, parts of which are now weedy, the spoon frequently fouling up until I reached the deeper water at the far end. Here the banks are seldom trodden and are vastly overgrown with head-high rushes, but the effort was rewarded by another small pike that swirled from the edge of the reeds to seize the spoon aggressively after a short backhand cast.

I finished the session in a bay of much deeper water, casting parallel along the east bank where the shallows suddenly fall sheer to 15 feet or so, and a thick patch of dark-green weed provides an ideal ambush for feeding pike to lurk in hiding. A few casts and the line appeared to drag as though entangled with weed, but as it neared the bank I felt a slight kick on the rod, dragging out a tiny fish that looked hardly bigger than the spoon itself, much less capable of swallowing it—a miniature pike already displaying the aggressive disposition of its elders.

I ended at lunchtime with the best fish of the day also lured from the weedbed: a pike of a little over 5 lb (2.3 kg) that was hooked only lightly. The spoon whipped out as it struggled in the landing-net, thus saving me the peril of removing it from heavily armed jaws.

JULY 22ND

While piking at the lakes a couple of days ago, part of my attention was diverted by a steady line of pigeons flighting along the brow of the hill fully half a mile away, the distant specks disappearing just over the skyline beside Roughground Copse, where I knew there was at least half an acre of barley flattened by the recent heavy rains. A few were still following the same path early this morning, and I set out just after lunch armed with the gun and decoys and hopes of a few hours sport to prevent further damage to the crop.

The weather was far from ideal, with bright sunlight and very little wind to keep the pigeons moving. However, creeping along the edge of the copse I was encouraged as about fifty rose from the laid area and a similar number clattered from a line of hedgerow oaks at the far end of the field where they had been digesting their ill-gotten gains. The barley has taken a severe battering from the wind and rain, the worst hit patch fortunately conveniently sited within shooting distance of the copse.

Within minutes I had placed the decoys and manipulated a clump of elder saplings to serve as a rough screen beneath the welcome shade of an oak, its

Less attractive in sunny weather. Setting up artificial decoys
on an area of laid barley.

situation commanding an uninterrupted view across the valley. Nothing happened for some time, the sun beating down mercilessly to distort the distant background woods in a quivering heat haze, the warmth bringing out swarms of biting insects—the one real bugbear of summer shooting, whose attentions can become almost unbearable on a really hot day. A team of swifts were doing their utmost to decimate the numbers high above the treetops, and a twittering of swallows skimmed back and forth over the sea of corn. Nevertheless, I continued to swat and scratch while waiting for the first pigeon to return—they had rather wisely decided to sit out the hottest part of the day.

I fired a shot in the hope of putting some on the wing, and as the report rolled along the valley, a small cluster scattered from a dead elm beside the marsh, a few drifting aimlessly towards the patch of barley. At 100 yards they spotted the decoys, and although some peeled towards them from the main bunch, they suddenly decided that something was wrong and passed over warily to where I crouched below the oak. I began the innings well, taking the nearest before it was lost in the canopy of leaf above me, and swinging hastily through the second as it veered away to present an easy crossing shot. Both fell where they were easily gathered, the first crashing through the branches to fall almost in the hide, bringing a shower of oak leaves trailing in its wake.

More pigeon now began to move, though almost without exception they refused to alight among the decoys. The decoys were obviously at fault, for having no dead birds to start with as normal, I had to fall back on a set of plastic dummies, which in bright sunlight produce an unnaturally harsh shine, attracting birds from a distance but not standing up to a closer inspection. Those birds coming in shied away at the last moment, following the path of the first arrivals towards the oak, where they intended to alight to give the decoys a more thorough examination. This suited my purpose well, and although overhead shots were sometimes lost in the leaf canopy, it was simply a matter of leaving them until the very last second, swinging up through an incoming bird and firing directly the stock hit my shoulder, the resulting crash through the branches showing whether or not the shot had found its mark. In the main it worked, most pigeon hitting the ground almost at my feet where they could be gathered without having to enter the corn.

For two hours they came, though not in great numbers, an odd bird or two arriving every few minutes to offset the ceaseless tormenting of the flies. Suddenly the sky became strangely dark, a disagreeable black cloud having rolled in low from the west shielded by the copse. The first real warning of the approaching storm was a vivid streak of forked lightning and a deafening rumble, closely followed by the urgent patter of the first heavy spots of rain falling like shot on the sycamore leaves. Needless to say, standing beneath a tall oak while a thunderstorm rages overhead is not the healthiest way of spending an afternoon, and by the time the storm really broke I was safely back home watching it unleash its full fury from the study window, following an untimely retreat from the copse with more pigeons than I was able to carry comfortably.

JULY 24TH

I have been waiting somewhat impatiently for a spell of fine weather to add to my supplies of vegetation used in taxidermy work. This provides the settings of natural habitat among which mounted specimens are installed. Until this afternoon I have been continually hampered by bad weather, an absolutely dry day being essential when the material is gathered to avoid the effects of mould and mildew. To further test my patience, the collecting season is very short, as each type of foliage requires to be harvested at exactly the right stage in its development so as to be preserved in a usable condition. If too young and tender, the plants will wither and decompose, but left too long they will become brittle when fully dried and many of the useful grasses will shed their attractive seeds. Correctly treated, suitable plants will withstand decay and remain looking at their best for a great many years, some even lasting for centuries.

The differing types of vegetation require different methods of preservation to retain the correct shape and natural looks, and if treated carefully will greatly enhance the overall appearance of a taxidermy case. The most widely used seeding grasses are relatively simple to prepare, gathered when fully dry and tied in bunches that are hung upside down in a moisture-free environment for a few weeks to prevent bending, following an immersion in turpentine to eliminate any minute insect pests that could cause future trouble when sealed in a case. The fronds of bracken, another plant with many decorative uses, will not lend themselves to such a method, and will wither and curl in an unsightly fashion unless squeezed firmly in a flower press or between sheets of weighted newspaper, which absorbs any excess moisture from the plant and retains its flat shape. Rushes can be treated in the same way, but their moisture content is far higher and they are best dried in a box of fine sand, the weight of the sand holding them in shape and eliminating any fears of mould. Unfortunately, much of a plant's natural colour is lost during the drying process, but with a little care it can be restored with oil or acrylic paint, and when dry, formed to its natural contours with a lightly warmed iron. Sprigs of gorse and broom are much less trouble, requiring only a few hours drying on the kitchen stove and a light wash of colour to restore their natural tones.

After collecting a few boxes of seeding grasses, I added a variety of rushes from the margins of Charles's carp lake, where I noticed two of the residents rooting around the base of a phragmite rushbed, their explorations sending up strings of tiny bubbles to burst silently on the surface. A family of young coot cheeped among the reedmace and a solitary common sandpiper paid a brief visit to a mudflat near the island, zig-zagging evasively over the steep bank as I was spotted beside the water.

My task was completed just in time. While returning heavily laden along the lane, yet another evening storm was brewing on the skyline over Rabbit Hill. I hope the weather will soon show signs of improvement: if it remains wet for much longer it will create many problems with the coming corn harvest.

110

JULY 27TH

Bandit appears to be making progress in leaps and bounds, but being still very young and delicate I am continuing to gorge her every four hours with as much food as she will take. It took her only a few days to outgrow the box, for now she likes to exercise her wings in preparation for flight and, in its confines, spent most of the time jumping up and down like an animated jack-in-the-box. I have now arranged a comfortable perch on the corner of my desk, where she can see what is going on around her and stretch her wings to their fullest extent. She spends almost the entire day with me, travelling on the passenger seat of the truck or perched on the desk, seeming to accept whatever happens with complete indifference and showing a definite interest in all that goes on around her. With feathers developing rapidly, she occupies most of the afternoon by preening, until my desk and papers are littered with down and feather wax. When a little flying practice is decided upon, she flaps up and down like an eccentric grasshopper until the air is filled with a miniature snowstorm of down. Apparently satisfied with its wide distribution, she ruffles her plumage back into place, tucks one leg into her flank feathers, and quizzically studies the house martins journeying back and forth to their nests below the eaves, paying no attention to the spasmodic rattling of the typewriter.

Unfortunately, it is not merely feather down that is distributed around the study. It is impossible to house-train a sparrowhawk, a wet cloth being essential for mopping up operations as her accuracy has not improved and she frequently misses the sheets of newspaper spread widely to take care of

Honeysuckle.

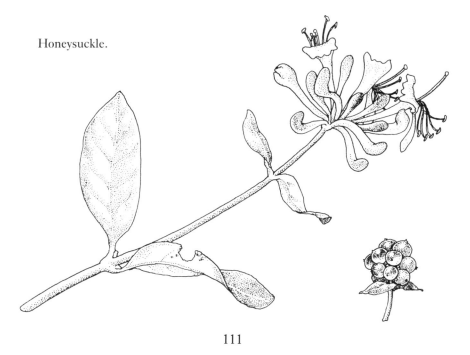

111

minor lapses in self-control. On one, not so minor, occasion, she caught me squarely in the back of the neck from fully four feet, remaining not in the least apologetic for such shameful conduct and scrutinizing me afterwards with a somewhat mystified expression as I departed, stiff-necked, to the bathroom. This certainly put me in my place, but twenty minutes later, she treated the taxman's bill in the same contemptuous manner—an act of notoriety that seemed a little more appropriate.

As Bandit's legs have gained strength, I have started carrying her on my fist for short periods around the house, getting her balance accustomed to the motion of walking. A couple of days ago I made the mistake of taking her outside while I checked a sudden commotion among the puppies in the back garden. I was surprised to discover she can almost fly. As I examined the pups her gaze fell upon a comfortable-looking perch in the form of a nearby fencing rail. She made an over-enthusiastic jump for it, but misjudged her landing abysmally and sailed right over, unceremoniously coming to rest in the nearby water tank, and from where she was quickly retrieved apparently none the worse for her misadventure. I decided on the spot that it was high time to fit her jesses, thereby affording some control over her future movements.

JULY 30TH

Frustrated by a fruitless attempt at the chub last night with the fly rod, I returned to the river during the heat of the afternoon with a tin of worms, to try outwitting them by more persuasive measures. A cautious inspection of the heavily shaded swim revealed a nice little shoal containing a couple of good fish keeping pace with the current below the trees. However, the only way of reaching them was by trotting a line from a grassy mound well upstream, the overhanging branches being far too thick to wield a rod above where they lay close by the bank.

Avoiding disturbance, I crept away and baited up with a small brandling worm gathered from the garden muckheap, adding no weight to the line but attaching a small quill float to keep the bait from snagging the riverbed. The current rushes fast over the sandy lie, and in only a few seconds the first cast had trotted through with no sign of a bite. Following a few more blank runs, I raised the float to allow the bait almost to brush the bottom. Reaching the centre of the swim, this time the little quill shot under and I tightened to the pull of a good fish. It lurched sideways for a tangle of ash roots jutting from the bank, but by leaning back as hard as I dared, I quickly steered it clear. Making headway against the pull of the current was difficult, but once hauled clear of the bank I was able to relax the pressure a little and encourage it gradually upstream to the shallow junction of a marsh drain, where it wallowed just in reach of the net—2½ lb (1.1 kg) of streamlined silver, its big, brassy-tinted scales reflected warmly in the afternoon sun.

As is often the case with chub, one fish is caught then all goes quiet. Trying several more runs without an offer, I wandered some way downstream to

112

another favourite lie beneath a line of spreading oaks, where the water would also be well shaded by a thick canopy of leaf. It was a struggle to get through the nettles, but I finally reached a suitable spot that allowed casting between two trees, the actual lie being almost in midstream and usually holding a small shoal of dace, although I fear the cormorants have taken their toll throughout the winter, the numbers seeming well down compared with previous years.

Besides the usual swarm of brilliant damsel-flies, one of their giant dragonfly cousins, the brown aeshna, was patrolling its stretch of the river hawking for flies, its double set of transparent gossamer-like wings vibrating audibly as it manoeuvred erratically above my float. Below it the float once more dipped under, this time to a small fish I thought was a dace but that proved to be a tiny chub, the anal fin a definite convex shape instead of the inward curving concave that denotes a dace.

True to form, there were no more takers despite covering the swim thoroughly. However, before leaving, I took a quick look below the furthest oak to see if any brown trout had taken up residence. Leaning from its branches I discovered a couple of less than 1 lb hanging along the down-stream edge of a trailing weedbed, but nothing of any size was apparent. I may return one evening with the fly rod to fish for my supper.

Greater burdock.

August

AUGUST 1ST

The arrival of August sees the first indications that the year is on the wane: the goal of reproducing another generation towards which all nature has striven has been achieved, leaving the countryside looking tarnished and unruly, and its citizens weary and exhausted. Much of the birdlife is subdued compared with the last few months, many having completed the wearisome task of rearing broods of youngsters and now becoming ragged and unkempt as the moult sets in. The woods and hedgerows have fallen strangely silent as their previously conspicuous occupants now skulk among the undergrowth, at best mere shadows of their former selves. The once resplendent cock pheasant, which crowed with such gusto in the spring, is now conspicuous by his absence and prefers to sulk in hiding as if ashamed to show his face, his fine feathers gone—a changed bird from the proud, ornate, and licentious character that lorded over his harem in the spring. Many other birds will soon be feeling the turning of the year, and during the month the first migrants will be leaving the southern shores, cuckoos and turtledoves showing the way, soon to be followed by the first members of the swallow and warbler tribes.

Although wildlife in its many forms is resting, it will soon be the busiest time of the year on the land as the corn harvest gets into full swing, and farmers pray for fine weather to allow all to be safely gathered to the barn. Much of the corn is ripe, the heavily laden ears hanging their heads and already providing food to the denizens of the fields. However, unfortunately this year, much has been laid flat by the heavy downpours and strong winds and some will be lost, leaving the flocks of hungry wood pigeons rather spoiled for choice.

The 'Glorious Twelfth' of August sees the opening day of the grouse season on the northern heather-clad moors, and it heralds the advent of the lowland shooting seasons. Little more than a fortnight later, the mallard will provide a welcome sight as they venture to glean the corn stubbles, and flighting geese send the pulse racing as their approaching voices are heard in the twilight of dawn and dusk. By then the days will have shortened noticeably, and a dawn ambush will not necessarily mean rising at an unearthly hour.

AUGUST 3RD

Rushed Bandit to the veterinary surgeon yesterday after discovering her in the throes of a fit soon after I had returned home from work. It was an extremely harrowing experience. One minute she was happily preening on her perch waiting to be fed, and the next her whole body was racked with intense convulsions, her wings flapping wildly as she careered around uncontrollably in evident distress. The seizure lasted for less than a minute, though obviously had a paralysing effect, for when it finished she lay gasping and barely able to stand, staring blankly forward and looking extremely sorry for herself. Not surprisingly, she showed no interest in her food, though it was well past the normal feeding time.

As usual the afternoon surgery was extremely busy, and by the time the vet managed to see us Bandit had undergone three more identical attacks, each one more frightening than the last. Fits are not uncommon among sparrowhawks, usually caused by some form of vitamin deficiency or imbalance, which I have been hoping to avoid by adding a vitamin supplement to her varied diet. The examination seemed to indicate some other cause, the possibility of epilepsy not being entirely ruled out.

Bandit was given an immediate injection of calcium boragluconate, the unavoidable stress of which brought on another violent attack. I feared she had not long to live.

Arriving home I placed her padded box in a darkened room where she would rest and not exert herself unduly, possibly prompting another attack. Although very tired and weak, she eventually managed to accept a little finely minced beef later in the evening in which I concealed a minute dosage of phenobarbitone prescribed by the vet. All I can do now is to provide her with as much food as she will take, together with complete peace and quiet to aid the slim chance she has of survival. Apart from this, I can only hope for the best, although the odds are stacked rather heavily against a complete recovery. Any recurrence of the fits will inevitably weaken her still further, and could even prove terminal.

I spent most of a very depressing evening by her side, feeling completely helpless and pondering on our short career together. It hardly seems possible that in such a short time Bandit has come to play such a big part in my life, and if I lose her now it will leave a huge void that will prove almost impossible to fill.

AUGUST 6TH

Bandit seems a lot brighter today and has begun to take an interest in life again, even though the last few days have been traumatic for both of us. Rising early each morning, I have been expecting to find her dead, but twenty-four hours ago she seemed to pass the crisis point and since then seems to be on the road to recovery.

On the day following her fits she was pitifully weak, appearing totally disorientated and hardly able to stand, huddling miserably with wings drooping loosely by her side. This lethargy was almost certainly a side-effect of the drugs, but at the time I feared she had suffered some form of brain damage during the convulsions, seeming unable to focus her half-closed eyes and staggering around in a most disturbing manner.

Feeding her proved the biggest problem. A sparrowhawk loses weight very rapidly and once low takes a very long time to regain condition. It was therefore of utmost importance to get her to take as much food as possible. During the day I attempted to feed her constantly, tempting her with a few morsels to keep up her strength, but the actual amounts taken were hopelessly small and seemed barely sufficient to keep her alive. Between feeds she was confined to the box and kept in the dark to restrict any unnecessary movement and to conserve her energy.

It was touch and go, but yesterday she gradually regained her senses and, typically female, began to take an interest in her appearance, preening and adjusting her feathers and even attempting to exercise her wings, but she soon became unbalanced in her weakened and unstable condition.

This morning showed a vast improvement, and following a hearty feed I was delighted to see her back on my study desk renewing acquaintance with the house martins, preening happily, and once again wafting copious amounts of feather down around the room. After such a horrifying experience, I could forgive her for anything. I can only hope there is no recurrence of the fits, and have stepped up her vitamin intake accordingly just in case this was the cause of the trouble.

AUGUST 8TH

A sweltering hot day with precious little breeze to temper the air, a brassy sun burning above feathery puffs of cumulus to tempt out hosts of butterflies to the purple flower sprays of the garden buddleia, whose fragrance invited continual visits from peacocks, tortoiseshells, red admirals, and an exquisitely dressed painted lady to sample its heady nectar.

The long-awaited dry weather has also brought out the combine harvesters in force, for although some winter barley has been cut during the infrequent dry intervals, the weather has hampered the corn harvest and much ripened grain stands awaiting rainless days and a drying wind. From mid-morning, when the dampness had lifted from the earth, the fields became a regular hive of industry and the air vibrated to the roar of heavy farm machinery. The droning combine, belching chaff and dust, gorged hungrily around the narrowing islands of standing corn, joined at intervals by the rattle and bump of tractor and trailer groaning beneath the weight of tons of golden grain. Following the procession came the steady rhythmic thumping of the baler, compressing the threshed straw into tightly bound bales ready to be carted later to the empty Dutch barn.

The gathering in of the harvest is allowing a welcome access to the fields again, and it was a real treat to be able to wander directly across the shorn stubble to feed the waterfowl at the end of the barley field, instead of the long detour laden with a heavy food sack that I have been humping around the headland for the last few weeks. Opening up the cornfields will also enable us to see how the gamebirds have fared through the summer as they forage the stubbles for spilt grain with their season's young, giving a fair indication of what lies in store when the first frosts of October have singed the leaves, and

Harvest—highlight of the year.

we search the dwindling hedgerows and rough places on early shooting days. The pheasants have coped rather better than expected despite inhospitable weather at hatching time, and I have encountered many a small brood around the fields. The majority are almost fully grown poults, but I have seen at least one late clutch of chicks barely able to fly—the replacements of an early lost clutch. I fear the partridges have not withstood the rigours of summer so well, as I have seen only a handful of youngsters on my travels around the farm. Some of the old birds have already formed small coveys of their own, their offspring almost certainly lost to the cold rains of an inclement June.

AUGUST 9TH

The clutch of red-breasted geese hatched right on time this morning, leaving only a late sitting of scaup eggs to come off before my incubation duties are over for another year. It hardly seems more than a few short weeks since I was awaiting the first birds to lay, but since early spring I have been turning the incubating eggs each morning and evening, and making regular inspections to check developments inside the shell, so that anything addled or infertile

117

could be removed before it contaminated the incubator by producing harmful gases.

The goslings were dry by nightfall and were moved to a brooder where they will be reared in much the same way as ducks, although being natural grazers, they will need a fair amount of grass added to the staple diet of chick crumbs. For the initial feed, I always cut the grass very finely with scissors, sprinkling it over the youngsters, which encourages them to pick it off and thereby learn to feed. Once they recognize it as food, the chopped grass can be given in increasing amounts and is much preferred to manufactured foods.

When the first feathers start to appear through the down, the goslings will be transferred to an outside pen on the lawn where they can graze freely, for if kept inside young geese will often resort to picking one another's feathers as a substitute for grass and an entire brood can be stripped to virtual baldness within a few hours. Presumably the feather down in some way resembles the texture of grass, but sheer boredom is another possible cause. Whatever the reason, once the feather-pecking habit has been formed, it can prove almost impossible to eradicate and in extreme cases the birds may have to be split up and reared singly if their plumage is to survive intact.

After shutting the brooder house for the night, I spent a few minutes identifying some of an unusually large swarm of moths hovering around the back-garden light. Just for a change, it was a pleasantly warm evening to tempt them on the wing, and among the many different species abroad most prominent were the large, buff-coloured drinker moths and a rather bedraggled poplar hawk, the latter dressed in a camouflage of natural greens and browns—an uncommon but welcome visitor to the garden. On the next suitable night I must rig up my moth lamp in the garden to see what it attracts, and whether I can add an odd specimen or two to my collection.

AUGUST 12TH

The grouse season opens today, but being in lowland Norfolk I had to content myself with a few hours at the pigeons, this time attacking a strip of laid wheat on top of the hill beside a quiet by-road, where a large area has been stripped of grain. Wheat ripens later than barley, and the birds find it more attractive, particularly at the succulent half-ripe stage when it is soft and palatable.

The weather—as ever—looked far from promising, with angry storm-clouds rolling continuously across the valley, again threatening rain. However, the strong south-westerly was at least in my favour, blowing directly towards the roosting firs half a mile over the hill. Pigeon invariably prefer flighting into the wind when travelling to a feeding ground, and the stronger it blows the better, carrying the sound of any shooting well downwind to disturb the roosting woods and to help to keep them moving.

I chose a spot beside a prominent oak amongst a line bordering the wheat, making a rough hide in the undergrowth that allowed a wide field of fire covering the area worst hit by the weather. I had to use plastic decoys again, but with no bright sun to create an unnatural shine, their pulling power is greatly increased in dull weather. It was already mid-afternoon, early enough to start in late summer, pigeon being at their keenest to feed in the early evenings. When decoying during the winter months the complete opposite holds good: the birds ravenous at first light after spending the long winter nights in a cold roosting wood.

There was hardly time to watch the flocks of young lapwings tumbling across the low meadows before the first two arrivals topped the brow of the hill, right on course for the decoys. They did not travel far, passing on their way within a comfortable 25 yards of where I crouched beside the oak. Their flightpath turned out to be the main line of approach and several pigeons, mainly singletons, trickled along the same route during the early evening, making for relatively easy shooting—apart from a few real corkers that were returning very high from another cornfield half a mile upwind. The few of these I connected with crashed down a long way behind on a field of open stubble.

Of those coming upwind from the firs, very few showed any reluctance to decoy, but any hesitating on the fringe were encouraged to commit themselves by my throwing a dead bird among the decoys, the flash of falling grey giving the impression of an earlier arrival alighting at the feast.

The flight was still going strong well into evening, when I had to return home to prepare Bandit's evening meal, but by then I had a good bundle of pigeons and, just before leaving, I added an old carrion crow to the bag as it sneaked silently along the row of oaks.

AUGUST 15TH

Feeling the need for some fresh air after spending the morning poring over a mound of largely unnecessary paperwork, I finally decided that enough was enough, swapping the pen for the fly rod and setting off to the river to try my luck.

Trevor, the dairyman, was already fishing just upstream of the chub lie, though with little success, and I made my way to the upriver boundary, intending to fish gradually downriver and finish up trying for a brownie under the oak trees.

After a cast or two across an eddy created by a protruding willow root, there was a tremendous splash downstream and I thought Trevor had fallen in. He had feared the same for me, but we were both wrong. A bullock, lumbering along the far bank, had lost its footing and was now wallowing in four feet of water, churning the bottom silt to a muddy soup as it tried to regain dry land. There was little we could do to help, except encourage it gradually downstream where the bank was less steep, and where it eventually hauled itself out unaided, seeming none the worse for its misadventure.

On the way back from this minor diversion I noticed a few dace rising in midstream, and although the ripples were small, I thought it worth trying my luck with a tiny dry fly. The rises moved gradually towards the far bank, so I positioned myself to cast slightly upstream within easy reach, missing an instant boil as the first offering touched the water.

This seemed to set the pattern for the following half hour, with frequent snatches at the fly that I missed time and time again, presumably through striking too slowly even though I had tried to hit them faster every time. The takes were like lightning, often directly as the fly settled on the water, but try as I might, I was always too late and seemed to be striking at nothing more than the phantoms of tiny fish.

Not one to resist a challenge of this nature, I decided the trout would have to wait until I did catch a dace. The capture of such elusive fish was rapidly turning into something of an obsession. By mid-afternoon my efforts were still unrewarded, despite experiencing a very near miss by actually flipping a tiny dace right out of the water.

Absorbed in total concentration, I was suddenly startled by a lone curlew passing overhead, its rich 'tour-lee!' causing me to miss yet another fish as I watched it round the bend of the river and disappear from sight, its wild voice echoing mournfully into the distance.

Time passed quickly. Trevor had long since given up and had returned to do the milking, but I resolved to stick it out until I had at least one dace to my credit. I kept expecting that just one more cast would do it, but another inevitable miss would make me try again, unable to rest for a moment although my arm ached with incessant casting.

I altered my tactics. The main problem seemed to be caused by the line bellying in the current, taking much of the power from the strike. I took a few paces upstream from where I had almost taken root, and cast directly to the fish, stripping the surplus line back quickly to keep it tight and hitting at the first sign of a ripple near the fly. In this way I achieved my first capture—a diminutive dace hardly the size of a decent sardine—but no less rewarding than the taking of a large trout.

A heavier rise in midstream prompted me to try again, and now that I had 'mastered' the technique, it was hardly more than twenty minutes before another lay gasping on the bank: a real specimen dace for this stretch of the river, getting on for ½ lb (0.2 kg). At that moment it seemed the equivalent of a fresh-run salmon!

Another 'sardine' was banked before I was forced to retire, having embedded my fly in a willow root on the far bank with an over-enthusiastic cast at a heavy boil well upstream. It was already past my normal mealtime, as the afternoon had flown by while I was absorbed with my efforts. I had to give the brownies a miss. Never before have I worked so hard for three such measly fish, but I can't remember having enjoyed myself so much for ages!

AUGUST 17TH

Whisper's puppies are now in the process of being distributed to their new homes, and it will be something of a relief to see them happily settled with their future owners, both for ourselves and Whisper, who is rapidly tiring of being treated as nothing more than a mobile filling station each time she is foolish enough to venture into the confines of the pen—the pups still keen to suckle even though fully weaned to solid food. The ravenous pack now consumes an enormous amount of food, wolfing down at least four square meals a day and still foraging around like portable canine dustbins in the never-ending search for anything in the least bit edible.

They have been growing more playful and boisterous with each day that passes, the back garden now erupting spasmodically to the yelps and howls of mock battles as they establish something of a pecking order amongst themselves and contest ownership of various toys and possessions. Like Snow White's dwarfs, their characters differ widely—introvert, extrovert, mischievous, good-natured, quiet, and noisy—but all are united by one common motivation: food! Just before the first pup was collected, I decided to take a few photographs of the complete litter, but getting all ten to remain reasonably still and in one place for a family portrait was much easier said than done. It was eventually only accomplished during the midday feed by lining them up with several strategically placed bowls of food.

Both children have doted on the puppies since birth, and were not particularly overjoyed when their future owners began arriving to collect their charges. My son, Michael, has become attached to the largest pup—the first-born—and my daughter, Jennifer, was apparently under the impression that we were somehow keeping the lot. However, with the three we already have, a total of thirteen dogs would obviously have been a bit too much to cope with.

I am hopeful the majority will go to good working homes; the German pointer grows quickly into a big strong dog that can be boisterous to say the least. It requires plenty of strenuous work and activity to keep it occupied, and it is only at its happiest when scouring the countryside for game.

AUGUST 20TH

Spectre has all but completed the summer moult and now looks neat and tidy in her slightly darker plumage. I have been reducing her food slightly over the past few days to begin cutting down the reserves of fat put on by months of rich feeding and the comparative lack of exercise. At the end of the summer gorge, Spectre weighed well over 2 lb and was in a pretty lethargic state of mind. However, with the removal of only an ounce or so she is beginning to react favourably, clearly needing little more than a refresher course before I can again take her out hunting.

It was a delight once more to feel her weight on the glove as we travelled to the nearby stubble field, intending to start off with a few straightforward flights to the glove to re-accustom her to what must again become a habit. Crossing the back lawn, we were dive-bombed by an angry swarm of house martins, most now feeding their second brood of chicks in the mud domes below the eaves. Once free of their attentions, Spectre displayed every sign of keenness, bobbing her head expectantly as we proceeded along the hedge as if expecting me to flush something for her to chase.

Dispensing with the need for a creance—a safety line attached to the

121

Keen to begin hunting again.
Spectre awaiting collection
in the mews.

jesses—I sat the buzzard on a fence post and walked twenty paces to call her to the glove. There she received a thorough scolding from an extremely irritable wren that popped out of the undergrowth close by, hopping ridiculously close along the wire fence to explain just what it thought of the presence of a large bird of prey that dared to invade its privacy. Spectre remained unimpressed by the wren's bravado, swivelling her head upside down to follow its movements closely, the tiny bird with the big voice weaving this way and that until finally it tired of pestering Spectre and returned to the safety of the thick bramble patch.

She was on her way before I had time to raise the glove, thumping heavily on my fist to take the offered sliver of rabbit meat, and feeling comparatively enormous after spending so much of my time with Bandit. The retraining seems almost unnecessary, but I will keep at it until returning to my call once again becomes second nature. The regular flying will also help to tone up her muscles. Once this has been achieved, the rest should be easy and with any luck we will be ready to resume pursuit of the moorhen—her favourite quarry—when the season opens at the beginning of September.

Following several more short flights at which she performed faultlessly, I cast her off 50 yards to a riverside oak, walking away a full 200 yards before calling her back. She came instantly, her broad wings almost brushing the golden stubble at the end of the strong downward beat, gliding effortlessly up to the glove where she took her fill. A few more days of this and she will be more than ready for hunting.

I only wish the same were true for Bandit, but I have reluctantly abandoned all hopes of even attempting to train her as there is still something definitely amiss. I am at a loss to explain just what it is. Although there are few visible signs, since having the fits she has not responded well, and I fear my original suspicions of brain damage may be confirmed. Sparrowhawks are notoriously difficult to train even when there are no additional problems, and it would be extremely foolish to attempt training a bird that is not one hundred per cent fit. All I can do is provide her with as much good food as she will take and avoid any stresses and strains of training, but I think that unless she shows a vast improvement, the best I can hope for is that she will survive and possibly be of some future use for breeding. I can at least console myself with the fact that there was nothing I could have done, but this is little consolation at the end of a project that seemed doomed to failure almost from the start.

AUGUST 23RD

It required something of an effort to drag myself from bed this morning and to peer blearily through the misted bedroom window to check the weather. It had just turned three o'clock. Outside, the stars were twinkling brightly in the inky blackness, promising a dry start to the day, and I was relieved to find the wind had dropped, giving almost perfect conditions for an early-morning fishing trip.

An hour before dawn, I met up with Andy Davison on the outskirts of

Wild angelica.

Norwich, from where we travelled to Hickling Broad, having planned an early session at the bream. Within minutes of arriving our gear was stowed safely aboard a boat, an outboard motor had been attached, and we were soon steering a course from the boatyard across the centre of the vast sheet of water in the gloomy halflight of dawn. Hickling Broad is a large inland water set among acres of tall phragmite reedbeds—the 'Norfolk' reed much favoured by thatchers—lying roughly ten miles as the gull flies to the north-west of Great Yarmouth. And gulls there were in plenty, the boat's progress disturbing large gatherings as we purred across the broad, together with rafts of dozing mallard and a few sleepy parties of coot.

Having covered almost a mile of water the engine was cut to allow the boat to drift towards a quiet corner, where we spent a few minutes searching for any movements of fish. Very little disturbed the flat calm, and switching to the oars, I finally rowed to the edge of a weedbed 40 yards from the bank, baiting up with a cocktail of brandlings and maggots after ground baiting a likely looking spot.

As the sun filtered weakly through a layer of light cloud to send its silver stream glittering across the featureless water, the broad came to life, two great wedges of greylags lifting from the far end to cleave a well-worn path in company with regular flights of mallard and tufted ducks. A few small bunches of teal swished over to their dawn feeding grounds. We were delighted to see Hickling's resident pair of cranes pass low over the reedbeds, at first looking like rather ungainly herons until their distinctive shape appeared in silhouette against the sky.

I was trying to capture the dawn with my camera when Andy suddenly noticed my stick float slowly gliding away. Thanks to his warning I was just in time to strike and to feel the kick of a fish: a beautiful bronze bream as wide as a dinner plate that was persuaded easily to the net after a short struggle. It weighed about 4 lb (1.8 kg). With renewed interest we stared religiously at our floats, but it was a long vigil before mine again rocked gently and finally slid under, this time to a bream half the size of the first and still gleaming in the tarnished silver of its youth.

Although regularly ground baiting the swim, there was no sign of the hoped-for shoals of bream. Instead, we were entertained at intervals by a majestic pair of marsh harriers, the large marshland raptors appearing almost buzzard-like as they quartered buoyantly across the wide Norfolk skies. They confidently rode a stiffening breeze that stirred the whispering reedbeds, in search of their prey. Rowing further from the shore, we dropped anchor where the wind put a ripple on the water, again lobbing out a few handfuls of groundbait in the hope of attracting fish.

With the sun warm on my back I began to feel drowsy, the gentle rocking motion of the boat and the mesmerizing effect of a bobbing float relaxing me fully. Pretty soon I was happily nodding off to the piping of curlews and the distant cries of the gulls, until Andy snatched at a tentative bite and reeled in a perch, his first for some time and one of the most striking of our freshwater fish. It had boldly striped flanks and scarlet fins, and threatening dorsal spines that it held erect while being unhooked. It was the first perch I have seen for many a day, the local River Wensum now sadly almost devoid of these sporting fish, even though they were once so common and so easily caught that they provided the mainstay of my boyhood fishing and many a delicious meal. Minutes later another perch came to Andy's net, larger than the first and of a deeper colouring—a very attractive fish on which to end our session. It had been a rather quiet morning, for among the several other boats that had by now joined us I saw no other fish taken. It hardly seemed to matter, the few fish we had caught merely providing a bonus to a very pleasant outing.

AUGUST 25TH

Parked under a sheltering roadside bank to photograph an army of Canada geese assembled on the barley stubble below Roughground Copse. It was early evening and the light was still good. Already the advance guard of eighty-odd birds had gathered for the evening feed, in company with a few late wood pigeons gleaning a last meal of grain from the headland below the oaks and a large congregation of lapwings, among which the telephoto lens revealed a respectable number of young birds of the year.

While setting up the camera, more skeins of geese laboured steadily from the western horizon, the first wave containing a further forty or so birds, their urgent bugle-like cries ringing louder by the second and building to a crescendo as they spotted their companions and set their wings for the long glide over the last leg of the journey, back-pedalling frantically with black paddles lowered to alight on the downwind edge of the serried ranks. A noisy party of Egyptian geese joined the throng, their hoarse and husky bellowings sounding somewhat incongruous compared with the close harmony of the Canadas. Like outcasts, they alighted some way from the main flock, immediately squabbling amongst themselves over the best feeding places. The constant activity prompted the West Lake greylags to take to the air in scattered bunches, and for some minutes the sky above the stubble seemed full of geese—a timely and exciting preview of encounters soon to come.

Considering that no harm has come to them since the season ended on the last day of January, the goose packs are already quite restless: the lookouts honked a warning as I parted the hedge to allow the lens to pick them up. Instantly, row upon row of long necks erected as one—like an untidy assembly of walking stick handles—but they stayed their ground and, eventually deciding there was no immediate danger, one by one the necks were gradually lowered to resume feeding. After I had taken a few photographs, a rough count before I left totalled over a hundred and fifty geese, although a few tail-enders were still arriving with the first of the mallard as I drove away.

When the fierce scarlet sunset had paled to dusk, the sky clouded from the west, leaving the still night air heavy and humid and a blue haze of rising mist wafting silently across the marshes. It seemed an ideal night to try out the moth lamp.

We have already lost well over an hour of evening light as the nights draw in. By nine o'clock it was fully dark, but by then I had rigged up a bright floodlight against the sitting-room window, positioning it to cover the spinney opposite and where it could be easily seen from the low marshes at the end of the adjacent field. For several minutes it attracted nothing but swarms of gnats and mosquitos, but presently the first moths began to arrive in increasing numbers. Within the hour the outside of the window pane resembled a set from a Hitchcock film, being smothered with myriads of night-flying insects. Among a confusion of tiny micro-moths the first interesting specimen to arrive was a newly hatched iron prominent, a rather late appearance for such a perfect specimen, its slate-brown wings streaked and fringed with rusty red. Many other species followed—brimstones, thorns, prominents, hook-tips, pugs, and carpets—all drawn unerringly to the light as moths to the proverbial flame. Hopping around among the fluttering invasion, I was lucky to add a few specimens to my collection of over four hundred, among them an attractive dark-phase melanic form of the peppered moth, a good example of which I have been seeking for some time.

The highlight of the evening was the appearance of a splendid garden tiger, whose chocolate-and-white forewings opened to reveal underwings and body of a brilliant scarlet blotched with black: one of the most colourful of the British moths and also among the largest. Equalling it in size was a female oak eggar, which remained on the windowsill gently fanning its wings until the light was extinguished. By this time the window and the wall beneath it were literally crawling with an amazing diversity of night-flying creatures, normally seldom noticed and seen as little more than dim outlines fluttering against the window panes, their unique beauty and delicate colours passing all but unnoticed during the secret hours of darkness.

AUGUST 27TH

Had another exciting evening at Charles's carp lake. On arrival, I ground baited a deep swim with small cubes of luncheon meat and then tackled up with a wedge of bread crust to stalk the margins while I allowed the fish time to find the food.

Charles had already warned me that the carp have learned to leave floating crusts well alone, and the first cast beside the island was treated with the contempt it deserved—two discerning fish knowing exactly what it was but returning at intervals to nose it around the surface as if deliberately trying to provoke a reaction on my part. One even had the nerve to slap it with its tail before they gave up the game and drifted off to amuse themselves elsewhere.

I tried the deeper end, where another couple of about 4 lb (1.4 kg) were nonchalantly patrolling the downwind edge and apparently taking something from the surface. Here the reaction was just the same, the smaller of the two even holding the crust gingerly below the surface while making no attempt to swallow it. I was tempted to strike, but could still see the white knob of bread in the clear water and left it alone. Moments after it reappeared on the surface, a really big fish slid from beneath the overhanging brambles, gliding slowly but purposefully towards the bait. I knew just what to expect, but much to my astonishment it barely gave the bait a second glance before engulfing it in its wide mouth with hardly a moment's hesitation. I was slow to strike, a clean take being the last thing I expected after the reactions of the smaller fish, and could scarcely believe my luck when the carp ploughed away to take me on a rapid circuit of the pond edges, where it tried to snag the line among the dangerously low brambles. I hung on like a limpet, fully expecting the line to snap as it twanged like a guitar string while fighting to keep the fish in open water. The struggle took several minutes as run followed run, the clutch screaming at each renewed effort. The tug-of-war finally ended with the largest carp from the lake this season, a stubby-looking mirror of 9¼ lb (4.2 kg). Hanging from its bottom lip was another hook and shred of line from a previous encounter, when some less fortunate angler had almost certainly ended up among the brambles.

There was barely time for a couple of quick photographs in the failing light before the heavens opened to release a persistent downpour that left me soaked to the skin after crouching for an uncomfortable half hour among the bankside bushes. Thankfully, the low cloud drifted slowly to the east allowing the sun's strong rays to bathe the marshes and causing a thick mist to evaporate from the sodden ground. Mallard took wing all along the river, appearing as dim shadows from the low ground and passing over chuckling to themselves towards a nearby corn stubble, where after much cautious circling, the bolder spirits planed down to land out of sight behind the hedge.

A sudden splash in the reedbed interrupted my thoughts of early-season flighting as a big fish rolled beside the bank. A well-aimed crust landed within inches, drifting slowly and somewhat dangerously among the reeds. It was a hostile place to be, with little hope of encouraging a fish from its depths. As a safety measure I tightened the reel clutch another couple of notches and resolved to haul for all I was worth if the bread was taken. When it eventually happened I was surprised to pull the fish out relatively easily—luckily only 2 lb (0.9 kg), for anything larger would almost certainly have broken my cast among the reeds.

Bubbles began rising from the baited swim as all surface movement ceased. I switched to luncheon meat lightly weighted on the bottom, pinching a lump of dough on a loop of line to serve as a bite indicator. It was a long wait despite steady strings of bubbles rising around the bait, the still evening air full of the gentle cooing of wood pigeons. One in a tall willow beside me stopped abruptly in mid-sentence as the threatening outline of a sparrow-hawk twisted silently along the copse.

After a couple of tentative twitches, the dough lifted to a steady run and I tightened the line to the last fish of the evening, a really immaculate mirror of exactly 4 lb (1.8 kg). It was a perfect specimen with which to finish, for I had certainly had enough: my clothes were sodden and uncomfortably cold as I hastened homewards in the failing light. The mallard were still seeking their supper in force, and all the way home I could hear their muted chattering from the autumn-scented stubble and the whistle of pinions circling overhead, the sound bringing a promise of exciting nights to come.

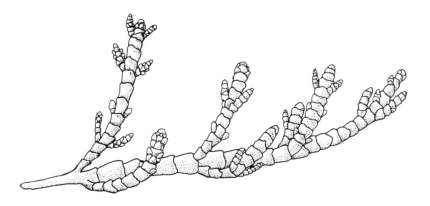

Marsh samphire.

AUGUST 30TH

Came across a family of spotted flycatchers at the duckponds this afternoon at feeding time, four well-developed youngsters perched singly on adjacent posts of the perimeter fence, guarded by a single parent that hissed a warning from the nearby undergrowth. I glimpsed its darting form among the willow-herb, but it preferred to remain cautiously out of sight. A brood of flycatchers appears as regular as clockwork at the ponds every year during the last few days of August, but I have yet to discover their nest, which must be sited somewhere quite close, probably concealed in a crack in an old alder or dead elm at the top end of the copse where the cover is at its thickest.

One youngster had perfected its trade of catching flies to a fine art, flitting upwards every few seconds to snatch a passing insect, its mandibles snapping together with a distinctly audible click. It seldom seemed to miss. The fledglings must gorge themselves quickly now, for any day they will begin the long and tiring trek to the heat of an African winter where, if they survive the perilous journey, they can capture flies to their hearts content while their birthplace is gripped in the relentless clutches of winter.

Many of the resident ducks have also turned their attentions to the flies and other minute aquatic life that now flourishes in and above the water to provide a welcome supplement to their diet. My favourites, the hooded mergansers, spend much time pursuing small shoals of roach fry and minnows that have drifted unwittingly via the feeder stream into the ponds, their underwater antics and sheer speed and manoeuvrability a delight to observe in the clear sun-dappled water.

September

SEPTEMBER 1ST

For once the weather forecasters had got it right, with heavy rains and violent gales lashing the countryside to mark the opening day of the wildfowling season. Continuous rain fell throughout the day, but by evening the sky had almost cleared and the wind moderated to a stiff westerly as I took up position on a high bank overlooking the river, finding shelter in the lee of a low hedge beside a convenient elder bush just sufficiently thick to screen me from any flighting fowl. The stubble-grazing geese have made a timely departure for pastures new, but I knew there would be duck in plenty on the wing, the nearby lakes always manned on the first night of the season.

Sure enough, a spattering of shots echoed along the valley from Bulrush Lake and minutes later the first parties of mallard came chattering upwind, although much too high to risk a shot. Allowing the leaders to depart unscathed, eventually a small wedge of mallard came beating against a sudden squall, a high overhead shot sending a fine drake planing down to thud heavily on the riverbank. A mile to the west another distant volley of shots put more on the wing, and soon the sky above the marsh was full of duck. Small, bewildered parties criss-crossed the dark stormclouds that had again swelled from the west to all but obscure the sun, which peeped bravely through a cleft in the blackness to scorch the earth with a brilliant silver fire, creating an awesome backcloth studded with the black forms of flighting fowl.

The vibrant cackle of greylags drifted on the wind from far away, getting steadily louder by the second as they moved along the valley to appear presently as two distant wavering lines rising and falling with the contours of the land. Together they must have amounted to a hundred strong, and it was with trembling fingers that I removed the light-load game cartridges from the gun and slipped a couple of BBs into the breech in case they should come my way. The cackling grew in volume, though it was soon clear they would pass well wide, allowing the strong tailwind to carry them along on a course for Bulrush Lake, and arching their huge wings for the steep descent to the water. Just short of range an over-enthusiastic shot turned them prematurely, and off they went again, yelping like a pack of hounds into the far dim distance.

Watching them melt slowly into the greyness, my reactions were put to the test as a flight of unseen mallard zipped over low. However, the gun held straight and another fine mallard bounced on the stubble behind me, the remainder breaking ranks and flaring skywards to leave me confused and with no time to fire a second barrel. The bird safely gathered, I waited in the hide until it was almost too dark to see, adding another mallard to the bag with a snapshot against the last of the light, although it was merely a bonus to the very sight of so many fowl flighting against the vastness of the sky, and the changing kaleidoscope of patterns of a dramatic autumn sunset.

SEPTEMBER 3RD

After two disappointing attempts at a wily old brownie in the river, this evening finally saw what had become a contest of wits brought to a successful conclusion. From its own point of view, the trout had chosen a particularly good lie, awkward to reach, at least 25 yards from open ground, and dangerously close to the spreading branches of an ash that restricted accurate casting. There also, the current runs quite swiftly, adding greatly to the difficulties of presenting a lifelike and attractive offering.

It was such a pleasant afternoon that I took Spectre along for the outing, placing her on a log beside the riverbank as I prepared to continue the battle with the trout. Nearby a combine hummed around a field of late-standing wheat, its monotonous drone a sound characteristic of advancing summer days when the last of the harvest is gathered in.

My very first cast caused a heavy swirl below the fly, but for some reason the fish came short, the brightness of the sun probably accentuating any shortcomings in its dressing. After another identical reaction a few casts later, all went quiet and I could only presume it had lost interest. There seemed nothing for it but to give it a rest until the evening, while I tackled the shoal of dace that were beginning to rise in midstream 50 yards upriver.

Spectre sat quietly while I cast, her head pivoting comically back and forth like a spectator watching the ball at a tennis match as she followed the path of the fly. It was some time before I actually made contact with a fish and by then she had lost interest, remaining totally unimpressed by the skilful handling and presentation that had brought about its capture, preening quietly and methodically through her new set of feathers. She allowed little more than a cursory glance as I snatched a glistening dace from below the willow stumps, although she scrutinized it rather more deliberately when it was lifted ceremoniously ashore.

The shadows lengthened as the sun sank gradually beyond Marsh Wood, taking the brassy glare from the water and allowing a sudden contrasting chill to descend with the first of the dew. The combine ground to a halt, the hush and stillness of evening emphasized abruptly as the first faint wisps of mist smouldered above the river. I gave an involuntary shiver as Spectre puffed out her feathers. The sky was clear ice-blue. It was to be a cold night.

It was high time to try the trout again. A swarm of insects danced low across the lie as I tied on a sedge fly—a really lifelike imitation complete with realistic wings and antennae that closely resembled those gyrating dizzily across the surface. The first two casts drifted wide of the swim, but the following alighted with the touch of thistledown well upstream and just short of the far bank. I let it drift before drawing it slowly across the lie, creating a small bow wave that induced a sudden splash as it was taken boldly. The first

131

powerful run ended deep among the weeds, but after hauling it out the fish came readily, a steady drag against the current with little sign of the expected struggle. It reached the net covered with weed, explaining the reason for such a one-sided battle.

I guessed its weight at not much over 2 lb (0.9 kg), an exquisitely spotted fish with perfect fins and tail. Already having a good supply of trout in the deep freeze, it seemed wrong to remove such a perfect specimen from the river, so after examining my catch I slid it slowly back to the shallows from where it rocketed downstream with a flick of its tail, and disappeared. We may now meet again, although I suspect it will be some time before it again succumbs to the temptation of an artificial fly.

SEPTEMBER 6TH

Spectre was raring to go when I returned home from work at midday, screaming in anticipation when she heard my approach along the gravel drive as if aware I had planned to take her hunting. We were soon on our way to give the moorhen a try on Spring Marsh.

A heavy shower had refreshed the land, but a light breeze gently rolled away the clouds to leave the fields trembling in the heat of a glorious September afternoon. Spectre was very keen to hunt, bating impatiently as we forded the gravelly stream from the duckponds to the marsh. A moorhen rose from the far bank of the river and scuttled off upstream. I held her back, knowing only too well she stood no chance. The bird would lose her easily among the tangle of the riverbank, where the undergrowth was dense with wild thickets of flowering willow-herb and impenetrable beds of rushes, among which the moorhen is very much at home and remarkably adept at shaking off pursuit.

The marsh smelt clean and fresh, the nose-tingling tang of water mint and wet rushes combined with the rich earthy smell of mud. The air was blowing moist from Marsh Wood, where a green woodpecker chuckled among the alders and a mousing kestrel drifted high above the adjoining water meadow. We began by searching the overgrown central drain away from the river towards Rabbit Hill, sending a snipe or two 'scaaping' from the boggy region halfway along and a heavily moulting redshank flitting from the edge of the reeds. When another moorhen burst from the sedges Spectre was off like a shot, but unfortunately for her it followed the path of the drain and dropped back to cover as she shortened the distance between them. Spectre banked up and hovered briefly overhead, suddenly twisting as her prey was sighted and thumping boldly into the chest-high reeds. Her stoop was far too late. When I reached her she was clutching nothing more than a handful of sedges, displaying a reluctance to relinquish her hold until I picked her up. She peered in disbelief at the talonful of sedges until I cast her forward from the glove to a lone oak at the far end of the drain. Here she took stand in the topmost branches and turned to face me while I worked out the remainder of the rushes towards her.

She suddenly stiffened and launched from the tree, and although I saw nothing come out, a short downward glide ended with a sharp pounce among a bed of nettles. She had obviously tried something. Her aim had also improved, but instead of the expected moorhen she was clutching an enormous frog, one of her more bizarre addictions that has remained since capturing one on her very first successful flight. Since then she has remained extremely partial to a frog and there was little chance of rescuing the unfortunate creature. Following a vain attempt, it was, as usual, swallowed whole in a series of neck-stretching gulps until the last webbed foot finally disappeared and her crop bulged full and round. This signalled the end of hunting for the afternoon, her appetite being sufficiently dulled to discourage further interest and now content merely to sit and digest her catch—not a particularly auspicious start to the season and hardly deserving of an entry in the game book.

SEPTEMBER 9TH

With a welcome invitation from Charles to fish his local trout water as a guest this afternoon, I was relieved to see the weather turn out reasonably well—at least dry and bright although the strong southerly wind was going to make life difficult. The lake has a reputation of providing comparatively difficult fishing, in itself consisting of almost 30 acres of clear water of varying depth, tastefully dotted about with small tree-covered islands and thick reedbeds lining the banks, which cover almost a mile.

Before setting out Charles took me on an enlightening tour of the 'stew ponds' where the trout are reared prior to release in the lake. He took a bucketful of floating pellets with which to feed the fish. At first glance little could be seen in the long netting-covered channels, but a scoopful of pellets thrown in and the surface boiled with fish, every last trace of the food snapped up greedily within seconds. We then fed the larger stews (two areas of water penned off from the lake itself), one of which contained something approaching four thousand small trout that made an unbelievable sight as they came up for food. Beside it a pen held far larger fish that were a delight to observe feeding at close quarters, including a magnificent brown trout that was in the region of 8 lb (3.6 kg)—an aggressive-looking cock fish with a noticeably upturned lower jaw or 'kype'.

In the confines of the stews the fish are ready to snap at almost anything, but once released they rapidly become a different proposition: shy, wary, and difficult to catch, with the freedom to roam at will around 30 acres of water.

With so much bank to chose from it was difficult to know where to start. This afternoon most of the fish were apparently hanging along the downwind north bank, but there a strong headwind made casting virtually impossible and Charles eventually installed me near a water inlet that feeds the lake from the bordering river. Even there casting was quite difficult, as a blustery side wind whipped up large waves and played havoc with my line. At times I felt the fly whiz past rather too close for comfort, but with a little practice I finally

A scoopful of food thrown in, and the surface brimmed with fish.

began to get the hang of it, working a green damsel-fly nymph around the turbulent area near the inlet pipe where a rainbow was rising from time to time. Nothing happened until I speeded up the retrieve, when a savage take showed I had aroused its interest. The fish proved extremely fit, going berserk as I slid the landing-net into the water and giving several more energetic runs before being netted, luckily firmly hooked in the scissors of the jaw.

I worked hard with no further contact until the early evening, when the wind dropped sufficiently to allow fishing from the productive north bank. Here the evening rise was well under way and it was now possible to make a respectable cast directly into the wind. A huge brown trout was repeatedly crashing out of the water fully a 100 yards out, but I contented myself by trying for a small rainbow rising a few feet from an outcrop of sedges. An accurate cast finally took it as the nymph passed through the ripples of a rise.

By the time it was beached the light had almost gone. As the mallard continued to flight in from the surrounding stubbles, I plodded reluctantly to the clubhouse well pleased with taking a brace the first time on a difficult and unknown water.

SEPTEMBER 12TH

At last I could see them: a long, thin, undulating line of geese lifting through the dense low-lying fog half a mile away, banking slowly round to set a course in my direction. I had almost given up hope, having been in position before first light—or at least what passed for it—for a dense fog had fallen during the night and the dawn was little more than a gradual lightening of the greyness with visibility down to 15 yards at most. Not a living thing stirred in the stillness, the only sounds the constant dripping of condensed fog from the trees behind me and the distant muted honking of the geese.

For the last two mornings a single flight of Canadas had crossed the centre of the stubble soon after dawn on their way along the valley, but this morning the fog had delayed their journey and possibly altered their plans. There was nothing for it but to wait and see.

Gradually the sun gained in strength, its orange glow beginning to penetrate the gloom and burning off the mist to bring the distant hedge into outline as a dark-grey smudge on the horizon. Nearby a cock pheasant crowed a challenge to the dawn, gliding heavily from his roosting tree to a clumsy landing, where he stood like a statue for several seconds surveying the lie of the land. He failed to spot me crouched in the hedge bottom and apparently satisfied that all was well, began to seek out his breakfast of crane flies among the grassy stubble.

The fog was a long while lifting—at first little more than a gradual thinning over the high ground, but finally the sun broke through enough to encourage the first wood pigeons to venture from the copse. A few passed over temptingly, but I held my fire for fear of alarming the geese I hoped must move soon, their voices ringing ever more stridently as they prepared for flight. But would they come my way? As if in answer, the flock at last took wing from the lake as the fog suddenly dispersed from the high ground: about forty all told, but slightly off course and looking as though they might pass just out of range.

There was no hope of changing my position, so I crouched lower in the dripping hedge, waiting until the very last moment before springing up to fire a single shot at the bird on the extreme left flank. It folded obligingly and crashed heavily into the hedge—a young gander, broad of breast and redolent of good living on the stubbles. It would certainly make good eating.

As the sun's intensity increased, the last of the fog retreated to the lowlands, revealing the treetops in Marsh Wood but leaving their trunks shrouded in a veil of mist. Across the stubble a silken carpet of gossamer strands sparkled all the colours of the rainbow in the gathering light, the work of a million young spiders bespangled with glistening dew. What sights we miss by sleeping our lives away during what is often the most beautiful time of the day.

SEPTEMBER 15TH

There was a distinct autumnal feeling in the air early this morning as I carried Spectre to Spring Marsh in the hope of opening our account with the moorhen, a deep brooding stillness and silence that hung heavily over the countryside. The mood was reflected by a despondent mist that smouldered low across the marsh and hung stubbornly among the riverside copses. Not a single bird sang along the hedgerow, the silence broken only by the distant cackling of unseen greylags and the harsh croaking of a carrion crow perched in a tall larch across the river.

I have seldom seen such an abundance of moorhen as there are about the marshes this autumn, and in a few weeks the sprouting corn will suffer unless we can make an inroad among their numbers. As yet, the jungle of summer growth provides all too many hiding places among dense thickets of willow-herb, wild teasel, and beds of nettles and rushes stifling the banks of the marsh drains. To add to our problems many moorhen also prefer to remain in the vicinity of the river within easy reach of safety.

Fortunately there are several convenient clumps of nettles situated about the open marsh to which the birds retreat. Entering the first one beside the bridge, three moorhen burst out simultaneously, although there was safety in numbers. Spectre was confused, allowing the birds a few moments grace before making up her mind which one to chase. She followed the last to break cover, though only half-heartedly, the moorhen outflying her easily over 50 yards before dropping to a tangle of sedges near the river. Arriving far too late, Spectre threw up into a tall ash above it to sulk. I left her at her vantage point and continued working the cover towards her, realizing that she stood a far better chance with the added height to lend her speed on any subsequent flight.

It was not long before another moorhen flushed from the edge of the nettles, following the path of the first that took it almost directly below where

Spectre waited. There was no need to call her. As it neared she dropped soundlessly from the ash to intercept its line of flight, the bird oblivious of her presence until it was far too late. The collision in mid-air sent them both spinning down among the sedges on the far bank of the boundary stream.

She mantled fiercely astride her quarry as I forded the stream, guarding it jealously as I gently lifted both to the open ground where she could take her reward. I always allow her to satisfy her hunger on the first kill of the season, and very soon the ground was littered with feathers and her crop bulged with fresh moorhen meat. The feast will put her out of action for a few days but will ultimately make her keener to hunt and add a little more conviction to future endeavours.

SEPTEMBER 17TH

There was a commotion high above Marsh Wood this morning as a small gathering of rooks tumbled about the sky in a state of high excitement. The object of their attentions looked somewhat heron-like from where I stood overlooking West Lake, but as it drew gradually nearer I recognized the familiar outline of our old friend the osprey, moving slowly south-east on its autumn migration trail. It was travelling at least 300 feet up, but as the rooks gave up the chase and drifted away, their mobbing was taken up in relay by a pair of lapwings that allowed the bird no peace. Arriving high over the lake, the osprey wavered uncertainly in the air as if recognizing a former haunt, and for a few moments it seemed as though debating whether or not to stop. The renewed protestations of the lapwings, however, seemed to settle its mind and it continued in a steady southerly direction. I watched it out of sight.

It is difficult to believe that a whole summer has come and gone since an osprey—possibly the same bird—paid us a visit in early April before the lake's summer residents had arrived. Since then most have paired, mated, laid eggs, and reared their young, and have now departed leaving the reedbeds and marginal scrub strangely quiet and empty, no longer filled with their voices from dawn to dusk and the hustle and bustle of rearing a family over. After weeks of skirmishing with their elders, the young terns have all departed to new fishing grounds, and the sand-martin colony looks cold and deserted along the south face. Here, rows of untenanted nesting holes now stand vacant apart from a sprinkling of late youngsters exercising their wings along the face of the cliff. Instead of their ceaseless twitterings the lake now rings with the calls of gulls and wildfowl, and reaching the far end of the causeway a virtual blizzard of gulls, mallard, and greylag geese erupted from behind a sandbank that had screened my quiet approach. Here they had been preening and bathing, the shoreline littered with feathers and gull castings and a few casualties from the flock—one the half-submerged corpse of a young blackback that bobbed in the lapping wavelets against the shore.

SEPTEMBER 20TH

Ken called in on his way home from work this afternoon with news that the dragline had just breached the narrow causeway separating Bulrush Lake from a new digging of several acres that has been excavated over the past few months. The gravel seam runs deep in the new working, and to aid the task of its extraction, a huge water pump has been pounding away night and day to keep the site relatively dry. Thus the difference in water levels was several feet, and when the wall between the two was breached, the outcome was likely to be spectacular.

The results were dramatic to say the least. Within the space of half an hour the level of Bulrush Lake had dropped fully six feet, which considering its size—about 600 yards long and covering almost eight acres—was almost unbelievable. The place was hardly recognizable. Many huge islands now loomed where previously there had been a solid sheet of water, and large areas of the bottom had been revealed, stranding much of the lake life on scattered mudflats and in shallow elevated pools. Along a shallow stretch

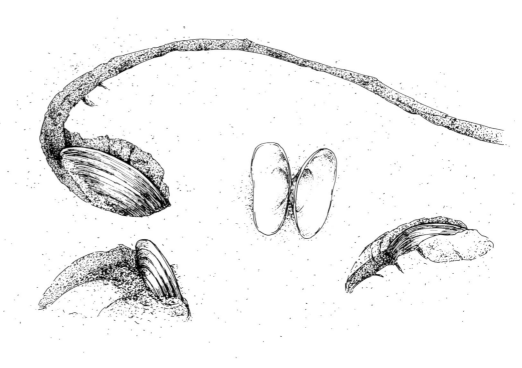

Swan mussels carving deep trails through the muddy lake bottom.

138

beside the farmhouse, a wide shelf now lay exposed, and venturing carefully across the mud it was interesting to note some of the life that had been left high and dry by the rapid lowering of the water. Swan mussels were in abundance—huge specimens that carved deep trails through the mud attempting to return to the water, and in a shallow pool beside the bank, we could see a few stranded fish darting timidly around in barely a foot of water.

The water level would evidently take several days to return to normal, and when Trevor, the cowman, arrived, he set to work with a spade cutting a channel to drain the pool, while I floundered around with a landing-net hoping to rescue a few of the fish. As the cloudiness settled, many more were revealed, crowding together as the water receded to a little pool where they formed a tight shoal—roach, gudgeon, a miniature pike, two tiny eels, and a small clan of perch varying from a few ounces to minute specimens smaller than minnows, yet still perfect replicas of their larger brethren.

Several feet of mud prevented us from reaching all the fish, although several were netted and safely returned to the remaining water. The rest will be lucky to survive, for I suspect the herons will not be long discovering the feast and a busy night is in the offing.

SEPTEMBER 22ND

I could hardly believe my eyes this evening when I wandered across to the ponds an hour before dusk to try for a duck. If there was one mallard, there must have been at least fifty taking off from the pens: little wonder the residents seem constantly hungry and the food bowls are always empty in the mornings. High time to thin a few out.

With so much time taken up with rearing the young fowl, I have rather neglected the ponds of late, so there was plenty of tall cover left in which to conceal myself to wait for their return. I chose a spot amidst a bed of prickly teasels almost on the riverbank, from where I could keep a convenient watch across the surrounding marshes.

The evenings are growing markedly colder now with a real nip in the air, but fortunately there are accordingly fewer flies to torment one with their constant attentions. A huge bat—probably a noctule—seemed to be finding a few as it hawked around the branches of the giant ash tree, even though its main interest seemed centred around a swarm of tiny moths fluttering about the leaf canopy high above my head.

As twilight approached, the resident tawny owl came hooting his way along the copse to his favourite lookout perch, pausing briefly on the rotten alder bough to swivel his head downwards, and meeting my eye before floating soundlessly away to continue his hunting along the riverbank. He should have lingered, for just moments later the dark form of a rat emerged from beneath an alder root and was soon tripping back and forth to a food trough laden with mouthfuls of pellets for its underground store. Its well-worn run passed by only a few feet from where I stood, and on one occasion it even had the cheek to sit up on its haunches and peer at me inquisitively, seeming not in the least disturbed by my presence. I must get the traps working again soon.

While debating whether or not to put an end to its pilfering, the harsh stutter of an incoming mallard sounded somewhere above. Glimpsing its reflection in the pond I swung up to take a very surprised drake with a snapshot as it flared away, folding it up just before it put a thick ash bough between us. It took a great deal of finding, for I failed to mark the spot where it crashed down amongst the nettles.

As the evening drew to a close, duck were moving constantly across Spring Marsh. Although I waited until dark, surprisingly few came back to the ponds considering the number I had earlier disturbed. However, I ended the vigil with a neat double between the trees from a small bunch planing down to the centre pond, both dropping within a few feet of one another on the far bank beside a very indignant emperor goose!

SEPTEMBER 24TH

Having risen far later than planned—always a bad start to the day—it was in attempting to shake off a feeling of mild depression that I found myself wandering rather aimlessly about the farm with no particular destination in mind and nothing planned to make good use of what remained of the day.

At first I could find little to lift the mood, for the end of summer always seems a depressing time of the year, with everywhere looking tired and overgrown as if awaiting the first frosts of autumn to restore some semblance of order to summer's disarray. Despite its withered appearance, autumn is obviously the most productive season with a beauty all of its own, and if one takes the trouble to look, there is much of interest to be found in all the wild places. Fruits, nuts, and berries are swelling to ripeness along the hedgerows as nature prepares a vast store to feed the masses throughout the coming winter months on a rich and bountiful fare. Clusters of elderberries are

Water mint.

darkening to a deep purple hue on the scattered bushes, and will provide the source of a heady wine if one can beat the birds that are already plundering the crop—as evidenced by the spattering of purple droppings scattered on the nettle leaves below the bushes. Rosehips and hawthorn berries are turning a vivid scarlet, the latter in profusion this year—a sure indication of an imminent hard winter as many old country folk will have you believe— though I tend to think it is the weather that has gone before rather than that which is to come that influences the productivity of the bushes.

In a quiet, sunny corner beside Blackthorn Copse, I discovered two beautiful peacock butterflies (already drowsy with blackberry juice) on a sheltered bramble patch, but the fruit tasted sour to my palate because of the lack of sunshine while it had matured. The bulk of the berries have yet to ripen, but with cold nights and rapidly shortening days, they will certainly be lacking much in flavour.

My wandering ended on the far bank of Bulrush Lake, whose water level is now rising again, and where my interest was aroused by the discovery of a few streams of tiny bubbles rising from four feet of water bordering a rushy island, as a small shoal of bream or tench rooted around the muddy lake bottom. I began to feel much brighter, returning home in a far more decisive frame of mind to tackle up the rods for an early-morning foray at the lake.

SEPTEMBER 25TH

It was a struggle to reach the bream swim before dawn, an uncomfortable journey carried out in almost total darkness and encumbered with a pair of rods, two nets, a bucket of groundbait, and a heavy shoulder bag through well over half a mile of tall dew-soaked vegetation. Fortunately I had the foresight to wear thigh waders and arrived relatively dry.

I could hardly have picked a better morning: dry, windless, and very mild, with the lake as calm as a millpond. By the time I had mixed up and cast out a few handfuls of groundbait—to which I added a sprinkling of maggots for good measure—a gash in the clouds to the east provided sufficient light to show a few bubbles rising below the mist just off the small reed-fringed island ten yards to my right, almost the same spot as they were rising yesterday.

I cast out the first rod baited with a small brandling worm and a couple of maggots on a size-ten hook, positioning the bait to rest just on the bottom while I unravelled a tangle of line on the second rod that had been caused by an argument with a particularly stubborn patch of brambles on my journey. Even before the last knot was untangled there was a bite, the float dipping gently a couple of times before sliding slowly away to the pull of a fish. Having taken a number of carp recently, the ensuing fight seemed weak—a dispirited floundering on the surface and with none of the deep, violent runs so typical of a carp. Soon the fish was broadside on, a fairly large bream considering the poor fight—about 4½ lb (2 kg). Anyway, it was a promising start.

With the fish safely in the keepnet, I got both rods working, the floats within a few feet of one another to enable both to be seen at once so that any

After the sun dissolved the mist, the swim went quiet.
Early morning on Bulrush Lake.

less positive bites would not be missed. The day was breaking fast, an intense crimson dawn lighting up the undersides of dispersing clouds and restoring rich colour to the landscape. Beside me, a thicket of great willow-herb added its late blooms to the banks, but it was somewhat overshadowed by the rich purple spikes of loosestrife that glowed warmly among the reeds. Two herons glided in silently from the west, their breasts stained crimson by the glow. They swerved erratically as I was spotted in what is normally a secluded corner. Watching their urgent departure, out of the corner of my eye I noticed the left-hand float glide slowly out of sight, lifting into a small silvered bream of a few ounces. It was quickly followed by another to the same rod, but as the sun dissolved the mist, the bubbles stopped rising and the swim went ominously quiet.

I gave it another full hour, but by then my patience was wearing thin. Leaving one rod to cover the swim, I used the other to fish a single maggot over a shallow bar 20 yards out, where a few small fish had started moving. They turned out to be small rudd, a few being taken on very delicate bites with a tiny size-16 hook before they too seemed to have had enough. I packed up at mid-morning with eight fish, the last a handsome perch that succumbed to a brandling as I was getting my gear together for the long trek home through the steaming tangle of undergrowth.

SEPTEMBER 28TH

Flew Spectre around Rabbit Hill on our way to the marsh. Instead of carrying her on the glove, when we reached the bottom of the hill I cast her up into the trees, from where she followed my progress from branch to branch as I searched out the wild bramble clumps and rough places hoping to find something for her to chase. This is my favourite form of hunting and Spectre seems to enjoy it immensely. She follows faithfully through the trees and at times sneaks slightly ahead in the hope of intercepting flushed game. It was rough going across the steep hillside through a mass of prickly briars, the bushes interwoven and their leaves already yellowing to match the sycamore leaves that are even now beginning to fall. It will not be long before the wood floors are carpeted with many rich autumn tints.

Having hunted the side of the hill, I had ejected nothing more exciting than a pair of blackbirds and a dunnock, when I heard Spectre's bells rattling away far ahead of me. She was clearly disenchanted with my efforts to produce something and had gone off hunting on her own.

Between the trees I watched her travel the entire length of the marsh, coming to rest in a dead elm overlooking a rough area of wilting bracken edged by a thicket of blackthorn that was laden with purple sloes. Something had aroused her interest. It was quite a walk, and several minutes had elapsed before I drew level on the far bank of a drain when she suddenly plunged out of sight among the tall bracken. A pheasant exploded from its edge, closely followed by two more: obviously late birds of the year though strong of wing. Spectre remained hidden, the only indication of her whereabouts the agitated tinkling of bells. I jumped the ditch and fought my way through the clinging fronds, finding her lying with one leg outstretched reaching deep among the bracken, where the tip of a wing showed she had caught another of the pheasants—as yet still out of season!

Protecting the poult with my glove, I quickly offered her a chick, feeling her grip weaken sufficiently to allow me to prise the locked talons apart to release the bird. I was relieved to find it unhurt. It was a young cock not yet in full plumage, and while Spectre was occupied with her dinner, I carried it out of sight and let it go. The bird sped away on blurring wings until it had crossed the river, no doubt thanking its lucky stars it had suffered nothing worse than the loss of a few feathers.

SEPTEMBER 30TH

Attending to the duckpond rats occupied most of the afternoon. Searching for the best sites at which to set my traps, I found much evidence of recent workings previously concealed by thick vegetation, mainly along the edge of the water. Now the corn has been cut and carted, and the stubbles cultivated, the rats are beginning to return to their winter quarters after a summer of plenty in the cornfields. The old holes have been re-opened beneath the alder stumps, and judging by the footmarks in the mud, a considerable number of youngsters have been reared. Unless I can thin them out effectively the pond will be over-run by the winter. The resident tawny owl no doubt accounts for a few, but the ground around the holes needs clearing to help him assist in their control.

I set the Fenn traps in wooden tunnels along a few of the main runs, for rats are unable to resist exploring any new hole on their territory and I find these traps especially lethal when baited with a little duck food placed below the trigger plate. The scent of food entices even the wariest to investigate.

With the task completed, I cleaned up and freed the springs of half-a-dozen well-used moletraps, for although appearing harmless, the creatures can create havoc in the spring by burrowing directly beneath nesting sites. The eggs then fall into the tunnel as the nest collapses, and it causes the duck to desert. There are several strong runs in an area near the water where worms are plentiful, one between two huge molehills so well used that it must be the local moles' equivalent of a subterranean motorway!

It is a pleasure to see the ducks acquiring their winter plumage again, for with the return of breeding attire will come the drakes' first attempts at displaying to renew the pair-bonding that has become somewhat relaxed during the period of summer eclipse. The eider drake has already begun cooing seductively as he assumes his striking black-and-white plumage, his self-confidence returning with the restoration of his full splendour. Mandarin and Carolina drakes—among the first to regain their colours—are beginning to strut and to parade before their partners instead of skulking unobtrusively among the reeds as they did during the misery of the moult.

October

OCTOBER 1ST

As we embark upon the final quarter of the year, great changes are occurring daily in the countryside as the nights lengthen and the temperature falls. Soon the first nose-tingling frosts will cause the leaves to wither and fall as nature's scythe gets to work among the vegetation. It is now the turn of the toadstools and other fungi to appear in the damp and misty conditions of the woodland floor and on decaying treestumps. On the close-cropped cattle pastures, the welcome parasols of mushrooms sprout from the earth in the early mornings, swelling so rapidly that one can almost see them grow.

The last of the birds prepare for long journeys to the warmer south, most prominent of which are the swallows, the power-lines a-twitter with their tiny bodies that resemble notes on a sheet of music whose score gains in complexity with each passing day. For long periods they sit idly contemplating what lies ahead as though reluctant to depart, but soon they will be off. Even now, as if to a pre-arranged signal, they suddenly all take to the air together for a practice flight to gorge themselves on the last of the insects. Luckily these are still in abundance, although many perish in the widespread cloak of spiders' webs that now adorn the hedgerows—most noticeable in the early mornings when their delicate lacework hangs like living jewellery bespangled with sparkling dew.

Finches and sparrows are now flocking into winter raiding-parties, starlings are beginning to congregate into large flocks that swish over to a communal roost before dusk, and rooks and jackdaws have massed in uncountable numbers to glean the last of the corn stubbles before the plough turns up the rich black earth ready for next summer's crop. Their throaty raspings fill the still autumn air. Nearer to home, the robin alone sings loud and clear in the orchard, where the apples are now fully ripe and wasps are busy with the abundance of windfalls.

The month of October sees the opening of the pheasant-shooting season, but few will be shot until the end of the month when they have fully earned their wings and learned their way around to provide early-season sport. They are flushed from fields of sugar beet and kale and along boundary hedgerows—the larger woods and coverts mainly being left as sanctuaries until shooting really gets under way after most of the leaves have fallen.

OCTOBER 3RD

On my last visit to the Mill Pools in early April, the daffodils were in their full glory and the surrounding woods were alive with spring migrants. Now the birds have deserted us and even that flower of the autumn, the rose-bay willow-herb, is well past its best, the downy seeds wafting on a chilly breeze that soughed through the willows as I took the path to the larger top lake. Beside one clump, a patch of yellow ragwort was crawling with the caterpillars of the cinnabar moth, completely untroubled by birds, their striking black-and-yellow banded bodies—nature's warning colours—telling of their distaste, having gorged themselves on a diet of the virulent ragwort.

This morning I decided to use only dry flies for the trout. In these small lakes the fish are easily tempted to sunken wet flies and lures, and the clear water would provide an ideal opportunity to gain a little more experience with the former, more exacting method, of which my fishing has been very limited.

The trout have lost none of their fighting spirit, the first small rainbow succumbing to a tiny pheasant-tailed nymph greased to float on the surface and worked slowly across where a fish was rising every few minutes. Seizing the nymph close in, it enabled me to see the complete take—a slow shadowing at first before putting in a sudden burst of speed, rushing at least six feet to snap up the fly before returning to deeper water. The whole manoeuvre took barely a second but was most interesting to see, for all one normally experiences of the actual take is a sudden bang on the line.

The fish made a mess of the fly, leaving it thoroughly water-logged and dishevelled. However, with another coating of flotant and a few flicks through the air, it was soon riding proudly on the surface again, taking a further fish only seconds later. As a result of a rough tussle, this time the fly was beyond repair, and I subsequently worked my way through a variety of patterns, some taken boldly, others ignored, until I was left with only a large crane fly—the daddy longlegs—of which there were a few naturals hatching from the surrounding grass and an insect or two drifting onto the lake. Once on the water they seemed too ungainly to rise again, floundering temptingly in the surface film before being snapped up by passing trout.

The artificial is one I had never used—a cumbersome though lifelike imitation with long trailing legs formed from the fibres of a cock pheasant's tail, knotted halfway along to form realistic joints. It definitely attracted fish, but striking time and again, I was left completely baffled, failing to make even slight contact with the most energetic of rises. A small rainbow began moving very close in. Hoping to discover just what I was doing wrong, I dapped it on the surface to see if I could get a reaction. When it rose again, I was surprised to see the fish actually strike it in passing as if attempting to knock it below the surface, coming back to snap up the submerged fly the second time around. When dry-fly fishing the temptation is to hit the boil. I was apparently striking far too early, not allowing the trout the chance to deal with so large a fly. It took a great deal of restraint, but by consciously counting to three after the rise, I found myself making contact at last, in this way taking my limit of fish by the early afternoon. Most enlightening: we live and learn!

Whisper and Spectre patiently awaiting an outing.

OCTOBER 6TH

Hunted Spectre again just after lunch, taking Whisper along for some much needed exercise and to help us search out some of the rougher areas of the marsh that, until now, have proved safe havens for the moorhen.

Whisper has a mind of her own and was almost uncontrollable at first, but after a few minutes of charging frantically around the stubble, she settled down to become quite biddable. She kept obligingly to heel as we crept along a high bank overlooking the marsh, where a few moorhen could be seen pottering along the banks of the centre drain until one chanced to look up and spotted us. Its warning croak sent them all scuttling back among the rushes, from where they are normally almost impossible to flush.

We retraced our steps to the duckponds, waded the stream, and continued along the open riverbank to cut off their escape route by working the drain away from the river. At its junction with the river, a small pike basked in the weak sunlight in a favourite lie beside a patch of gently swaying weed, but Whisper blundered across the adjoining mudbank and when I looked again it was gone, a muddy swirl marking the spot where it had lain.

Urged to get on, Whisper was soon quartering the ground enthusiastically, her sensitive nose thrusting this way and that among the rushes to discover an exciting variety of scents, but suddenly she burst out and raced ahead, flushing the first moorhen well out of range. I tightened my hold on Spectre's jesses. A string of oaths brought Whisper slinking back with her tail at half mast to where she finally settled down to work beside us, in a short time freezing rigidly in her classical point. There was something just ahead of us.

She held the stance well until we were in position and, when told to flush, she put out another moorhen not more than ten yards away. This was the chance we had been waiting for, but though appearing ungainly in the air, the bird's speed was deceptive and it was a long chase across the marsh until Spectre managed to snatch it just before it dropped in the edge of Marsh Wood. Bringing up the rear, Whisper eventually caught up, making in slowly towards the pair but prudently remaining at a safe distance. She has learned a healthy respect for the buzzard who, although normally quite harmless, is not averse to lashing out with her talons if approached too closely when she has taken prey. She is far from willing to tolerate interference from an inquisitive hunting companion.

OCTOBER 8TH

The sky cleared following a night of rough gales and heavy rain, but it was still blustery as Ken and myself set out to feed the pheasants on the farm, first loading up the truck with a few bales of straw and a sack of rough wheat cleared up from the floor of the barn.

The first pheasant shoot is only a few weeks away, and although very much on a small scale, it can provide an enjoyable informal day or two early in the season, even though bags are never excessive. Now that most of the stubbles

Feeding the pheasants. A scattering of straw attracts the pheasants
but conceals the corn from sparrows.

have been buried by the plough, food is getting harder to come by in the
fields, and by regular feeding of suitable areas what few pheasants there are
can be gathered together to offer a few respectable drives. At each feeding
spot a bale of straw is strewn loosely on the ground and the corn scattered
amongst it, encouraging the birds to scratch around for the grain. This keeps
them occupied and remaining in the vicinity for long periods, leaving less
time for them to wander off elsewhere. They are thus more likely to be found
at home on shooting days. Covering the corn with straw also discourages the
hordes of sparrows that would otherwise soon discover the easy source of
food.

Feeding along the sheltered side of Bluebell Copse, I noticed that last
night's gales had removed sufficient leaves to reveal an undiscovered magpie's nest—a huge fortress of sticks and mud at the very top of a spindly
blackthorn bush. This was obviously one that had been hidden among the
leaf canopy when I searched the copse in late spring. Not ten yards from it in
the fork of an ash was a drey of the now ubiquitous grey squirrel, an
unwelcome intruder that has now completely ousted the indigenous and far
more attractive little red squirrel over most of the county. A common sight

149

along the autumn hedgerows a number of years ago, it is now some time since I have seen a red, though the grey is extremely widespread and far from uncommon. The 'tree rat'—as it is rather disrespectfully labelled—is much despised by forester and gamekeeper alike, causing wholesale damage among the young plantations and destroying many a nest of eggs and nestlings of both songbirds and game. The only point in its favour is that its bushy tail comes in very useful for tying trout flies!

While a few pheasants are reared to supplement numbers, the farm shoot relies mainly on wild stock that, taking the weather into account, seem to have coped well this year. On our travels we came across several sunning themselves in the lee of hedges and others already busy among the acorns brought down by the gale, a windfall shared with the jays. The latter have a habit of burying the acorns underground for leaner times ahead, but I suspect very few are ever found again and in this way many an oak tree is unwittingly planted.

OCTOBER 10TH

After sharing an abortive dusk on Spring Marsh waiting for the duck to flight Ray came round for the evening, and over a few frames of snooker we discussed the possibility of giving the pike a try at Wood Lake early in the morning.

Despite yesterday's high winds and rain—the reason I had invited Ray for the flight—it was a pleasant morning: humid, misty, and with hardly a breath of wind to stir the rushes as we tackled up a pair of rods apiece along the deep east bank running parallel to the wood. The water drops almost sheer to about 20 feet, and I have previously taken pike here well into double figures.

Using two rods each deadbaited with smelt and tiny mackerel, we had hardly settled down when I noticed Ray's nearest float gliding away in a confident run, although when he struck at what was probably a small fish it let go almost immediately. However, his second chance came only a few minutes later, and with no mistake this time he was soon guiding a pike of a few pounds towards the bank.

My first opportunity came while untangling an absolute bird's nest of line that had slipped from a new spool on my smaller rod, the bait lying apparently out of action only a few feet from the bank. Concentrating on the umpteenth knot, I became aware of something pulling the line steadily through my fingers. Abandoning my task I tightened up and struck. A splash on the surface showed I had somehow made contact, yet it proved to be little bigger than Ray's previous catch.

By the time both rods were working again, the mist had lowered and thickened to almost obscure the far bank. Strangely enough, the conditions prompted the duck to move. For some time, small bunches were circling provocatively above our heads, preceding a gaggle of shadowy greylags that moved above the murk, whiffling down to graze on the centre of the marsh. However, the sun broke through and a light breeze blew away the last of the mist, when they cackled away along the valley to the west.

The pike remained in a feeding mood and Ray, fishing further out, had several runs before taking another, this time an even smaller fish of barely 1½ lb (0.7 kg). I added to the catch after moving 50 yards along the bank, where I had tucked myself up cosily among the rushes and was beginning to doze when the float slid away, stopped briefly, cocked up on one end, and then was off again before I could reel in the slack line to strike, feeling a lively kick as the hooks went home. It turned out to be the best fish of the morning, although nothing of any real size had turned up and there was no sign of the big fish I have occasionally seen sunning itself along the margins on hot summer afternoons.

OCTOBER 13TH

I took another brace of moorhen with Spectre, this time from the marshy ground bordering Bulrush Lake where we had not yet been this year. The first was an easy flight at a bird ejected from a refuge in the top branches of a holly clump near the farmhouse—taken in a long stoop from a hedgerow oak—and the next an exciting chase across the full length of the marsh that ended deep in Blackthorn Copse before Spectre finally caught up with it following a wild pursuit through the bushes. She is certainly taking her toll as repeated flying improves her condition and enhances speed and manoeuvrability in the air.

Feeding her up on the glove on the way home, we passed by a rough area of scrub on the south bank of West Lake, where a giant bed of thistles had attracted a small flock of goldfinches. Goldfinches love thistle seeds and, by advancing slowly, I was able to get quite close. The acrobatic little finches were preoccupied with stripping the hanging seedheads of their bounty, clinging upside down and working away totally oblivious to our approach.

The term for a gathering of goldfinches is a 'charm', an apt description, for charming they certainly were, flitting daintily from plant to plant twittering most prettily. It was evidently a family gathering, for I was close enough to note that all but two lacked the black-and-white heads with the crimson blaze across their faces that signifies an adult bird. The youngsters or 'greypates' are noticeably duller overall but sport the brilliant golden patches on their wings that gives the bird its name.

For some minutes we watched them feed but Spectre, having finished her meal and impatient to be on her way, bated lustily towards a nearby elm and the little flock went twittering across the water, not stopping until they eventually regrouped to feed on another patch of thistles beside the shore 200 yards away.

OCTOBER 15TH

Whisper was scratching at the back door asking to be let out late last night, so before retiring to bed we took a breath of fresh air to see what all the fuss was

151

about. She had picked up the scent of a hedgehog crossing the back lawn, but seemed put out when it rather unobligingly forced a stalemate by rolling itself into a defensive ball of spikes.

The midnight air was certainly fresh, with clusters of stars winking like diamonds in the velvety blackness of a clear, moonlit sky, and underfoot the grass was crisp and white with the makings of a sharp ground-frost.

By dawn everything sparkled, with frost remaining in the lee of hedges until mid-morning when a reluctant sun burned it off, leaving the leaves singed and blackened on the lower branches of the orchard ash. Giving the snowy-owl pen its weekly tidy up, I discovered a thick skin of ice on their pool, but having replenished the water the female was soon splashing boldly in the tub having her daily bath, seeming completely insensitive to the cold.

Both owls are now in fine fettle after the moult. Most of this time the female has spent demurely tucked away in her nesting-box, thoroughly embarrassed by her shabby condition. During her absence her mate has been getting well above his station, taking full advantage of her temporary indisposition to prance bravely around the pen as if he owned the place. She has, however, now returned to rule the roost in her customary belligerent manner, and he has once more been relegated to the lowest of the low.

Both birds watched attentively from a nearby log as I cleared up a heap of castings beneath a favourite roosting perch, a couple of which surprisingly showed traces of rat fur. The owls have apparently been busy during the long nights and it seems the rats have not chosen their winter quarters with much deliberation. It is at least encouraging to see them eating something other than their staple diet of day-old chicks, for I have been trying unsuccessfully to vary their rations—particularly at breeding time—but both display a reluctance to try anything new. A varied diet might just possibly increase their chances of breeding. The pair are certainly full of good intentions at breeding time, but though provided with a roomy aviary, plenty of nest-boxes, and a surplus of good food, as yet nothing has come of it. My hopes of obtaining a youngster for training have so far amounted to nothing. There are obviously some things I cannot help them with!

I have yet to hear of anyone successfully training a snowy owl for hunting, but I see no real reason why this should not be achieved. With something like a five-foot wingspan, it would certainly be an impressive bird to fly, possessing the strength to match its size and an obvious capability of taking rabbits and hares. The snowy's strength is colossal—as I once found out to my cost. Forced to catch up the birds for penning one winter's night, as I grasped the female firmly in both hands, she somehow contrived to return the gesture, inserting her inch-long talons straight through my thickest hawking glove: a painfully illuminating confirmation of her awesome power. Locked in a mutual and rather intimate embrace with her was an experience I would have gladly forgone, and it was with great relief that we finally parted company. Against such strength, even the strongest of hares would have stood no chance. Perhaps next year ... ?

152

OCTOBER 18TH

A raw autumnal start to the day, a ground frost, and an impenetrable fog lingering well into the morning. It therefore seemed quite fitting that such conditions should see the arrival of the first flock of fieldfares and redwings from across the North Sea to emphasize the fact that winter is just around the corner.

I was feeding the ducks as they came chattering out of the gloom, obviously hungry after their travels, for the flock wasted no time and descended as one to the single holly tree on the high bank, now laden with a bumper crop of blood-red berries. The resident mistle thrush was understandably put out, for he has zealously defended the tree against all comers since the berries began to turn but alas, this time the odds were too great and his strong-arm tactics were overwhelmed by the invaders' sheer weight of numbers—all his rushing back and forth and harsh scoldings to no avail as the newcomers raided his winter store.

In complete contrast, by lunchtime the fog had miraculously lifted and a sympathetic sun burned from an almost cloudless sky. I watched what must be our last swallow sweeping languidly about the garden looking for flies, but it seemed a wasted effort and it is high time the bird was on its way to warmer climes.

Looking lost and forlorn, it took a brief rest on the telephone cable beside the house, twittering a sad little song as it preened its feathers. So small and fragile, it seems hardly possible the little traveller will soon be winging its way the many hundreds of miles to the heat of South Africa along the hazardous course that negotiates many obstacles, not the least of which is the daunting task of crossing the interminable arid vastness of the Sahara Desert. What will drive it on its way will remain a mystery to me, and what strength and single-mindedness is needed to undertake such a journey, clearly not a task for the weak of will.

It took to its wings again, circled the garden twice, and flitted rather more purposefully across the field. I doubt if I shall see it again this year, but with luck on its side it will surely return to build its nest among the rafters in the tumbledown barn across the road next spring. *Bon voyage*!

OCTOBER 21ST

Piking again with Ray, a grey dawn finding us chugging upstream along the River Thurne from Martham Ferry to fish an area of the Norfolk Broadland that has the reputation of holding large fish. It was barely light enough to tackle up when we made a brief stop at the junction of Candle Dyke, but after a few casts other boats began to move and we decided to up anchor and find a quieter spot. We travelled to Heigham Sound and then via the twisting Meadow Dyke to Horsey Mere, which has produced some real specimen pike over the years.

Duck were continually swishing over at first light—mallard, teal, pochard, and tufted—and later several noisy skeins of greylags battled against the breeze across vast acres of reedbeds that stretched as far as the eye could see. Along Meadow Dyke the bream were feeding, bubbles rising in continuous streams in front of the boat, but ignoring them we arrived at Horsey Mere and followed the path of an inviting creek to a little bay sheltered among the reeds that looked quite 'pikey'. Though choked with weed, we moored at the edge and cast out a couple of rigs each to cover the water with deadbaits of smelt, mackerel, and a small and rather unwholesome trout that I lobbed into a small cove at the far end.

The forecasted rain held off, and very soon the reeds were bathed in mellow sunshine, our sheltered mooring very peaceful with just sufficient breeze to put a nice ripple on the water. It was most relaxing, and it was not until some time later while listening to the chiming of bearded tits deep among the phragmites that I suddenly noticed one of my floats had disappeared, the one baited with the trout. Snatching up the rod I reeled in and struck, feeling nothing but a solid resistance that seemed like weed. I dragged it heavily towards the boat until I detected a tiny kick that could only be a small jack pike. I declined Ray's offer of the landing-net until the float neared the boat, when a massive head surfaced momentarily, fixed me with a glassy stare and surged powerfully away, passing directly beneath my other rod to cause a few moments of confusion until Ray quickly reeled it in. Having weighed up the situation, the fish showed its strength at last, putting in several forceful runs towards the weeds, but I turned it short and after a few more lively spurts headed it towards Ray's outstretched net.

He had a struggle to haul it aboard—a long and lean fish, dark of colour and with a proportionately large and wicked-looking head. We guessed its weight at around 15 lb (6.8 kg). In fact, it pulled the balance down to 18 lb 6 oz (8.3 kg), a splendid way to begin our first piking session on Horsey.

Setting off some time later, we did a thorough tour of the area, stopping to try the likely looking spots, but most were choked with summer weed and we eventually made our way to Hickling Broad via the Sound, anchoring along the downwind edge to fish another sheltered cove. Here we waited a long time before Ray's line started stripping from the spool to a take. However, having hooked the fish and felt a couple of strong runs, it gained a weedbed and threw the hooks, a real disappointment after such a long wait.

We decided to explore the area more fully, returning to Martham Ferry and then setting off in the opposite direction to get the lie of the land and to earmark any likely spots for a future trip when the weed has died down. Returning homewards quite late, the little outboard motor suddenly coughed, spluttered a few times, and finally died. We had run out of petrol.

As Ray had been piloting the boat all day he somewhat sarcastically suggested it was now my turn to drive! Luckily he was only joking. Faced with a row of at least two miles against the current, we finally took an oar apiece and after a Herculean effort against the flow, arrived exhausted at the boat-yard as the sun was staining the western sky to a vivid orange while it dipped gradually to rest.

OCTOBER 22ND

I was returning home from Farm Wood after a successful hunting trip with Spectre this afternoon when pandemonium broke out on the hillside cattle-pasture opposite the farmhouse. The cows were acting very strangely, cavorting wildly around the field and evidently in pursuit of something. At the tip of the spearhead of animals I recognized the red-brown streak of a fox, its white-tipped brush streaming out behind it in the wind and obviously in a great hurry. What the animal was doing in the open fields at such an hour was difficult to imagine, but it looked rather small and was probably a cub of the year not yet used to the ways of the world.

The stampede continued across the grass, the cows making a comical sight as they chased hell-for-leather with their udders swinging and tails erect until the fox found refuge by darting through the boundary hawthorn hedge where its pursuers were unable to follow.

For some time the cows stood bellowing, snorting, and peering longingly into the hedge contemplating its disappearance. Meantime the object of their attentions slinked gratefully away at a more sedate pace towards Rough-ground Copse, on its way receiving another fright as a covey of partridges exploded noisily from its path. Even on gaining the copse there was little peace to be found. Its arrival was announced by a jay that screeched blue murder while following it out of sight over the brow of the hill. It will certainly think twice before venturing abroad in full daylight again.

The cows were a long time returning to their grazing, and even then a few went back periodically to where the fox had disappeared for a cautious sniff at the ground.

OCTOBER 25TH

Just for a change I hunted Spectre over the high ground overlooking the valley, our journey taking us to the furthest point of the farm across open grass fields studded with hedgerow oaks and fading stubbles now partly ploughed up for the autumn drilling. A multitude of lapwings have returned to the uplands, and together with the first sprinkling of golden plovers, they took to the air in a vast flock as a hare was disturbed from its form on a rough area of plough. Spectre hardly gave it a second glance as it skipped away, its white scut flashing as it pelted the full length of the field to pause briefly and risk a fleeting backward glance before disappearing through the hedge.

With Spectre following from tree to tree, in due course we arrived at Long Meadow—a narrow pasture that stretches along the farm boundary bordered by mature woodland already bedecked with the tints of autumn. The actual boundary is marked by a tiny beck carrying water from the high ground, in places smothered with brambles and ferns and a favourite haunt of wood-cock. True to form, one burst from the water's edge, proving much too quick for Spectre as it twisted elusively through the maze of treetrunks and was soon out of sight.

155

Reaching the end of the meadow well ahead of me, Spectre scattered a small bunch of wood pigeons from where they had been searching the wood floor for fallen acorns below a muster of elderly oaks. She swayed precariously on a contorted limb among the topmost branches, but was soon off again, having discovered something of interest a few yards further along the wood. Another pigeon laboured heavily from the brambles, this time a weak bird that lumbered slowly away through the trees with Spectre diving in pursuit, gaining well until the pair passed out of sight between the massive trunks and I was forced to stop and listen to see which way the chase had gone.

Presently her bells fell silent. She had either taken her quarry or given up the chase. I stumbled over the carpet of leaf litter and fallen boughs until I heard the bells again. I spied her deep in a bramble bush surrounded with floating white feathers, mantling over the dead pigeon. It was an ailing bird: thin, wasted, and lacking the normal healthy lustre to its feathers, so I took it away before Spectre could begin feeding, swapping it carefully for a joint of fresh rabbit from my hawking bag. I seldom risk using wood pigeons as hawk food even at the best of times, for they can harbour all manner of diseases, particularly so in the case of such an obviously sickly bird.

OCTOBER 28TH

An unwelcome visitor has been busy above the garden during the night. While exercising Whisper across the grass field, she ranged about widely with her nose glued to the ground until she suddenly skidded to a halt, freezing on point to indicate something of interest a few feet ahead of her. Thinking she had winded a pheasant squatting in the long grass, I called her off, but she ignored me and inched carefully forward, her hackles raised apprehensively and belly almost brushing the ground. Reaching tentatively forward she snatched up something in her mouth and brought it back to me with an enthusiastic wagging of her tail. It was a pheasant all right, but only its foot, and having presented me with her find Whisper immediately ran back to the spot and retrieved another. My suspicions were confirmed when I followed her to a depression in the grass, where a neat pile of intestines and a scattering of feathers showed where a fox had taken a leisurely meal. The stiff wing and tail feathers were severed neatly at the roots, so typical of the work of a fox. It had wasted nothing.

Nearby on a freshly turned molehill, a set of relatively small padmarks were visible in the sandy soil, probably made by the same fox seen a few days ago that has found easy pickings where the birds have taken to rather foolishly roosting on the open ground, where they stand little chance and are easily picked up at night by a prowling fox.

Later in the afternoon I watched several young pheasants from my study window settling down in the stubble for the night. It seems they are determined to lose more of their number before they acquire the habit of roosting well out of harm's way in the trees, for the fox will almost certainly return for another easy meal.

156

As an afterthought I returned with Whisper to hunt out the stubble just before dark, flushing no less than seven pheasants all jugged down together, which scattered towards the Roughground Copse. They should at least find some sanctuary there, giving them a better chance of survival instead of tempting providence on the open stubble.

OCTOBER 30TH

Delivered the third and final batch of young waterfowl to Trevor this afternoon, a motley bunch of late developers together with the final clutch of scaup that are always the last to go. To be truthful I was glad to see the back of them at last, since the rearing season creates a great deal of extra work and is very time consuming.

Catching them up from the orchard was quite a performance as the cover is thick at one end of the pen, but I finally got them all aboard the truck and arrived at Bungay on the Suffolk border just after lunch. Trevor was the customary half an hour late, but in no time at all had them sexed and sorted in his holding pens.

Trevor collected a female snow goose that I needed to pair with a widowed gander in the orchard.

I had decided to collect another couple of unrelated pairs of red-breasted geese to increase the orchard flock sufficiently to keep the grass in trim, and on the way to catch them up Trevor showed me a couple of versicolor teal—a small, South American species—lying dead in the corner of a pen, one of which had been dragged halfway down a mole run. It was obviously the work of a weasel, for the little predators will often utilize mole runs as a means of travelling around unobserved. This is one of the reasons the presence of moles in a rearing pen is to be discouraged. He is hoping the culprit will return to the carcases, and has set traps nearby in the hope of catching it before it kills again.

With the geese safely boxed we went to another large holding pen containing literally hundreds of mixed young waterfowl to catch a female snow goose that I need to pair with a widowed gander in the orchard. I was surprised at the number of mandarins and Carolinas there were among the flock, for my own birds were rather lazy this year, producing only a single clutch of eggs apiece in place of the normal two or three.

I completed the homeward journey well before dark, releasing the new birds immediately to accustom them to their new surroundings before nightfall. There was much excited cackling on both sides as they introduced themselves to the residents, but pretty soon they were all grazing peacefully together, the youngsters noticeably more subdued of plumage and less prominently marked.

I always heave a sigh of relief when the last of the birds have gone, for my work is now cut to basic feeding duties. Even so, I have no doubt I shall soon be looking forward to doing it all again next year.

November

NOVEMBER 1ST

It was a typically uninspiring start to November, with dull, grey, and drizzly skies, though to be fair the month can still produce pleasantly sunny days at times, which are much appreciated for their novelty. It is an in-between time of year, the summer almost forgotten but without the fresh and bracing atmosphere that winter brings. Everywhere there is evidence of staleness and decay, the countryside beginning to look thoroughly washed-out and colour-less when the multicoloured leaves have faded. The once resplendent trees are rapidly shrinking to mere skeletons of their former selves, and following the recent frosts, another strong wind will send the bulk of the leaves spiralling earthwards to transform the landscape dramatically, stripping the trees to their bare bones and adding to the general untidiness of nature's most slovenly season.

But all is not a picture of gloom and despondency. On the dwindling stubbles a few tenacious wild flowers still raise their heads defiantly against the weather: the beautiful scarlet pimpernel rubs shoulders with clumps of miniature field pansies and bright blue speedwell, the tiny flowers all the more precious for appearing in such unfriendly times.

On the shooting scene the time is fast approaching for the hallowed game coverts to be broached for the first time as the cover dies back, providing the cream of driven-pheasant shooting, and on rough nights the duck flight well on the wind and a wedge of geese may come along to offer a chance, even though they have grown wary and often wait until the very last moment of the day to flight in from their feeding grounds.

Food is becoming shorter in the wild. On the way to prospect West Lake for a future piking expedition, I disturbed a couple of cock pheasants below an oak cramming their crops with acorns, together with a pair of blackbirds scratching hungrily among the deep leaf litter. Above the valley a vast flock of rooks lifted from the high ground, where they have taken to digging up the young corn now greening the autumn drillings.

The first cormorants have returned to the lake to earn their winter living from its waters. Four launched clumsily from the causeway where black-headed gulls were already gathering for the night, the beginning of a seemingly never-ending stream that glides low over the house each afternoon on their way to roost. By evening there must now be well over two thousand present, their squabblings audible very late into the night.

NOVEMBER 3RD

I joined the beating line for a day out on an estate a few miles from home. The estate, covering some 3,000 acres of mixed arable and woodland is no stranger to me. I spent a season working with the beaters a few years back when I was getting some very large bags of wood pigeon over decoys from the same ground during the winter months.

When I turned up at the keeper's house just before nine the sky was overcast with a hint of drizzle, but the rest of the team were in high spirits. Among them I recognized many of the old regulars who seem to turn up year after year for their weekly day out whatever the weather. All country people at heart, they have much in common: a love of the open air, an appreciation of the countryside and its sport, a very necessary sense of humour, and above all an enthusiasm to see game fly well to test the guns—although some of the elder among them probably owe at least part of their longevity to an ability to find the easiest way through the thickest coverts!

There were to be eight drives in all, mainly across the more open ground for partridges, but with an odd bit of woodland taken in to vary the bag with a few early-season pheasants. Such was the case of the first drive, culminating in Church Wood. Forcing our way through a tangled maze of firs and interwoven brambles, we could hear the pattering of feet as pheasants fled before us across the fallen leaves prior to breaking out through the treetops. Their arrival at the far end of the wood was announced by a spattering of shots from guns placed well below in a narrow valley.

The rest of the morning's work was over comparatively open ground. We were ferried somewhat uncomfortably from drive to drive in a covered trailer to work out crops of sugar beet, parsnips, and potatoes. Our line was advancing each time in wide semi-circles with the flanking beaters carrying conspicuous white flags that were waved frantically each time a covey rose to keep them moving forward to where the guns were waiting. At times it was impossible to hold them in, particularly against a headwind, when they proved unstoppable despite vigorous waving of the flags. Others were difficult to flush as we struggled through vast tracts of sugar beet that were soaking wet following a heavy shower in the late morning. At the end of the long fourth and final drive of the morning, we bumped back in the trailer along a rutted track to the keeper's house—a steaming huddle of men and dogs who were more than ready for lunch.

The afternoon was dry. Suitably restored, we set off again under a brightening sky. The wind had if anything increased, making the job of steering the coveys all the harder. During one upwind drive several pheasants climbed high and broke back over our line, but enough went forward to keep the guns on their toes. The highlight of the afternoon was a drive from a young plantation where partridges have been reared, but although we flushed large numbers, almost without exception all went the wrong way, bursting out on the right-hand flank to avoid the guns despite frantic efforts by the flagmen to keep them on line.

We finished at three o'clock, allowing ample time for the birds to re-group and settle down before dark. It had been a really pleasurable outing, and though admittedly I would have rather been on the other end of the line, it gave an exciting preview of things to come. It certainly gives one a far greater appreciation of the efforts necessary to put good sporting birds over the guns.

NOVEMBER 6TH

A still, quiet, and rather depressing day, with no sign of the sun and a hazy grey mist hanging around the fields throughout the daylight hours, which have shortened considerably now the clocks have been altered. An eerie silence hung about the countryside, magnifying the little betraying sounds of wildlife: a blackbird turning the leaves in the hedge bottom, the far-off shriek of a heron, and the tap-tapping of a nuthatch on a bare bough of the long-dead elm.

On my wanderings I stopped to examine an old nest in a thicket of twisted briar, only revealed now that the leaves have thinned. I recognized it at once as the work of a bullfinch with its unmistakable platform base of thin twigs and rootlets, and neat lining of hair.

Presently, a tiny scrap of a bird came hopping its way along the hedgerow, the first of a family procession of long-tailed tits that seemed unafraid and afforded me only the briefest glance as they progressed, flitting from twig to twig among the hawthorns, on the way examining minutely the underside of each leaf for hidden insects and spiders. Seen close up, they are one of our most delightful birds, the combination of pink, white, and black blending most attractively, with their long tails accounting for well over half the length. I counted fourteen all told, and they kept pace with me as I wandered down to Charles's carp lake to see if the fish were still moving. The remains of the hedgerow leaves now have but a tenuous hold: even the minuscule weight of the tits jarred the twigs enough to dislodge them to crackle dryly to the ground.

The carp were not moving. As the water cools they become inactive and cease their ecstatic summer rolling on the surface. Instead, they retreat to the muddy depths where they spend the colder months in a semi-torpid state. Catching them now will not be easy.

NOVEMBER 8TH

With the first pheasant shoot arranged for today, it was a relief to find the weather had changed—a fresh southerly springing up during the night to dispel the thick fog of the preceding two days, when visibility hardly rose above 50 yards. This morning was clear, bright, and breezy as we assembled in the farmyard at nine o'clock.

The sandpit beside Long Meadow was to be the first drive, the walking guns also bringing in a few acres of high ground to where we lined out the bottom of the hill. A few partridges often gather on the summit and, sure enough, a tight covey of redlegs approached just after we had taken up our stands. They hugged the contours of the land until the last moment when one peeled from the bunch to provide me with the first shot, sizzling overhead before the first barrel sent it plunging into the boundary beck. The rest broke ranks and whistled through the line barely above head height, far too low to offer a safe shot.

As the dogs came into sight over the brow of the hill ahead of the walkers, the first pheasants started coming forward, breaking obligingly over the line in ones and twos. The four I took—three hens and a cock—crashed deep into the boundary wood at our rear. Halfway through the drive the unexpected happened: a frustrating flush of at least a dozen birds rose *en masse* to pass directly over, all remaining dangerously low. I allowed them to pass. They will undoubtedly fly much better next time through.

The sugar beet was a real disappointment. Fed regularly, a nice showing of pheasants has been seen there most mornings but though we worked it to the last inch only an odd one or two were found—a brace of partridges and a couple of hares being the main additions to our bag. The beet are still very thick with leaf, providing an abundance of cover for hiding birds.

After two more drives it was time for lunch. By the time we reappeared from the local pub the wind had turned bitterly cold, lending speed to the quarry at the next venue, Rabbit Hill, where a small strip of kale has been left on the summit to provide some necessary cover. Standing well below on the open marsh we were treated to some really testing shots as those disturbed from the kale passed over the hilltop gaining height to hurtle over our stands on the valley floor. A tall hen gave me my first opportunity, coming directly towards me, lifting all the while. It was going like a rocket. Throwing the gun to my shoulder I gave it an impossible lead, swung hard, and was relieved to see it crumple at the second shot, bouncing 60 yards behind on the grazed turf at the far end of the central dyke. In terms of quality the drive proved to be the best of the day, with everything coming out fast and high, even though a few had escaped on the right-hand flank much too wide for Ken, who was standing helplessly at the end of the line.

The rest of the afternoon was spent hunting rough marshland and areas of dense scrub where pheasants tend to congregate as the day draws to a close. Still thick with vegetation, it took rather longer than expected, but a respectable number of pheasants were added to the tally by the time we had finished. We had planned to round off the day with an evening flight at Bulrush Lake, but the days are very short now and by four o'clock darkness was already beginning to close in. The duck will have to wait until another evening.

NOVEMBER 10TH

There had been a cruel hoar-frost in the early hours. Arriving at John Wilson's carp lake at half-past six, the dawn sky was just beginning to reveal the consequences of a clear, cloudless night. Everything was icy white. Mist smouldered across the water like smoke from a dying bonfire as I crept around the oldest of the two lakes, casting in a handful of hemp seed at a few chosen swims in the rather forlorn hope of getting the carp to feed.

Remarkably, despite the cold, a couple of fish were rolling around on the top when I returned to the new lake in almost full daylight. As John had suggested, I made a long cast with a floating crust between the bank and an island, first lobbing in a handful to get them interested. The fish were slow to react, and at first I received rather more interest from a flock of cheeky black-headed gulls that dived down to snap up the crusts, their natural wariness overcome by the pangs of hunger. It was a toss-up as to which I would catch first, but half an hour later, as John was walking the dogs around the lake, there was a sudden splash at the bait. Fishing at distance I struck hard, feeling that wonderful surge of power on the end of the line that could only be a carp. The sensation restored warmth to numbed fingers, flexing my arm as the fish strained the rod and kicked away deep. This process was repeated several times before I could manoeuvre it closer. Nearing the bank the carp appeared to be swimming rather awkwardly. The reason became apparent as it was lifted clear of the water. It was foul-hooked in the chin—a fish of about 8 lb (3.6 kg)—an extremely lucky start. John arrived right on cue with his camera to take a few shots before it slid back to an icy home.

I gave the swim a little longer but the struggle had put everything out of sight. The only interest, now the gulls had drifted away, was shown by an enterprising mallard drake that seemed to appear from nowhere each time I cast out afresh. It was time to try the old lake.

With the sun rising laboriously above the fir woods, it seemed even colder beneath the trees. Creeping along the leaf-strewn pathway, I crossed the footbridge to discover a beautiful fly agaric below the ferns, the sun sparkling on the frosted red cap of this most toxic of toadstools.

With two rods in action I float-fished the bottom, one baited with a chunk of luncheon meat and the other with some borlotti beans John had given me to try. The beans did the trick. Although missing the first positive bite while unpacking my sandwiches, I was prepared for the next—a small common of about 2 lb (0.9 kg) that was reluctant to come ashore, the skirmish again fouling up the swim.

I made another move, this time to the small, tree-clad island lying below the tall south bank. Fishing only a rod length out, it seemed a long vigil as I shivered in the deep shade below the alders where the sun could not penetrate, while before me at the far end of the water the golden silver birches were bathed in its welcome rays, which only served to accentuate the cold. To busy myself, from time to time I scattered a little hemp around the floats but it was not until I poured out a reviving cup of coffee that the left-hand float wagged very gently sideways. Snatching up the rod I struck when the float toppled as the bait was lifted from the bottom. The fish was on—and not a small one either! It was some time before I caught sight of it, for the carp bored away deep, hugging the bottom. When I did eventually gain the upper hand it gave a few tense moments by trying to snag me on a willow trailing dangerously close. I slipped the net under before it could try again, another lucky catch, as the hook was barely holding in its bottom lip: an ideal end to a splendid morning, a mirror just short of 11 lb (5 kg). It must have been my lucky day.

NOVEMBER 12TH

Another cheerless November day—grey, bleak, wet, and cold, with a bitter blast chasing flurries of sodden leaves around the garden and bringing down the last of the apples. During a brief dry spell I hurried across to feed the ducks, disturbing a miserable bunch of lapwings from the hill above the house that lifted reluctantly to be swept about the sky like tattered rags. The truce was short-lived. Reaching the garden, another downpour swept almost horizontally across the fields, forcing them down again, the wretched group mustering in untidy rows with shoulders hunched and heads to wind in a sad and dispirited-looking huddle.

With the outside chores completed, it was a real treat to be tucked up cosily in my study as the rain drummed relentlessly against the window. It was an ideal day for concentrating on some long-overdue taxidermy work, with nothing to lure me outside. The subject was a beautiful barn owl, a road casualty already mounted and installed in a case but still awaiting a garnish of foliage and a sealed-glass front to keep out the dust and to protect the specimen from the attention of insects.

Barn owls all too frequently fall victim to cars. Their habit of dicing with death by hunting the short grass of roadside verges often has fatal consequences, and in this way many find their way to me, most of them remarkably undamaged. Luckily this one was virtually unmarked: a splendid adult female of perfect plumage and colour, the upperparts a rich golden-buff and a breast of the purest white.

Owls of all species are a pleasure to work on, the forward-looking faces and large eyes lending themselves readily to expression. This one I had mounted in an alert pose, crouched on a log with wings slightly parted as though disturbed in the act of taking off. The groundwork was already completed: a rough, papier-mâché base constructed from thin strips of paper pasted over a contoured base of light-gauge wire-netting, the mâché glued, dusted with sand, and stained to form an earthlike texture into which bunches of dried vegetation can be fixed when fully preserved and coloured to their natural tones.

To form the appropriate habitat I used a mixture of gorse, moss, dried grasses, bracken fronds, and a few attractive yarrow seedheads, seating each bunch firmly in the groundwork and adding a spot of glue to hold it in position. I was quite pleased with the result, for I consider the case settings as important as the specimen itself, adding much interest if tastefully carried out and the plants blended to create an interesting picture that, if correctly installed and cared for, will last for many years.

The case settings are almost as important as the bird itself. Putting
the finishing touches to the barn owl case.

NOVEMBER 15TH

Spectre was full of beans this morning, a long and cold night adding an edge to her appetite and sharpening her instinct to hunt. She was ready to chase almost anything, even stealing rather more than a casual glance at the tame waterfowl in the garden, and displaying her keenness by chasing a wren in and out of the hedge as we went down the lane beside West Lake towards the marsh. She did not give up until the wren found a safe refuge deep in a clump of holly. It was still swearing as I took her back on the glove, for in such a mood she is liable to go off hunting on her own and could end up almost anywhere, possibly crossing the river if something were to attract her attention. It was certainly not ideal weather for swimming.

The remaining moorhen have now grown distinctly wary, the very sight of her approaching shadow or the faintest tinkling of distant bells sufficient to send them all scuttling for the nearest cover. The marsh is generally cleared in seconds.

Nearing the river, I forced a path down the steep bank through a withered forest of shoulder-high bracken and willow-herb, holding her aloft above my head to give her a chance should something come out as I beat my way through the rubbish. Skirting the edge of a bramble patch, a cock pheasant took us both by surprise, exploding noisily from the undergrowth almost at my feet. Spectre needed no prompting, launching into the air close behind and sweeping down the slope, closing so fast that the bird was confused into seeking shelter in the nearest bed of nettles, instead of using its greater speed to outfly her which, once moving, it could have done with relative ease. Realizing the mistake, it once again took wing—but too late! With a final burst of speed, Spectre hurtled in for the kill and struck, the pair spinning down among the nettles in a confused tangle. Following a dramatic tussle she at last stood over it, broad wings hooding the prey and surrounded by a mass of burnished feathers. It all happened so quickly. At last—a pheasant in fair flight! Quite a feat for a lowly buzzard. A real red-letter day for her diary. It will make a splendid change in place of the moorhen stew she normally provides.

NOVEMBER 18TH

Two days of almost continuous rain has saturated the earth, the run-off from the fields transferring the clear slow-moving river Wensum that normally wends its way benignly through the water meadows into a swirling, brown torrent that sweeps branches and other debris picked up *en route* relentlessly downstream. At noon, the river overflowed its banks at Spring Marsh, and by early evening a silver sheet of water covered most of the marsh. Yet still it continued to rise. The conditions were ideal for an outing after the duck.

I was almost too late for evening flight. A wary flock of greylags had already settled on the water with a few scattered parties of duck as I attempted a cautious crossing of the marsh, trusting to memory to avoid the danger of the many criss-crossing dykes. It is remarkable how a flood can alter the whole appearance of an area of land I know so well, and each step was taken carefully despite wearing thigh waders, for nothing less would serve to get me to a high point beside the river. The goose sentries regarded my approach with suspicion. Cackling excitedly, the entire flock suddenly lifted with a great roar of wings, climbing steeply towards the western glow and curling gradually back on their path to yelp vibrantly across the sky in a long string following the course of the river. There was little chance of them returning.

Continuing towards the river, little wisps of snipe rose temptingly from shrinking islands still above the flood, but these I left alone as already the first returning duck were beginning to circle the marsh. Wading carefully, I at last gained sanctuary on another small island beside the river. Here, crouched low among the rushes, I faced the setting sun, but in no time at all the light began to fail. I watched the wary duck and listened to the gnawing of voles along the riverbank, and snipe dropping back unseen to the water's edge.

A single mallard broke from a bunch and glided straight over, giving an easy chance, although the first shot passed inexplicably wide. The second brought it tumbling heavily to the island. The shots disturbed a host of fowl upriver, mainly mallard, apart from one close-knit bunch of a dozen teal that sizzled past just too wide for a shot. For some minutes the sky seemed full of duck, and even though I was well concealed, most kept out of range until I was taken unawares by a bunch from behind. I recovered just in time to get off a double as they flared skywards, the first thudding beside me and the second slanting away into the darkness to splash heavily far out in the floods.

After gathering both there was barely enough light to probe a safe retreat from the marsh. I was thankful to reach the bottom of Rabbit Hill without incident. The evenings are now very short, with duck still moving around in the darkness as I made my way back home.

NOVEMBER 20TH

Spent another cold morning's piking on West Lake. For the third time this month dawn found me huddling on the causeway, but as the sun now seldom bothers to put in an appearance much before seven o'clock, it did not mean rising too early. I was already shivering beside the water before it peeped shyly over the rim of the world to flood the sky with gorgeous shades of apple green, streaked with delicate pastel pink. I cursed myself for not thawing the deadbaits earlier, for they were still partly frozen and difficult to attach to the hooks with numbed and frozen fingers. The first one went sailing at least 50 yards over the lake after parting company with the twin sets of treble hooks. Forced to settle for less distance, soon both floats were bobbing merrily away in the ripples 20 yards from the bank.

Then, in the far distance, came the cries of wild swans! They were very faint at first but unmistakable. Bewick's—seven of them, all the way from Russia, beating a steady line out of the early eastern glow. I could hear them coming a couple of miles away, so quiet was the morning. Passing 1,000 feet

Netting a stocky, well-conditioned pike of 10¾ lb (4.9 kg).

above the lake, they were welcomed by a friendly bunch of Canadas resting at the far end, and even my tame barnacles added to the chorus, though in rather less musical fashion. The aristocrats did not falter in their stride, beating effortlessly from horizon to horizon until swallowed completely in the vastness of the sky.

I was soon pacing up and down the causeway in an effort to keep warm, leaving the reel-bale arms open in case I should get a run. However, with no sign of action I gathered the rods together to seek a more sheltered spot out of a wind increasing both in coldness and intensity. I found just what I was looking for: a sunny and secluded corner sheltered by a bank of spoil on its upward edge. The water was encouragingly deep, and bordered with banks of tall rushes and stunted alders. It looked promising in terms of sport.

The baits now fully thawed, I pumped out a herring and a smelt, positioning both within yards of the opposite bank on either side of a jutting peninsula, spending the next few minutes watching the antics of a small flock of siskins in the alders. A long wait followed, but beside water there is always

168

something to occupy the time. The sun was warm on my back as I lay among the reeds to observe a great-crested grebe diving repeatedly not far from the bank, once surfacing close with a small silver fish in its beak. On the nearby sandbank a cantankerous pair of herring gulls disputed ownership of a titbit of food, and a brilliant kingfisher streaked past in a great hurry, screaming shrilly as though late for some appointment.

And then the float was off, stopping and starting and performing a merry dance before it went off to a definite run. I gave it ten feet before striking, but it was only a small fish of about 4 lb (1.8 kg) that threw the hooks as I tried to beach it—a very pale, sandy-coloured pike typical of West Lake's murky waters.

Casting across the wind I heaved out the still-intact herring as hard as I dared, placing it accurately beside the bare branches of an overhanging alder. This time there was hardly time to settle down. A calm patch appeared among the wavelets as a spreading circle of herring oil came to the surface. Something was after the bait.

As the slick widened the float suddenly took off to cruise steadily along the far bank before turning back abruptly and slipping below the waves. I knew at once this was a better fish. It towed solidly away, remaining deep, but once turned came readily to the shore until it spotted me and put in a lusty surge that made the reel scream as it tore off line. Being firmly hooked, it eventually co-operated: a stocky, well-conditioned pike that was covered in thick slime, and fairly short in length considering an unexpected 10¾ lb (4.9 kg).

NOVEMBER 23RD

We had our first taste of winter this morning. Snow fell during the night—just a sprinkling—but sufficient to cover the ground and remind us that winter is just around the corner. Its arrival seemed to bring about a sudden urgency among the birdlife, and all morning I noticed little flocks occupied in the desperate struggle to find food, a full belly being their only protection against the weather.

A pair of pheasants scuttled from the feedstack on Rabbit Hill from their scratchings amongst the straw with a sizeable flock of small birds—mainly chaffinches—that fluttered reluctantly no further than to the nearest bushes to wait anxiously for me to leave and thus to allow them to return to the serious business of filling their crops with food. Among them I spotted two gorgeous bramblings, both males in winter dress, a species not commonly noticed unless one bothers to look closely among the confused winter flocks of finches.

Wood pigeons rattled noisily from every ivy-covered oak, forced to resort to a bitter meal of berries now their main food supplies are temporarily under cover of snow. Many more were flocking to the field of oilseed rape on the farm boundary, where tender young leaves still showed green and welcome above a dusting of snow, to attract the hungry hordes.

By midday much of the earth had reappeared, at least on areas thawed by an unwilling sun, the snow lingering stubbornly where the ground remained frozen on the shaded sides of hedges and along the valley floors. Screened from the south by a tall line of conifers, the owl pen and orchard stayed in deep shade all day. The geese looked cold and miserable, standing on one leg and shifting weight from side to side to allow each leg to be drawn up alternately and warmed briefly in their flank feathers. The snowy owls seldom suffer from cold feet. With fully feathered legs and toes, they have no such problem. Having eaten, both were comfortably fluffed up and looking quite at home in weather agreeably hospitable when compared to the harsh conditions prevalent in their natural arctic home.

NOVEMBER 25TH

Daylight came very slowly. Hardly before the last of the owls had thought of retiring to their daytime roosts, Ken and I were in position on a pasture above the farm, listening to the gentle hootings of two tawnies in the giant oak beside the cowhouse. It would be some time before the geese moved.

For over a week about a hundred greylags had grazed the pasture, and as some were beginning to turn their attentions to a nearby field of winter barley, it seemed a good time to ambush them on the early inward flight. They were almost sure to turn up at first light.

Even then it was seven o'clock before they moved, the temperature dropping alarmingly as the first pigeons ventured from the Farm Wood roost and we heard geese chattering in the half-light making ready for flight. Following a short debate, a large skein finally lifted clear of the lake, approaching the field from downwind to make us crouch even lower in the hedge, cackling excitedly all the way but topping the hawthorns well wide to scout the field for danger prior to landing. We both lay still, hoping they would circle again before committing themselves and this they did, swinging widely round for another cautious circuit before coming in to land. The second approach was perfect, the stirring spectacle of at least seventy yelping geese strung out widely across our front. They advanced at a comfortable height until, awaiting the very last moment, we both sprung up, leaving the geese no chance of veering off. I took the leader as they stalled, saw it crumple and switched to another easy overhead shot as the rest scattered in confusion. Ken also made a promising start, two more plump greylags hitting the ground behind him.

Warmed by the action, we decided to sit it out a while longer. Another half hour and we were both feeling chilled to the bone, blowing on frozen hands and stamping feet to restore some heat when a sudden metallic honking dispersed all thoughts of the cold—Canadas!—a small wedge coming our way from the marshes!

This lot looked to be moving well off course. A quick dash under cover of the hedge gave more hope of intercepting the line, but at the last moment they side-slipped on the breeze, whiffling down to my left almost directly over where we had been waiting! I was lucky enough to scramble two more down as they crossed the hedge but Ken, several yards to my right, could manage only a single, folding up the flanking bird but unable to get off his second barrel.

But enough was enough. Seven fine geese for seven shots, an ample amount to stock up the game larder. With any luck the cold weather will allow the geese to be kept for a week or two before eating. Suitably treated, there is nothing to rival the flavour of a well-hung wild goose.

NOVEMBER 28TH

With nothing planned for the morning, it seemed worth giving the pigeons a try on a few acres of late-drilled wheat. A reasonable number had been feeding on the corn over the past few days, possibly only a couple of hundred, but they were concentrated at a particular spot at the top of the hill beside three prominent oaks. There a patch of heavy land had defied all attempts to break it down to the fine tilth necessary for a good seedbed. It had formed into unworkable sticky clods that covered the grain rather sparsely, and left a fair amount exposed to attract the pigeons. If the weather held, the situation looked promising.

My hopes were dashed when I awoke to a steady rain, but I was out before daylight just the same, determined to at least go through the motions as soon as the weather cleared. Luckily, after a damp and drizzly dawn, the sky cleared sufficiently to set up shop below the furthest of the three oaks, situating the decoys well upwind in a wide crescent pattern, and settling down as comfortably as the conditions would allow with my back propped against the doubtful shelter of the craggy trunk.

A great deal of pigeons moved at first light. Prospecting the field, they skirted the decoys hesitantly at first, reluctant to drop down to the muddy ground. A few glided towards the oaks for a closer look, and during the first hour I dropped about a dozen before they were stopped by another storm sweeping in from the north. It was sleet this time, culminating in a wild flurry of hailstones. With it came a freshening wind. I turned up my collar and hung on in the hope it would clear away the clouds and allow the pigeons to move again.

The air turned bitter when the storm was over, but in spite of the cold, I shot well above form as a constant flow of pigeons working from the valley woods quickly provided a good set of natural decoys. With well over forty set out, new arrivals dropped in steadily throughout the morning, the majority decoying really well once the wind had begun to dry out the surface of the field.

There was a brief lull as another shower of hail darkened the sky, now with a little snow thrown in by way of a change, giving me a chance to tidy up the decoys and to collect the birds dropped at long range showered all over the field. By the time an exhausting pick-up was complete, the black clouds had rolled away to the south and a welcome sun had broken through to dry the land. This was a great improvement. Now the pigeons really piled in, turning up from all directions to pitch fearlessly across the front of the hide, their flightpath funnelled easily by an accurate upwind siting of the decoys.

By noon I was low on cartridges, but by this time the flight had slowed down considerably and finally ceased altogether as the elements again threw their worst at me, as I cowered uncomfortably below the oak. Rain turned to sleet and finally snow before it passed, but it was now too late to matter. I had taken well over a hundred. The pigeons had obviously had enough.

They were not the only ones! I was cold, wet, tired, and hungry, and now faced with the job of humping a hundredweight and a half of pigeons across almost half a mile of sticky ground. It had been a terrific day while it lasted!

NOVEMBER 30TH

A perfect day, spent among good company, and in the splendid surroundings of a typical Norfolk estate. It was a day of bright skies and high cloud that allowed mellow sunshine to highlight the rich autumnal tones of the country-side, the rolling parkland and wood floors a blend of russets, gold, and many shades of brown. Above this, the last stubborn leaves still clung to the less-exposed branches of the mature woodland. Above all hung the excitement of a formal day's pheasant shooting.

A brisk south-westerly did nothing to cool enthusiasm as we gathered near the hall to set out for the first drive of the day, the team of guns, beaters, and dogs all eager to get under way and flushed with anticipation of the day that lay ahead.

Although not really cold, the south-westerly was to influence almost every drive, the downwind stands being by far the more productive. On the first couple of drives I drew comparatively quiet upwind pegs, most birds curling up above the woods and allowing the wind to sweep them over the line. I dropped three hen pheasants before missing an easy overhead cock bird as it appeared skimming over a stand of tall pines. It was my favourite type of shot but I attributed the lost chance to being stiff and cold.

The following drive I shall always remember. Standing downwind of a steep hill, where splendid mature oaks tower intimidatingly high, I was treated to the sight of pheasants flushed before the beaters, rocketing from the far end of the wood, gliding down and gaining speed above the trees, and lifting sharply as they broke out to sweep over my peg with the wind hard in their tails. My first shot crumpled a real corker, coming in a long glide from far away and hurtling over at a terrific pace. I brought the gun up, swung through hard, and fired, relieved to see it fold cleanly and crash far behind in a cascade of feathers. There is nothing like a successful shot at the start of a drive to instil confidence, and by the time the beaters appeared at the end of an exciting drive, several more had been taken in an identical fashion, the last a rewarding shot at an unusually dark bird that came side-slipping along the wood to provide a really testing target.

For the last drive before lunch I was drawn beside a stand of massive beeches, my position quiet until the drive was almost over, when four ill-advised cocks came forward one by one. The last climbed into the wind in the opposite direction, but changed its mind at the last moment and curled back to sail over high. My final shot of the morning sent it spinning among the beeches to bounce on a springy cushion of mast. I gathered it where it had fallen beside the others, its wings outstretched and its metallic armour glowing warmly against a carpet of rustling tawny leaves.

Following a break for lunch and a couple of busy boundary drives, the remainder of the afternoon was spent in heavily wooded parkland where the wind was kinder, allowing us to hear the exciting sounds from the wood, which for me adds much pleasure to the proceedings: the tap-tapping sticks of approaching beaters; the sudden rattle of wings as birds take flight; and the shouts of 'Forward!' that rang repeatedly through the trees, hailing the appearance of a pheasant bursting over the treetops to rise sharply as the waiting guns were spotted, the sun glinting on the bronze plumage of autumn-coloured birds.

All too soon the sun sank lower in the west and the air chilled. The day was almost over. Time had flown by all too swiftly. I finished the day in a narrow ride separating two long coverts, at first entranced as two roe deer bounded from cover and bounced away across the adjoining fields before the first pheasants appeared skimming above the leafless oaks. It was a time for tricky snapshots through the tracery of overhead branches, but I held the gun reasonably straight and there was another half a dozen to collect when the drive was done. It had been a glorious day of almost two hundred head, the sights, scents, and sounds all consigned to the memory to be relived long after the keeper's whistle had signalled the completion of the final drive.

December

DECEMBER 1ST

As we turn the pages of the year's final chapter, we are presented with what looks a dismal picture of lifelessness and decay as the land is laid bare by sharp frosts, sudden wintry showers, and the bitter winds of December. One could almost be forgiven for thinking that everything is death and destruction, but the rot is only skin deep—a transient period of dormancy while hidden forces are at work rebuilding the reserves ready to burst into vibrant life again once the first hint of spring summons the countryside from its long winter sleep. At the moment such miracles seem a long way off.

It is a time for noticing little things previously overlooked in the lushness of warmer times. To the keen observer all is now an open book, and there is much of interest to be discovered. Old nests, suspended drunkenly among the skeletons of trees and now brimming with fallen leaves, show where many a family of birds has been reared, some close by where we passed in the summer completely unaware of their existence. The ubiquitous grey-squirrel dreys are now exposed, seemingly more and more each year: untidy accumulations of twigs, leaves, and grasses lodged in the fork of a tree and now standing out like a sore thumb among the bareness of the branches. If we tap the trunk one will occasionally pop out to scurry away through the treetops or hug a wide trunk where it immediately becomes as one with the tree until a betraying breeze ruffles the long hairs of its tail.

Clearing the duckpond inlet channel, I came across the anvil of a song thrush—a single, sharp flint among the frosted nettles projecting upwards where many a hapless snail had ended its life dashed heedlessly against the stone. The scattered remains are mostly from yellow—or pink-banded snails, of which the bird is so fond. I had heard its tappings many times, but never bothered to look.

The morning remained bright and clear, the mantle of crisp hoar frost shrouding the low marshes surviving well into the morning before the sun could burn it off. Before then, I had seen another movement of Bewick's swans, twenty-six this time, a wild excitement evident in their voices as the journey's end was neared. Minutes later, a drake goosander came winging upstream, passing unawares and close enough to see the sheen on the dark bottle-green head and even the delicate blush of pink suffusing its white breast. It is a species I have often considered adding to my collection of ornamental fowl, but the price is prohibitive and the birds are difficult to maintain in captivity. For the present I must content myself with occasional sightings of the few that grace the valley during the winter months. Oddly enough, they are almost exclusively males.

DECEMBER 3RD

A howling gale prompted me to try an evening flight near Marsh Wood, for under such conditions duck often move across the corner of the wood and, given a strong headwind, low enough to offer a shot or two. Concealed in a thicket of dead willow-herb, I opened the score with a few pigeons heading homeward to a warm fir-tree roost deep in the sheltered heart of the wood, their crops bulging roundly with ripe acorns. It was long after their bedtime when the duck began to flight, but the wind was in the wrong quarter, the south-west, and most passed well over the boundary, the few flighting overhead lifting far too high for a shot.

Just before dark something startled me by whizzing low over my head. It was a woodcock, flitting owl-like across the marsh, closely followed by a second, and at intervals three more. The woodcock have certainly arrived in numbers this year.

The woodcock is a real mystery of a bird. It is often glimpsed only in the twilight of dawn and dusk as it travels to and from its feeding and resting places. It is an elusive character, spending the daylight hours in damp, secret haunts among leaves and twigs that carpet the woods and coverts, its plumage in perfect harmony with the tones of the wood floor. It ventures out only when day is done to search for earthworms and other invertebrates, which it locates by probing soft areas of boggy ground with a long, skewer-like bill. Each November our handful of residents are supplemented by varying numbers from across the North Sea, a mass migration sometimes resulting in a 'fall' of woodcock as they turn up exhausted on our shores. Here, they hide away to rest and to recover before spreading out to find winter homes among the woods, where they provide much excitement on shooting days, for no bird is prized more for its reputation of being an elusive target.

Its 'pin' feathers—trophies much sought after by the shooting person— are situated at the base of the first primaries, and are still occasionally used for artist's brushes, having an extremely fine and flexible tip much favoured for delicate work.

The bird is also reputed to carry its young between its legs in flight if threatened with danger, but although a few witnessings to this extraordinary habit have been recorded, it is still a matter for conjecture that would make it unique in the wader world. It is encouraging to see so many woodcock about. The past few years have seen rather lean times hereabouts for the bird. Possibly it has had a good breeding season. It will be interesting to see if many are found in the woods on late shooting days.

DECEMBER 6TH

I was witness to a murder this morning. Parking in the lay-by opposite the duckponds, I spotted a small group of great black-backed gulls huddled on the field of winter barley 50 yards from the road: five smart adults in conspicuous livery of contrasting black and white, accompanied by two mottled-brown youngsters, a solemn bunch looking strangely out of place resting beside a group of fresh molehills.

Suddenly the nearest gull sprang into action. A quick sideways dash ended with a vicious stab at the earth where something had attracted its attention. In its wicked beak was a small, dark object that it tossed into the air, stabbing and shaking it like a cat with a mouse until the rest joined in what soon developed into a noisy free-for-all. The binoculars revealed a mole, the ill-fated creature soon reduced to battered bundle of black fur when all hell broke loose as two of the giants fought a tug-o'-war in an attempt to establish ownership. The winner attempted to escape by running off and lifting heavily into the air, labouring unsteadily away in the direction of West Lake. The rest shadowed it closely, dive-bombing and shrieking until the fracas passed from sight below the steep west bank. I could still hear the dispute as I crossed the stubble to feed the ducks.

A few black-backs always winter hereabouts. Away from their normal coastal haunts, they often frequent refuse tips to scavenge a living among the waste, but being of an omnivorous and somewhat opportunist nature, they will eat almost anything. A hungry gull is not above attacking a weak or injured bird or animal if the chance arises. Years ago, while pigeon shooting, I saw a marauding group attack a full-grown rabbit suffering from myxomatosis, the unfortunate coney only cheating an even more agonizing death by escaping in a nearby burrow. Never before have I seen one capture a mole.

DECEMBER 7TH

The silence was shattered by the alarm clock half an hour before dawn, and I lay for a few minutes listening to the wind and rain buffeting the window pane, a warm bed inviting me to get up at a more reasonable hour instead of venturing forth into the cold, dark world outside. And all for the sake of a Christmas goose. On the previous two mornings several flights of Canadas had passed over the barley stubble adjoining the garden and last night, full of good intentions, I set the alarm to allow me to be in position well before first light, in the hope of ambushing the geese as they journeyed along the valley *en route* for a fallow stubble half a mile away.

Suppressing the desire for more sleep, within fifteen minutes I had risen, clothed myself, gulped down a welcome mug of tea, and was trudging resolutely across the stubble, the chilling rain full in my face and leaning heavily against the strong northerly wind. Out here it was a different world, the branches of bushes and trees thrashing wildly in the wind as the first faint glimmer of dawn began to lighten the eastern horizon. Above me, however, the sky was still black and impenetrable with stormclouds.

I had already constructed a rough hide in the hedge last night, and just as I reached its sanctuary the rain stopped. As I stood adjusting the hide and waiting for the dawn, chattering parties of mallard passed over unseen in the inky blackness, and once the fluted piping of a drake as a little bunch of teal whizzed past quite low. Their flickering outlines could be glimpsed only for a moment before they too were swallowed in the gloom. As the sky lightened almost imperceptibly, I could just make out the first clamour of goose talk in the distance as they prepared for flight, their voices rising and falling as they encouraged one another to take to the air. Presently, an altered tone drifted on the wind, an urgent clamour as the first flight took to their wings. Straining my eyes in the gloom I was just able to make out a thin line of geese, about a score all told, winging their way purposefully against the wind in the general direction of where I crouched in the hide of hazel fans and dead grasses. Although at first appearing to head in my direction, the line of geese was gradually pushed off course by the wind, eventually passing my position wide by at least 100 yards. The next flight of about a dozen birds followed the same route, boring resolutely into the gale. The wind was obviously having an effect on their flightline. As I was debating whether to move further along the hedge to intercept them, I heard the main bunch take to the air, their voices increasing in volume and urgency as they approached the stubble. This time I was in luck. At least seventy huge Canadas advanced, strung out in a wide V, the exact centre of the spearhead winging dead on line. Waiting until they were almost overhead, I swung up the gun to blot out the leading bird, swinging through as I fired and having the satisfaction of seeing the massive bird fold up before taking another as the flock back-pedalled in the air. Both birds crashed well behind on the adjoining plough, their white bellies facing upwards to pinpoint where they had fallen: a good right and left, and well worth the discomfort of braving the elements of a rough December dawn.

DECEMBER 10TH

A cutting, cold, east wind chilled my fingers as I rather clumsily put up the trout rod and tied on a blue dog-nobbler. It was freezing cold, but I had made the journey to the Valley Lakes on what would be my last opportunity of the year and vowed to stick it out, at least for a respectable couple of hours or so. As expected, there was very little movement on the water in the shape of rising trout, and the entire lake looked cold and deserted, except for two more hardy characters flogging away resolutely at the far end of the lake.

The first hour further confirmed my suspicions, for although dutifully dragging the depths with all manner of coloured lures, the nearest I came to a fish was a couple of tentative pulls while slowly retrieving the first casting of a yellow nobbler well below the surface. Having almost churned the water to a froth without success, I moved along the bank 30 yards or so to a more exposed area where the wind had put a steady ripple on the water. This achieved the desired result. A few moments later I felt a savage pull from six feet down—that long-awaited electrifying kick that restored a little warmth and meant a fish at last. Striking upwards to set the hook, I felt the trout bore deeper in a long sideways run, 20 yards from the bank. It felt like a good, strong fish. Following a few short runs, I was surprised to see it surface almost played out and ready for the net, a dark-coloured cock fish of just $1\frac{1}{2}$ lb (0.7 kg), rather smaller than anticipated.

With renewed hope, I continued at the same depth, the next two casts rewarded by two more almost identically sized fish, both brought safely to the net after a short tussle. And that was it. I had obviously made contact with a wandering shoal. Although continuing well into the afternoon with a variety of lures, there was no further response, and as the wind was growing steadily stronger and colder, I decided to call it a day: the humid, sultry days of midsummer trouting at the lakes now but a pleasant memory in the failing light. An old cock pheasant fluttered into the nearby alder belt as I made my way to the fishing hut to weigh my catch, rousing and fluffing his feathers to keep the cold at bay. I wished him well, not envying him the long night at roost on an exposed branch of the leafless alders.

DECEMBER 14TH

Having completed all the necessary chores around the garden, I was pleased to find myself with an hour or two to spare before the early dusk of winter brought the day to a close. Spectre was screaming in anticipation whenever she heard me pass the mews, a gentle but persistent hint that she was in good condition for flying. With this in mind I decided to hunt her in the early afternoon, when a bitter north-easterly caused her to ruffle and to fluff her body feathers as I carried her to Bulrush Marsh. I hoped to find an odd moorhen or two skulking along the tangled hedges edging a small marshy pond that contained a couple of tall sallows growing directly from the water.

Passing Blackthorn Copse, Spectre displayed a readiness to hunt, bobbing her head excitedly, and eventually bating towards a tall oak set in the boundary hedge that commands a good view of the pond. I allowed her her freedom, knowing full well that she would fly only as far as the oak and take stand in its top branches waiting for me to work out the remainder of the hedge towards her. Searching among the withered bramble patches and holly clumps in the hope of disturbing something, by the time I arrived beneath her I had evicted nothing apart from a foraging pair of hedge sparrows. She was still peering below, awaiting the chance of a flight. Continuing 20 yards along the hedge, I called and waved her over my head to her usual stand in a tall dead elm at the far side of the pond. Beating steadily to the elm, Spectre suddenly checked in mid-air and curled back on the wind, gaining momentum and swooping purposefully for a small thicket of blackthorn. Something had evidently moved ahead of us. This proved to be the case, as she suddenly dived and struck in the edge of the thorns, but emerging empty-handed, proceeded to bounce up and down along its edge. A cock blackbird protested from the centre of the thorns, but thinking her prey was something larger, I quickly took her up and cast her back to the elm, from where she would get a good view of anything flushed. I then raced to the far side of the thicket hoping to eject her prey. Halfway along, a moorhen burst from hiding and made for the pond, with Spectre gliding from her lookout branch to give chase, missing the bird by inches as it splashed headlong into the water. Spectre threw up above it to alight in the tallest sallow, but it was several

178

minutes before I finally flushed the moorhen from a tangle of dried rushes at the water's edge. This time there was no mistake. A fast chase across the open meadow and the bird was taken cleanly in the air, the pair spinning to thump on the soft meadow grass to end an exciting chase.

DECEMBER 16TH

Starlings! Thousands of them! In fact, there must be tens of thousands. Each afternoon their numbers build up steadily until an hour before dusk, when a seething mass darkens the sky to sweep this way and that above the stubble like plumes of dense black smoke. They alight in a scavenging mass until something disturbs them and they take to the air with a great roar of wings and swerve about the fields like a vast flock of waders on the foreshore. Sometimes the dizzy hordes descend to the orchard, and within seconds the bare boughs of the apple trees are suddenly filled with animated black leaves. The muck spreader has been at work on the stubble, but the birds ignore the fact, feeding busily until they all suddenly disappear just before dark to a communal roost. With a great swish of wings the flock travels a mile across country to a warm pinewood, causing considerable damage by roosting *en masse*, their sheer weight of numbers snapping off twigs and small branches and even killing the trees as their droppings smother the ground if the roost is used over a long period. It is some indication of their numbers when such a small bird causes such widespread destruction.

I heard a dog fox barking on the field above the house this evening, his treble barks answered by a rival across the river. Both were moving slowly up the valley, possibly to a rendezvous with a favoured vixen. Their cries sounded rather eerie ringing around the valley, carrying far in the stillness of the night and setting the farm dogs barking. The only other sounds of the night were the harsh cries of a heron passing over in the darkness to its nocturnal fishing ground, and the occasional hooting of a tawny owl at the top of the orchard.

DECEMBER 18TH

At the end of a rather gruelling day, I collected the fourten and set off for the duckponds in the hope of a mallard at evening flight, and to spend an hour or so generally unwinding. A fourten is not the ideal fowling piece in view of its restricted range, but in a situation where noise must be minimized to avoid disturbance to the resident fowl, it fulfils its role admirably and is a pleasant little gun to use once handling has been perfected.

As I stood concealed beside a laurel clump on the riverbank, columns of thick marsh mist rose slowly to blanket the distant fir woods, and with little or no wind, conditions were far from ideal. Nevertheless, I decided to wait until darkness called a halt. A few late wood pigeons drifted into the tallest of the firs and a continual column of black-headed gulls made their way on tired wings to the nearby lake, but the light began to fail with not so much as a whisper of duck wings until a shot half a mile upriver put a few birds on the

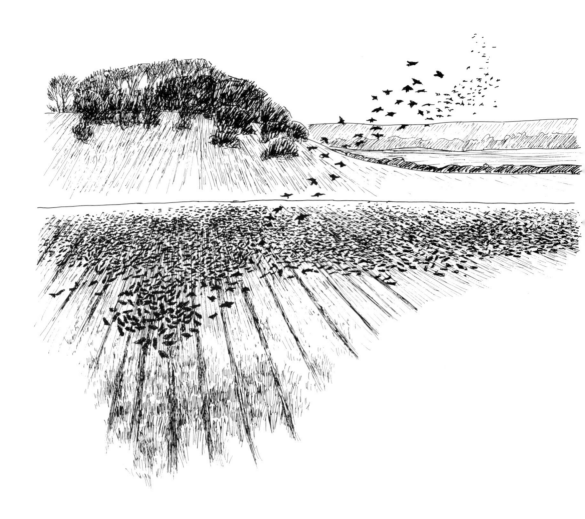

Highly gregarious in winter, a seething mass of starlings drifts
like a plume of smoke over the stubble.

wing. Most passed over very high like flickering shadows, but presently a little group of five birds began to circle the ponds looking for a feeding place. I crouched closer to the laurels as a single bird detached itself from the bunch and planed down over a tall ash tree, just in range of the little gun. At the single crack it folded neatly and thumped down to a bed of last summer's nettles beside me: a fine fat drake in immaculate condition, its rich colours glowing warmly in the half-light of dusk. More duck were now in the air, and by remaining patient as the birds wheeled and circled tantalizingly just out of range, I was rewarded eventually as a pair arched their wings to drop to the water. Taking the first as an easy overhead shot, there was just sufficient time to click another cartridge into the chamber and take the second as it fought to regain height over the ash tree. This bird was rather less co-operative than the first, splashing down in a shower of spray ten feet out from the river bank. I raced downstream ahead of it and waded out into the strong flow of the shallows to cut it off and to prevent it from being swept away, but by this time it was almost completely dark and difficult to see where I was going. My first discovery was a deep hole cut by the water's flow, which resulted in both boots being filled with icy water, but I did manage to retrieve the duck without further mishap. An enjoyable little evening's sport, marred only by the sensation that both my legs felt as though amputated just below the knee— but such are the hazards of duck flighting.

DECEMBER 21ST

On the way to feed the ducks I hunted Spectre from the small carp lake to the duckponds, taking in the rough tangled slope that runs down to the riverbank that has become one of the last strongholds of the moorhen now that she has taken almost a score from the adjoining marshlands. It had been another mercilessly cold night, patches of white hoar frost still lingered along the hedge bottoms and a bitter little breeze had sprung up from the north and begun to rustle the reeds. The carp lake looked extremely cold and forbidding. With a thin skin of ice glassing over part of its surface, it made me shiver just to think of its occupants lying well out of sight at the bottom of the deepest holes.

Apart from a cock pheasant whirring out 50 yards ahead, the bank seemed empty, but as we stood debating where to try next, a moorhen launched from the boughs of an ivy-covered alder, where it had found some temporary cover among the creepers. Spectre wasted no time, but having learned its lessons well, the moorhen headed straight for the river, plunging boldly in and remaining submerged until a widening ring of ripples showed it had found safety beneath the far bank. The buzzard hovered briefly above it. Realizing her chance was gone, she mounted steadily into the breeze, gaining height to make wide circle of the duckponds and the surrounding marsh. Lost from sight behind the trees she seemed a long while gone, and I was relieved when she at last returned to glide to the top of her favourite alder, standing high above the centre pond where, after a brief shuffling of her feathers, she tucked up one leg and settled down to scan her surroundings.

Strangely enough, she has never interfered with any of the waterfowl, and they in turn ignore her, seeming to accept her presence, although a wild hawk passing over the ponds causes instant panic. The usual flock of black-headed gulls turned up as I fed the ducks, shrieking down boldly to snap up scraps of bread thrown on the water for the ducks.

I noticed Spectre shifting on her perch. Without warning she suddenly dropped from the bough, wings closed and tail upturned, the wind whistling through her bells as she fell like a stone. The gull saw her drop far too late, a clever snatch taking the gull from the air almost before it had seen her coming, and long before it had time to take evasive action. The fatal glide ended in an undignified heap as Spectre bounced off the perimeter fence—she was so intent on her prey that she failed even to notice it in her path: one of her rather more inglorious moments.

DECEMBER 23RD

It was sheltered in the wood. Outside a raw wind and driving rain were sweeping across the fields and rattling the branches high above me, but here, deep among the ivy-draped alders, the wind was hardly able to penetrate and the air at ground level was comparatively still. I always find something deeply satisfying about being tucked cosily in the depths of a wood when all around is lashed with gales. Farm Wood is wild, completely overgrown, and unmanaged. No one but me ever goes there, and then only when the pigeon begin using the wood as a winter roost, often turning up early to top up their crops on a wealth of ivy berries before finding a comfortable perch for the night.

The signs were promising, an encouraging amount of preened feathers and droppings lying below the trees showing the wood had been used for some time. I made a rough hide below a clearing by draping an armful of bracken over a fallen trunk, turned up my collar against a vicious little breeze, and leant back on a handy tree-stump to await events.

Within minutes the first pigeons came beating upwind over the trees, a bunch of half a dozen with the rain in their faces. They swept in confidently before my single shot scattered them on the wind, apart from one that tumbled through the branches to crash at my feet on the carpet of sodden leaves. Its crop was bulging with pieces of sugar beet churned up by the harvester. There was little hope of a second barrel, but hardly had they gone than another bunch came labouring along the path of the first. This time I managed two shots, the second a fruitless stab among the branches as the remainder whisked back on the wind. This one also had its crop crammed with sugar beet. It might be worth searching the fields with an eye to a day's decoying.

Undeterred by the shooting, small parties turned up at regular intervals throughout the afternoon, many passing directly over a small gap in the branches to my right where, picking each shot carefully, I managed to keep up a good average of birds for cartridges fired. I took mainly singles, there being seldom time to get off a second barrel.

The afternoon was all too short. By four o'clock the wood was in twilight and the pigeon stopped coming, but just as I was collecting the last of the fallen, an old carrion crow came croaking low over the alders to its roost in the tall fir behind me. It saw me too late, its avoiding action to no avail as a hurried shot sent it parachuting through the tops of the alders, the end of another ardent egg-thief. I have seen it steal into the wood on many an occasion at dusk.

DECEMBER 25TH

Christmas morning and, according to the weatherman, the mildest for forty years. It was grey and misty outside. Not a thing stirred, neither car nor plane nor distant rumble of farm machinery, in fact nothing to spoil the complete stillness and silence except the distant croaking of a passing heron and the gabble of duck talking down by the river as I strolled across to give the waterfowl an early-morning feed. After doling out the usual mixture of pellets and wheat (no Christmas dinner for them!), I paused against a convenient tree-stump to examine the flock of nearly a hundred fowl, almost every one now in full colour apart from the fleet of tiny ruddy ducks and a couple of garganey teal. The goldeneyes are looking superb, two gorgeously coloured males interrupting their feeding to display lustily to their partners. So did the immaculate trio of hooded merganser drakes, who erected bold headdresses of black and white, and puffed themselves up importantly before their future spouses. As yet their efforts are receiving little or no reaction.

It was while carrying out a rough head count that I spotted a movement in the entrance tunnel of a nesting-box situated above the water, and seconds

I paused to examine the flock of fowl.

later was intrigued to see a mallard duck sneak sheepishly from the tunnel, hastily joining the flock to feed and seeming in such earnest that I was prompted to wade out to examine the box. On lifting the lid I discovered a clutch of eight eggs nestled on a copious bed of down, their shells shiny and smooth with long hours of incubation. They must surely be infertile. The duck obviously did not share my feelings. After a quick wash and brush up she returned to the box to continue her duties.

Keeping watch from a discreet distance I was joined by the resident robin, who hopped almost to my feet to accept a crust of bread and eventually perched on the nearby woodpile to deliver his melancholy little winter song. It sounded very beautiful, but rather sad.

DECEMBER 28TH

Still feeling the effects of the excesses of the past few days, I took Spectre out for a short hunting trip. The raw wind of the morning had moderated only slightly but it was good to be out again—a brief respite to restore equilibrium before the gruelling process of seeing in the New Year begins.

I set off down the road with Spectre close behind, scattering a chuckling flock of fieldfares gorging the last of the berries from the roadside holly. She was in a mischievous mood, seeming rather pleased with herself for causing such confusion and flying from rooftop to rooftop until we reached the far end of the village. Here she alighted rather precariously on a television aerial, swaying alarmingly back and forth until I called her off. Even then she refused the glove, sweeping past to mount high into the wind, evidently taking great delight in playing me up. Sweeping high over the adjoining stubble, she put to wing the massive flock of starlings, many thousands strong, feinting down-wards as if to attack and scattering them in all directions before they curled away to re-group in the bare branches of Roughground Copse.

Spectre continued to play, riding the wind with scarcely a wingbeat and mewing loudly overhead, her stiff primaries spread like upward curving fingers as she tested the updraught, allowing each gust to push her higher still. I have complete faith in her now, and she followed me thus past Blackthorn Copse to the marsh where, getting back to business, she drifted to the dead elm and invited me to hunt the nearby hedge.

Not hopeful of finding much, I worked it half-heartedly towards her. I had barely started when she suddenly slipped from the bough, a silent downward glide ending with a brave stoop among the brambles. Nothing came out.

Running to the far end I found her spread-eagled uncomfortably across the thorns, her talons reaching deep into the bush. She seemed to be holding something! I was delighted to find her locked to a pheasant, a dark melanistic hen of which there are several about the farm. Another unexpected candidate for the cooking pot. She is certainly earning her keep!

DECEMBER 31ST

Following a gentle stroll about the farm getting on terms with a few late pheasants, I saw out the last of the daylight hours beside the river on Spring Marsh awaiting the final flight of the year, and though the chances of a duck were remote, it was enough just to be there to see the curtain come down on yet another year in one of my favourite places. And a fine performance it was too. After a day of light westerly winds and unseasonal sunshine, a blanket of cloud lying to the west above Marsh Wood cleared to reveal a splendid sunset, the thinning clouds stained to pink as all colour was drained from the landscape. The first ducks planed down on sickle wings, coloured black as pitch against the dying embers of the year. They were feeding far upriver, but somehow it mattered not to get a shot, I was content enough just to watch the last blaze of red and gold finally dissolve into darkness as a chorus of greylags came chortling upriver—a wide string seen as little more than flickering shadows as they bid a last farewell. Our paths will surely cross again.

It seems hardly possible that a full twelve months have passed since I began to pen these notes. Where has it gone? A year composed of little triumphs and failures, excitements and disasters, that go to make up what is the infinitely varied pattern of the country way of life. The year has turned full circle once again—one more gone, one less to go, a rather sober note on which to bring this diary to an end. Curiously enough, I always feel a certain tinge of sadness as each year draws inevitably to its close. But enough of this! Tomorrow is a fresh start. Another brand new year is only hours away. What will it bring? The winter solstice has passed. Already the ducks are courting, the days even now beginning to lengthen, and my old friends the herons renewing interest in the dilapidated structures of the heronry. A prehistoric shriek rung out from Marsh Wood as one settled in the top of a larch. Shouldering the gun reluctantly, I trod the path for home.

Open seasons for game, wildfowl, etc.

(all dates inclusive)

Red grouse—August 12th to December 10th.

Black grouse—August 20th to December 10th.

Ptarmigan—August 12th to December 10th.

Capercaillie—October 1st to January 31st.

Partridge—September 1st to February 1st.

Pheasant—October 1st to February 1st.

Snipe—August 12th to January 31st.

Woodcock (England and Wales)—October 1st to January 31st; (Scotland)—September 1st to January 31st.

Wild duck and geese—September 1st to January 31st, except in or over areas below high-water mark of ordinary spring tides where the season is extended to February 20th.

Moorhen, coot, golden plover—September 1st to January 31st.

Rabbits—no close season.

Hares—no close season over much of the country, but on moorlands and unenclosed non-arable lands, hares may only be shot between December 11th (July 1st in Scotland) and March 31st.

Other birds classed as vermin, i.e. magpies, jays, carrion crows, etc.—no close season.

If in doubt refer to the Wildlife and Countryside Act 1981.

Fishing seasons

Coarse fish (roach, perch, dace, rudd, chub, pike, tench, carp, bream, barbel, eels, etc.)—June 16th to March 14th inclusive.

Brown trout—April 1st to October 29th inclusive.

Rainbow trout—April 1st to October 29th inclusive in rivers and unenclosed waters controlled by the water authority, but in the case of totally enclosed, privately owned waters, there is no official close season and opening dates vary according to fishery rules.

While the above is correct in water controlled by the Anglian Water Authority, it must be noted that open and closed seasons for fishing vary throughout the country.

Index

Page numbers in *italic* refer to illustrations.